ECOCRITICISM

Ecocriticism explores the ways in which we imagine and portray the relationship between humans and the environment across many areas of cultural production, including Romantic poetry, wildlife documentaries, climate models, the Hollywood blockbuster *The Day After Tomorrow*, and novels by Margaret Atwood, Kim Scott, Barbara Kingsolver and Octavia Butler.

Greg Garrard's animated and accessible volume responds to the diversity of the field today and explores its key concepts, including:

- pollution
- pastoral
- wilderness
- apocalypse
- animals
- Indigeneity
- the Earth.

Thoroughly revised to reflect the breadth and diversity of twenty-first-century environmental writing and criticism, this edition addresses climate change and justice throughout, and features a new chapter on Indigeneity. It also presents a glossary of terms and suggestions for further reading.

Concise, clear and authoritative, *Ecocriticism* offers the ideal introduction to this crucial subject for students of literary and cultural studies.

Greg Garrard is Professor of Environmental Humanities in the Faculty of Creative and Critical Studies, UBC Okanagan. He is the author of numerous essays on animal studies and environmental criticism, and co-author of *Climate Change Skepticism: A Transnational Ecocritical Analysis* (2019).

THE NEW CRITICAL IDIOM

SERIES EDITOR: JOHN DRAKAKIS, UNIVERSITY OF STIRLING

The New Critical Idiom is an invaluable series of introductory guides to today's critical terminology. Each book:

- provides a handy, explanatory guide to the use (and abuse) of the term;
- offers an original and distinctive overview by a leading literary and cultural critic;
- relates the term to the larger field of cultural representation.

With a strong emphasis on clarity, lively debate and the widest possible breadth of examples, *The New Critical Idiom* is an indispensable approach to key topics in literary studies.

Trauma
Stef Craps and Lucy Bond

Children's Literature
Carrie Hintz

Pastoral
Second edition
Terry Gifford

Fantasy
Lucie Armitt

Intertextuality
Third edition
Graham Allen

Literary Geography
Sheila Hones

Metafiction
Yaël Schlick

Ecocriticism
Third edition
Greg Garrard

Fictionality
Karen Petroski

For more information about this series, please visit: www.routledge.com/The-New-Critical-Idiom/book-series/SE0155

ECOCRITICISM

Greg Garrard

Third edition

Routledge
Taylor & Francis Group

LONDON AND NEW YORK

Designed cover image: Xinzheng, Getty

Third edition published 2023
by Routledge
4 Park Square, Milton Park, Abingdon, Oxon OX14 4RN

and by Routledge
605 Third Avenue, New York, NY 10158

Routledge is an imprint of the Taylor & Francis Group, an informa business

First edition published by Routledge 2004

Second edition published by Routledge 2012

British Library Cataloguing-in-Publication Data
A catalogue record for this book is available from the British Library

Library of Congress Cataloging-in-Publication Data
Names: Garrard, Greg, author.
Title: Ecocriticism / Greg Garrard.
Description: Third edition. | Abingdon, Oxon ; New York, NY : Routledge, 2023. |
Series: New critical idiom | Includes bibliographical references and index. |
Identifiers: LCCN 2022041904 (print) | LCCN 2022041905 (ebook) | ISBN 9781032004051 (hardback) | ISBN 9781032004020 (paperback) | ISBN 9781003174011 (ebook)
Subjects: LCSH: English literature--History and criticism--Theory, etc. | Nature in literature. | American literature--History and criticism--Theory, etc. | Conservation of natural resources in literature. | Environmental protection in literature. | Philosophy of nature in literature. | Wilderness areas in literature. | Climatic changes in literature. | Ecology in literature. | Ecocriticism. | Criticism--Great Britain. | Criticism--United States.
Classification: LCC PR143 .G37 2023 (print) | LCC PR143 (ebook) | DDC 820.9/36--dc22/eng/20220906
LC record available at https://lccn.loc.gov/2022041904
LC ebook record available at https://lccn.loc.gov/2022041905

ISBN: 978-1-032-00405-1 (hbk)
ISBN: 978-1-032-00402-0 (pbk)
ISBN: 978-1-003-17401-1 (ebk)

DOI: 10.4324/9781003174011

Typeset in Garamond and Scala Sans
by Taylor & Francis Books

CONTENTS

ACKNOWLEDGEMENTS

The third edition of *Ecocriticism* was researched and written on the traditional unceded territory of the Syilx Okanagan people. Chapter 7 explains what this means, literally, ethically and personally. I am grateful for the support of my admin assistant Lacia Vogel and the work of my research assistants and graduate students at UBC: Rina Garcia Chua, Claire Halston, Caitlin Voth, Leah Wafler, Steph Hendricks, Madeline Donald, and, especially, Yazdan Gordanpour, who helped prepare the manuscript and secure permissions. I did most of the work in a studio flat at UBC's Woodhaven Eco-Culture Centre in Kelowna, BC, which was an enormous boon – especially given the peppercorn rent. I've come a long way, baby, since 2004, learning from too many students, friends and colleagues at Bath Spa University, UBC, ASLE, EASLCE, ALECC and ASLE-UKI to list them all here – but I thank you nonetheless. In revising for this edition, I benefitted from specific, much-needed advice from Joni Adamson, Camille Dungy, Allison Hargreaves, George Handley, Erin James, Jennifer Ladino, Alexa Weik von Mossner, Francisco Peña, Kate Rigby and Scott Slovic. Richard Kerridge is, as always, *il miglior fabbro*, as well as a beloved friend. Reviewing nearly two decades-worth of ecocriticism and environmental writing, and then writing about 65k words of new material in less than a year, whilst teaching regular classes and being Associate Dean of Research and Graduate Studies, was an absurd undertaking that would have been impossible without the love, tolerance, encouragement and superior organisational abilities of my wife Verity. She is the best.

Preparing this new edition left me humbled and overawed by the intelligence, ingenuity, imagination and hunger for change of the writers, creative and critical, who are rising to the challenge of environmental crisis. The last decade, especially, has been stunningly fertile. It is not enough; perhaps never will be enough. But it gives me hope.

Precisely because he did not insist on it, I wish to acknowledge Tim Seibles for his generosity in allowing me to quote from his poem 'Fearless.'

Arna Bontemps, 'A Black Man Talks of Reaping'. Reprinted by permission of Harold Ober Associates. Copyright 1963 by Arna Bontemps

Lucille Clifton, 'surely i am able to write poems' from *The Collected Poems of Lucille Clifton*. Copyright 2004 by Lucille Clifton. Reprinted with the permission of The Permissions Company, LLC on behalf of BOA Editions Ltd., www.boaeditions.org.

Excerpts from 'Thrushes' from COLLECTED POEMS by Ted Hughes. Copyright © 2003 by The Estate of Ted Hughes. Reprinted by permission of Farrar, Straus and Giroux. All Rights Reserved. Published by Faber and Faber Ltd. outside the USA and the Philippines.

'Urban Renewal XIII', copyright 2006 by Major Jackson. Reprinted by permission of W.W. Norton and Co.

'The Purse-Seine', copyright 1938 by Robinson Jeffers and renewed 1966 by Donnan Jeffers & Garth Jeffers; from THE SELECTED POETRY OF ROBINSON JEFFERS by Robinson Jeffers. Used by permission of Random House, an imprint and division of Penguin Random House LLC. All rights reserved.

Excerpts from 'Rearmament' from *The Selected Poetry of Robinson Jeffers* by Jeffers, Robinson. Edited by Tim Hunt. Copyright © 2001 by Jeffers Literary Properties. All rights reserved. Used by permission of Stanford University Press.

Excerpts from 'Shoal' from *NEW SELECTED POEMS* by Les Murray. Copyright © 2007, 2012, 2014 by Les Murray. Reprinted by permission of Farrar, Straus and Giroux. All Rights Reserved. Australia and New Zealand rights held by Margaret Connolly and Associates. Outside USA, Canada, Australia, New Zealand, Les Murray is published by Carcanet Press, Manchester, UK.

Preface to the Third Edition

The term 'ecocriticism' was coined by William Rueckert in 1978 (ch.1); the Association for the Study of Literature and the Environment (ASLE) was formed in 1992; and Cheryll Glotfelty and Harold Fromm's field-defining *The Ecocriticism Reader* was published in 1996. Google Scholar, tracking only material available online, yields 'About 31,700 results' in response to 'ecocriticism' as a search term. David Mazel, suspecting that ecocriticism 'actually boasts a much longer history' than the lifespan of the term would suggest, presented *A Century of Early Ecocriticism* in 2001. Such a wealth of scholarship could be presented in many different ways. Lawrence Buell's *The Future of Environmental Criticism* (2005) presents the ecocritical insurgency of the 1990s as a 'first wave' that canonised nature writing, Romantic literature and eco-poetry; sought to protect Nature from the misrepresentations and depredations of human cultures; and saw 'science as a corrective to [the] critical subjectivism and cultural relativism' (2005: 18) of postmodern theory. Later 'second wave' ecocriticism adopted a more ambivalent relationship to science; emphasised the interpenetration of the domains of nature and culture; aligned itself with the environmental justice movement (ch.2); and valued a wider range of literature, not all of it explicitly concerned with the natural environment. In 2009, Scott Slovic and Joni Adamson described 'a new third wave of ecocriticism, which recognizes ethnic and national particularities and yet transcends ethnic and national boundaries' (p.7). This wave would encompass eco-cosmopolitan, multi-ethnic, transnational and queer/trans ecologies. Though Buell acknowledges that '"palimpsest" would be a better metaphor than "wave"' (p.17) given the way that each development builds upon, rather than superseding, the last, Greta Gaard argues that the 'wave' metaphor itself 'erases' ecofeminism, which has made important contributions to the field throughout its history (2010: 644). She also criticises the first edition of this book (*Ecocriticism* (2004)) for 'misrepresentation' (p.644) and 'omissions' (p.645) of major ecofeminist works, and calls for a 'different metaphor for describing the developments of ecocritical history.' In a similar vein, Elizabeth DeLoughrey and George B. Handley's

'Introduction' to their seminal *Postcolonial Ecologies* questions the way that previous editions of this book traced an American-centred 'genealogy' of environmental thought, in the identification of Rachel Carson's *Silent Spring* (1962) as marking the beginning of modern environmentalism, for example. They thereby 'call attention to an implicit production of a singular American ecocritical genealogy that, like all histories, might be reconfigured in broader, more rhizomatic, terms' (2011: 15). Their terminology here recalls the distinction presented by Gilles Deleuze (1925–1995) and Félix Guattari (1930–1992) in *A Thousand Plateaus* between tree-like and 'rhizomatic' images of thought (1987: 5–7). For the former, we might picture an oak tree, a tap-rooted plant like a dandelion, or the 'tree of life' metaphor of popular evolutionary biology; for the latter, creeping plants like poison ivy and stinging nettles, or the strange networks created by lateral gene transfers amongst unrelated, mainly unicellular, organisms (p.10). For all these authors, tree-like, or arborescent, structures are considered hierarchical, ethnocentric, patriarchal and all-encompassing, whereas rhizomic ones are open, infinite, heterogeneous and anti-hierarchical.

In this edition, 'Beginnings: Pollution', 'Pastoral' and 'Wilderness' are introduced using a tap-root structure, which is clear to the reader and fits the evidence, while the 'Positions' and 'Apocalypse' chapters convey the multiple roots of, respectively, contemporary environmentalism and apocalypticism using what Deleuze and Guattari call a 'fascicular' or bundled structure (pp.5–6). 'Animals' is organised around a typology of representations, including anthropomorphism and zoomorphism, and the chapter on 'The Earth' discusses 'Images', 'Data' and 'Narratives' of our planet. A chapter on 'Indigeneity' replaces the 'Dwelling' chapter of previous editions (with the loss of its discussion of Georgic). It argues that Indigenous people themselves have always participated – albeit unequally – in the colonial constructions of Indigeneity imposed upon them, making it a uniquely reflexive or 'loopy' trope. In this way, the third edition reconciles clarity and accessibility with critiques that have questioned the way that an introductory text can seem definitive when it is, on the contrary, intended as an opening.

NOTE ON TERMINOLOGY AND TYPOLOGY

This edition adopts the University of British Columbia's 'Indigenous Peoples: Language Guidelines' with the exception that it follows eco-critics south of the border in using the term 'Native American'. 'Indigenous' is used in contexts where specific group names (e.g. Syilx, Navajo) are not appropriate or available. As the Guide observes, 'specificity adds context and clarity, which makes for a richer story' (p.8). (http://assets.brand.ubc.ca/downloads/ubc_indigenous_peoples_langua ge_guide.pdf) The names of racialised groups are capitalised, i.e. Black, White. The word used for beings that are not human is contentious because 'Nature' is a questionable concept for ecocritics and the term 'non-humans' implies lack or failure, hence hierarchy. I use the portmanteau adjective 'other-than-human' and Val Plumwood's 'Earth Other' (ch.2) instead. Bolded names with dates are presented only for deceased individuals.

SERIES EDITOR'S PREFACE

The New Critical Idiom is a series of introductory books which seeks to extend the lexicon of literary terms in order to address the radical changes which have taken place in the study of literature during the last decades of the twentieth century. The aim is to provide clear, well-illustrated accounts of the full range of terminology currently in use, and to evolve histories of its changing usage.

The current state of the discipline of literary studies is one where there is considerable debate concerning basic questions of terminology. This involves, among other things, the boundaries which distinguish the literary from the non-literary; the position of literature within the larger sphere of culture; the relationship between literatures of different cultures; and questions concerning the relation of literary to other cultural forms within the context of interdisciplinary studies.

It is clear that the field of literary criticism and theory is a dynamic and heterogeneous one. The present need is for individual volumes on terms which combine clarity of exposition with an adventurousness of perspective and a breadth of application. Each volume will contain as part of its apparatus some indication of the direction in which the definition of particular terms is likely to move, as well as expanding the disciplinary boundaries within which some of these terms have been traditionally contained. This will involve some re-situation of terms within the larger field of cultural representation, and will introduce examples from the area of film and the modern media in addition to examples from a variety of literary texts.

1

BEGINNINGS

POLLUTION

Beginnings are always debatable, but for the sake of simplicity we will assume that modern Western environmentalism begins with the prologue to Rachel Carson's *Silent Spring* (1962), 'A Fable for Tomorrow'. Carson's fairy tale opens with the words, 'There was once a town in the heart of America where all life seemed to live in harmony with its surroundings' and, invoking the ancient tradition of the pastoral, goes on to paint a picture of 'prosperous farms', 'green fields', foxes barking in the hills, silent deer, ferns and wildflowers, 'countless birds' and trout lying in clear, cold streams, all delighted in by those who pass through the town (1999: 21). Images of natural beauty emphasise the 'harmony' of humanity and nature that 'once' existed. Thus the fable at first presents us with a picture of essential changelessness, which human activity scarcely disturbs, and which the annual round of seasons only reinforces. However, pastoral peace rapidly gives way to catastrophic destruction:

> Then a strange blight crept over the area and everything began to change. Some evil spell had settled on the community: mysterious

DOI: 10.4324/9781003174011-1

maladies swept the flocks of chickens; the cattle and sheep sickened and died. Everywhere was a shadow of death.

In the ensuing paragraphs, every element of the rural idyll is torn apart by some agent of change, the mystery of which is emphasised by the use of both natural and supernatural terminology of 'malady' and 'spell'. Carson describes the collapse in bird populations in impassioned terms: 'On the mornings that had once throbbed with the dawn chorus of robins, catbirds, doves, jays, wrens, and scores of other bird voices there was now no sound; only silence lay over the fields and woods and marsh' (1999: 22). The 'silent spring' of the title alludes, on one level, to this loss of birdsong, although it also comes to function as a synecdoche for a more general environmental apocalypse.

The founding text of modern environmentalism not only begins with an overtly poetic parable, but also relies on the literary genres of pastoral and apocalypse, pre-existing ways of imagining the place of humans in nature that may be traced back to such sources as *Genesis* and *Revelation*, the first and last books of the Christian Bible. *Silent Spring* initially suggests that the mythical eco-catastrophe of the fable might be supernatural, and emphasises this by including an epigram from Keats's poem 'La Belle Dame Sans Merci', in which the magical power of a beautiful woman blights the environment: 'The sedge is wither'd from the lake, / And no birds sing' (p.7). But then the fable concludes: 'No witchcraft, no enemy action had silenced the rebirth of new life in this stricken world. The people had done it themselves' (p.22). The rest of the book sets out to prove that such an apocalypse was already under way all over America, and that the doom befalling this mythical town of the future could be seen as a composite of lesser tragedies happening in 1962.

The real culprits, according to Carson, were the new organic pesticides such as DDT, aldrin and dieldrin that had been introduced after the Second World War and had already proven successful in killing pest insects. *Silent Spring* marshalled an impressive array of scientific evidence to show that this very success was a serious threat both to wildlife and to human health, confronting the utopian claims of agricultural scientists on their own ground. Carson's scientific claims have since been largely confirmed, leading to increased public awareness of pesticide pollution, firmer state regulation and development of less persistent agricultural chemicals. On the other hand, intensive agriculture is the main cause of collapsing insect populations in Europe and North America today, so the silent spring Carson imagined may still be in store for us.

Environmentalist claims like these make crucial contributions to modern politics and culture, yet for the student of the humanities they can be difficult to assess on their own terms. Academia is organised into relatively autonomous 'disciplines' and scientific problems require scientific expertise. Nevertheless, the rhetorical strategies, use of pastoral and apocalyptic imagery, and literary allusions with which Carson shapes her scientific material are amenable to 'literary' or 'cultural' analysis. Such analysis is what we will call 'ecocriticism'. This book is a critical introduction to the field of ecocriticism today.

Let us look at some provisional definitions of the subject. The first is from *The Ecocriticism Reader* (1996), a foundational anthology of American ecocriticism:

> What ... *is* ecocriticism? Simply put, ecocriticism is the study of the relationship between literature and the physical environment. Just as feminist criticism examines language and literature from a gender-conscious perspective, and Marxist criticism brings an awareness of modes of production and economic class to its reading of texts, eco-criticism takes an earth-centred approach to literary studies.
>
> (Glotfelty and Fromm 1996: xix)

Cheryll Glotfelty goes on to specify some of the questions ecocritics ask, ranging from 'How is nature represented in this sonnet?' through 'How has the concept of wilderness changed over time?' to 'How is science itself open to literary analysis?' and finally 'What cross-fertilization is possible between literary studies and environmental discourse in related disciplines such as history, philosophy, psychology, art history, and ethics?' Note how the questions posed by ecocriticism in Glotfelty's account follow a distinct trajectory: the first is very narrow and literary, tending to favour studies of Romanticism such as Jonathan Bate's *Romantic Ecology* (1991). The questions grow in scope as the list continues, with several of the later ones suggesting gargantuan inter-disciplinary studies resembling Simon Schama's *Landscape and Memory* (1995).

Glotfelty compares ecocriticism to feminism and Marxism, and it is true that ecocritics generally tie their cultural analyses to a 'green' moral and political agenda, though not always the *same* agenda, as the next chapter shows. Ecocritics share their overt political commitment with other scholars within the humanities and social sciences, whereas scientists are expected to avoid voicing positions that might compromise their objectivity. Increasingly, ecocriticism is seen as one of the disciplines gathered in the 'environmental humanities' (Emmett and Nye 2017).

A more recent definition comes from Cheryl Lousley's excellent survey of ecocriticism:

> Ecocriticism describes and confronts the socially uneven encounters and entanglements of earthly living, from petro-capitalism to cancer stories to the poetry of bird song. As a political mode of literary and cultural analysis, ecocriticism aims to understand and intervene in the destruction and diminishment of living worlds. Ranging in its critical engagements across historical periods, cultural texts, and cultural formations, ecocriticism focuses on the aesthetic modes, social meanings, contexts, genealogies, and counterpoints of cultural practices that contribute to ecological ruination and resilience. A core premise is that environmental crises have social, cultural, affective, imaginative, and material dimensions.
>
> (Lousley 2020: 2)

Her definition is at once more precise and expansive, as befits a more mature field, and it emphasises 'socially uneven encounters and entanglements' rather than an 'earth-centred approach.' Lousley's 'core premise' highlights that ecocriticism does not claim to have all the answers. Instead, it works alongside numerous other academic disciplines that seek to understand and remedy 'environmental crises.'

From the point of view of academics, ecocriticism is dominated by the Association for the Study of Literature and Environment (ASLE), a professional association that started in America but now has branches in many other countries. It organises regular conferences and publishes a journal that includes literary analysis, creative writing and articles on environmental education and activism. Having once championed nature writing and Romantic literature, ASLE is now centred on environmental justice, and its members research the broad range of cultural processes and products in which, and through which, the complex negotiations of nature and culture take place.

Indeed, the widest definition of the subject of ecocriticism is the study of the relationship of the human and the non-human throughout human cultural history. It can even involve critical analysis of the term 'human' itself (ch.6). This is, as Timothy Clark points out, both invitingly broad and, potentially, 'arbitrary and formless': 'After all, the "environment" is ultimately *everything* and it becomes a merely empty exercise to connect everything with everything else' (2019: 59). This book will narrow down the subject by focusing on Anglophone literature and visual culture, principally those of Britain and North America.

Ecocriticism is unique amongst contemporary literary and cultural theories because of its relationship with the science of ecology. Ecocritics may not be qualified to contribute to scientific debates, but they must nevertheless transgress disciplinary boundaries and develop their own 'ecological literacy' as far as possible. I therefore provide brief discussions of some important environmental threats faced by the world today, climate change in particular. Even this modest crossing of disciplinary boundaries challenges the assumption that ecological problems are scientific problems rather than objects of cultural analysis. When *Silent Spring* was published, the agro-chemical industry reacted by criticising the book for its literary qualities, which, they implied, could not coexist with the appropriate scientific rigour. Are we undermining Carson's scientific authority if we read her book using literary-critical tools? John Passmore helpfully distinguishes between 'problems in ecology', which are properly scientific issues requiring the formulation and testing of hypotheses in ecological experiments, and 'ecological problems', which are 'features of our society, arising out of our dealings with nature, from which we should like to free ourselves, and which we do not regard as inevitable consequences of what is good in that society' (Passmore 1974: 44). To describe something as an ecological problem is to make a normative claim about how we would wish things to be, and while this usually arises out of the claims of ecological scientists, it is not defined by them. A 'weed' is not a kind of plant, only the wrong kind in the wrong place. Eliminating weeds is obviously a 'problem in gardening', but defining weeds in the first place requires a cultural, not horticultural, analysis. Likewise, 'pollution' is an ecological problem because it does not name a substance or class of substances, but represents a normative claim that too much of something is present in the environment, usually in the wrong place. Carson investigated a problem in ecology, with the help of wildlife biologists and environmental toxicologists, to show that DDT was poisoning wildlife, but *Silent Spring* undertook cultural not scientific work when it made the moral case that it *ought* not to be. The great achievement of the book was to turn a (scientific) problem in ecology into a widely perceived ecological problem that was then contested politically, legally and in the media and popular culture. Thus, ecocriticism cannot debate problems in ecology, but it can help to define, explore and resolve ecological problems in this wider sense.

One 'ecocritical' way of reading is to see contributions to environmental debate as examples of rhetoric. I have already suggested that Carson deploys both pastoral imagery and apocalyptic rhetoric, and will return to these subjects, but there are many other applications of formal rhetorical analysis. For example, Ralph Lutts attempts to account for the impact of *Silent Spring* by drawing attention to its underlying analogy between pesticides and another kind of pollution that was strong in popular consciousness in 1962:

> She was sounding an alarm about a kind of pollution that was invisible to the senses; could be transported great distances, perhaps globally; could accumulate over time in body tissues; could produce chronic, as well as acute, poisoning; and could result in cancer, birth defects, and genetic mutations that may not become evident until years or decades after exposure. ... Chemical pesticides were not the only form of pollution fitting this description. Another form, far better known to the public at the time, was radioactive fallout. Pesticides could be understood as another form of fallout.
>
> (Lutts 2000: 19)

Carson combines ancient ways of imagining nature with the contemporary language of 'fallout hysteria', with a view to establishing particular normative claims about pollution. Detailed rhetorical analysis shows how *Silent Spring* is constructed in order to achieve certain political results: not only the concrete measures described in the final chapter, but also a subtle revision of the concept of 'pollution' from visible smoke to imperceptible chemicals.

Terry Eagleton explains that reading discourses (including literary ones) as rhetoric means that we are interested in:

... the kinds of *effects* which discourses produce, and how they produce them. Reading a zoology textbook to find out about giraffes is part of studying zoology, but reading it to see how its discourse is structured and organised, and examining what kind of effects these forms and devices produce in particular readers in actual situations, is a different kind of project. It is, in fact, probably the oldest form of literary criticism in the world, known as rhetoric.

(1996: 205)

Ecocriticism undertakes rhetorical readings of environmental discourses. The field of environmental communication is similar, but uses social science methods to analyse discourses, represented by large data sets, at a broad scale, whereas ecocriticism uses literary critical methods, typically close analysis of small numbers of examples. Today, some ecocritics combine both methods (ch.9).

I will be reading culture as rhetoric, not in the strict sense understood by rhetoricians, but as a way of interpreting the production, reproduction and transformation of large-scale metaphors. Each chapter will examine one such metaphor in terms of its origins, key examples, possible political effects and relationship to social interests. Some, like 'pastoral', are established literary tropes, whilst others name more heterogeneous materials provisionally unified under a single title. I refer to the chapter headings as 'tropes' because they are all, in some sense, ways of imagining, constructing or presenting nature in a figure. Each trope, including the introductory example of 'pollution' in this chapter, gathers together permutations of creative imagination: metaphor, genre, narrative, image. The basis upon which each trope is defined and limited is worked out in each chapter (see Preface), with the proviso that, as ecocritics like to say, 'the map is not the terrain.' Other tropes such as 'health', 'utopia', 'mother Earth' and 'justice' would also reward study. This tropology is intended to be enabling, not limiting.

In rhetorical analysis, the meaning of tropes is closely related to their wider social context. They are therefore not fixed entities but develop and change historically. 'Pollution', for example, derives from the Latin 'polluere' meaning 'to defile', and its early English usage reflects its theologico-moral origins: until the seventeenth century it denoted moral contamination of a person, or acts of defilement such as masturbation. This spiritual definition was gradually transformed into a material, 'environmental' one between the seventeenth and nineteenth centuries, to the point where today only the latter is widely known. People learned to fear their detritus, though even now, pollution retains some of its old aura of moral, as well as material, taint. In Chris Jordan's moving photo series 'Midway: Message from the Gyre' (2009), the images of dead, disintegrated albatross chicks killed by plastic pollution juxtapose the bleached fragility of the birds' bones with the jaunty colours and awful persistence of lighters and bottle caps. 'Midway' is factual reportage that also inspires feelings of grief and shame in viewers. Such patterns of historical continuity, as well as change, will appear in later chapters.

By the early seventeenth century, 'pollution' had begun to acquire connotations of physical impurity, and in 1661 John Evelyn published *Fumifugium,* a pamphlet attacking 'The inconveniencie of the aer and smoak of London,' even then laden with coal smoke. The dominant view, though, remained that pollution came exclusively from malodorous *natural* sources: marshes, rotting animals, horse manure, and even human exhalations. As Peter Thorsheim explains in *Inventing Pollution* (2006), by 1800 Londoners were burning one tonne of coal per person every year, and yet they continued to believe that sulphurous coal smoke protected them from miasmatic illness. Over the course of the century, influenced by 'scientific understanding, political ideology, and popular culture' (p.6), the modern conception of pollution was invented:

> In contrast to earlier ideas that traced polluted air to miasma and cautioned those with respiratory ailments to avoid rural areas, keep a safe distance from houseplants, and even inhale coal smoke, during the late nineteenth century many came to see smoke as pollution and to believe that nature was essential to health.
>
> (p.26)

Scientific progress was vital to this change, yet it followed from – and reinforced – the dissemination of Romantic ideas of the beneficence of nature by Victorian enthusiasts such as **William Morris** (1834–1896) and **John Ruskin** (1819–1900). Given that London's smoky yellow fog was the first atmospheric phenomenon to be *recognised* as melding weather and pollution, nature and culture, it makes sense for Jesse Oak Taylor to represent the novels of this period as 'climate models' that live 'at the intersection of literary and meteorological atmosphere' (2016: 10). As he puts it:

> Atmosphere is a concept manifest in works of literature, the air we breathe, and the skies overhead. Climate is a concept manifest in ideas, politics, cultural forms, bioregions, and weather patterns.
>
> (p.8)

When the term 'smog' was coined in 1905, combining 'smoke' and 'fog', it did not 'simply emerge at the intersection of nature and culture, it emerge[d] *as* that intersection' (p.3). Compare Taylor's claim with William Rueckerts's seminal *Literature and Ecology: An Experiment in Ecocriticism* (1978), which suggests that 'poems can be studied as models for energy flow, community building, and ecosystems' (Glotfelty and Fromm 1996: 110). Rueckerts warns against 'simple-minded analogical thinking,' (p.109) and yet the relationship he proposes between poetic and physical 'energy' is only ever metaphorical, whereas a contemporary scholar such as Taylor bases his argument on specific historical evidence and treats literature and science as distinct but integral partners in historical-environmental change (ch.8).

Just insofar as rhetoric alters the course of history, it takes sides in social struggles between genders, classes and ethno-racial groups. Cultures are not shaped equally by all their participants, nor are the many world cultures equally influential, and even tropes that might potentially confront or subvert environmentally damaging practices may be appropriated. Thus wilderness (ch.4), which advocates see as symbolising resistance to an industrialised, materialistic world view and social order, is also regularly depicted in advertisements as the 'natural home' of four-wheel-drive Sports Utility Vehicles. The terrible fuel economy of SUVs suggests that 'wilderness' has an ideological function in this case, helping to justify the conspicuous consumption of a privileged class and nation. Similarly ambivalent roles for environmental tropes recur throughout the book.

In ordinary usage, 'rhetoric' suggests language that displaces literal truth: it is all 'hot air.' The sense intended in this book, however, is emphatically interested in literal meaning. Unsurprisingly, many other fields of literary study emphasise the importance of language, as distinct from physical reality. Feminist literary theorists argue that apparently real or 'natural' categories such as gender difference are better understood as 'cultural constructions' that tell women how they *ought* to be, whilst pretending to say simply how they *are*. On this view, 'femininity' is not a natural or necessary consequence of being genetically or anatomically 'female', but rather a set of culturally prescribed behaviours. Feminist theory is therefore, in Kate Soper's terms, 'nature-sceptical' (1995: 34, cf. 119–48), in that it largely or wholly detaches the female sex from a 'constructed' feminine gender identity that lives only in language and culture. Judith Butler goes further in *Bodies That Matter* (1993): while she denies 'claiming that discourse causes sexual difference,' (p.1) she states that the *discourse* of 'sex' has 'the power to produce—demarcate, circulate, differentiate—the bodies it controls' (p.1). Following Butler, transgender theorists contend that biological sex difference is also a cultural construction, and that sex is 'assigned' (rather than discerned) at birth according to normative conventions. Soper disagrees with Butler, pointing out that 'It is precisely this conception of the body as a natural organism that must inform the idea of its being "produced" (confined, disciplined, distorted ...) by discursive formations and social and sexual norms and powers' (p.134). For Soper, nature-sceptical challenges to repressive stereotypes implicitly invoke human nature (as that which is oppressed) even as they dispute it.

'Constructionism' is a powerful tool for cultural analysis – I used it above in my discussion of the construction of 'pollution' – and yet it implies that 'nature' is only ever a cover for the interests of a privileged or embattled social group. The challenge for ecocritics is to keep one eye on the ways in which 'nature' is always in some ways culturally constructed, and the other on the fact that nature really exists, both the object and, albeit distantly, the origin of our discourse. Lawrence Buell calls this 'a myth of mutual constructionism: of physical environment (both natural and human-built) shaping in some measure the cultures that in some measure continually refashion it' (2001: 6). 'In some measure' sounds vague, but imprecision is unavoidable given the complexity of those reciprocally 'shaping' networks of nature and culture. Soper, likewise, advocates what she calls 'critical realism' about both humans and environments:

Bodies and landscape may be said to be culturally formed in the double sense that they are materially moulded and transformed by specific cultural practices and in the sense that they are experienced through the mediation of cultural discourse and representation. But they are not artefacts of culture, and it is no more appropriate to think of bodies and sexualities as the 'construct' of cultural practice and discourse than it is to think of the landscape as 'constructed' out of agricultural practices or as the discursively constituted effect of Romantic poetry.

(p.137)

Critical realism is my epistemological framework in this book, though I also question it in places (ch.7).

Ecocritics dispute the idea of science as wholly objective and value-free, so do not need to defer to ecology. Unlike other cultural critics, though, they cannot simply disregard scientific understandings of the world. To help them navigate these issues, ecocritics increasingly turn to the nearby field of Science and Technology Studies (STS), which:

... takes a variety of anti-essentialist positions with respect to science and technology. Neither science nor technology is a natural kind, having simple properties that define it once and for all. The sources of knowledge and artifacts are complex and various: there is no privileged scientific method that can translate nature into knowledge, and no technological method that can translate knowledge into artifacts. In addition, the interpretations of knowledge and artifacts are complex and various: claims, theories, facts, and objects may have very different meanings to different audiences.

(Sismondo 2010: 11)

I draw on STS research to illuminate climate science in chapter 8, 'The Earth'.

Buell's 'mutual constructionism', neat and useful as it is, nevertheless retains the metaphor of 'construction' itself, which can't help suggesting something like a building or a machine: an autonomous, intentional work of human minds and hands. Termites build enormous mounds, yet, biologists apart, few readers would think of them as 'social constructions'. STS scholar Ian Hacking observes in *The Social Construction of*

What? (1999) that 'construction' has become a dead metaphor, and comments:

> Anything worth calling a construction has a history. But not just any history. It has to be a history of building.
>
> (p.50)

This book explains how 'nature' has been, and continues to be, socially constructed. Pre-colonial Aboriginal Australians inhabited their landscapes as their home ('country' is the modern Aboriginal English term), and, guided by that perspective, practised forms of 'fire-stick farming' that rebuilt much of the continent into more congenial ecological patterns (Pyne 2019: 50). Settler colonial society, enculturated to see nature as a hostile enemy or economic resource, suppressed wildfires in Australia once they had the technological means, and their choice, too, changed the landscape: it built dense forest (pp.160–7). As Buell puts it, since 'human beings are **biocultural** creatures constructing themselves in interaction with surroundings they cannot not inhabit, all their artifacts may be expected to bear traces of that' (emphasis added, 2001: 2). The problem with the 'construction' metaphor is that it obscures, or mystifies, the natural basis of all human culture and exalts only our own powers as a species. We can forbid Indigenous 'fires of choice' (Pyne 2019: 52) in arid regions, but we cannot evade the natural consequence: far larger, fiercer 'fires of chance' (p.52). The anthropocentric implications of 'construction' are not easily avoided by a substitution of terms, but I tend to use 'shaping', 'elaboration' or 'inflection' to describe the complex transformations and negotiations between nature and culture, or between real and imagined versions of nature.

Returning to pollution with this in mind, we might observe that the rhetorical history of the term exists in an uneasy relationship with the truth claims of ecologists and environmental toxicologists. Techniques of chemical analysis have developed to the point where unimaginably small amounts of chemicals can be detected in the environment, while toxicologists warn that 'there is no relationship between toxic effects and our ability to detect a chemical' (Baarschers 1996: 47). Baarschers is critical of environmentalist 'hysteria' about chemicals in the environment at levels far below observable toxicity, and he is right to say that 'chemicals' are widely perceived as inherently dangerous and evil (p.42); few people understand any toxicology; and our personal risk assessments are subjective and incoherent (p.229). The false idea, or 'factoid', that 'synthetic' chemicals are inherently more toxic than the innumerable 'natural' ones, for instance, is an indirect legacy of Romanticism. Sociologists argue, though, that rather than divorcing the 'real risk' (as determined by toxicologists) from the 'perceived risk' felt by the public, we ought to see perceived risk as, ironically, a consequence of increasingly sophisticated surveillance. The more accurately the expert measures hazards, the greater the gap between official estimates of risk and my own assessment based on personal experience, a process of alienation Ulrich Beck describes as 'expropriation of the senses' (1999: 55). We can no longer assess risks by ourselves, and industrial safety scientists render risks less knowable and more fearful the more they try to dismiss them. At the same time, whole new types of pollution emerge even as industrial smoke and soot are eliminated: noise and light are considered pollutants, and anthropogenic carbon dioxide is classified by the US Environmental Protection Agency (EPA) as a pollutant despite the colossal amounts of it circulating in the atmosphere naturally.

Pollution is, then, disturbing and disorientating. We seem to be surrounded by threats we cannot perceive, avoid, or quantify, no matter how diligently we seek facts rather than 'factoids'. Ursula Heise sums up her authoritative survey of sociologists' accounts of risk in *Sense of Place and Sense of Planet* by saying it is a 'concept that encompasses far more than its technical or actuarial definitions to include complex cognitive, affective, social, and cultural processes without which it cannot be conceived, defined, or investigated' (2008: 130). Social theories of risk can benefit, she argues, from the methods of literary study, such as the identification of 'narrative templates' (p.122), or tropes, as I'm calling them, that frame and filter risk perceptions. Heise's explanation of why ecocritics should understand risk theory and vice versa underscores the interdisciplinarity that characterises the field:

> Not only is risk theorists' exploration of the ways cultural worldviews and institutions shape risk perceptions fundamental background knowledge for anyone interested in the forms that environmental art and writing have taken at different historical moments and in various cultural communities, but, inversely, literary critics' detailed analyses

of cultural practices stand to enrich and expand the body of data that an interdisciplinary risk theory can build on.

(p.136)

Like Jesse Oak Taylor, Heise shows how ecocriticism can contribute constructively to the diagnosis and resolution of ecological problems.

'Pollution' has seeped into our culture in many forms across a range of media. To help 'anatomize' it, Lawrence Buell sets out four criteria of 'toxic discourse' as a cultural genre: a 'mythography of betrayed Edens' (2001: 37) based, like Carson's parable above, in pastoral; horrified, 'totalizing images of a world without refuge from toxic penetration' (p.38) originating in the post-war fear of radioactive miasma from nuclear weapons; 'the threat of hegemonic oppression' (p.41) from powerful corporations or governments as contrasted with threatened communities; and the 'gothicization' of squalor and pollution characteristic of the environmental exposé. The legal drama *Erin Brockovich* (2000), based on a successful lawsuit of California power company Pacific Gas and Electric (PG&E), exemplifies several features of toxic discourse: the town of Hinkley is said to have been a 'real nice town' before it was contaminated by hexavalent chromium, but now the pollutant is understood to be everywhere. The company is only ever represented by creepy lawyers who seek to disclaim responsibility for the community's ills. The $333 million settlement functions in the movie as comeuppance for the company's misdeeds, even as financial compensation is acknowledged as unable to redeem physical suffering and death.

Texts preoccupied with toxicity, and even some movies, have moved beyond such stereotyped moral melodramas, and ecocriticism has developed sophisticated theoretical frameworks to engage with them. The most influential is Rob Nixon's *Slow Violence and the Environmentalism of the Poor* (2011), which brings a postcolonial ecocritical perspective to bear on a range of fictional and nonfictional witnesses to environmental destruction, mainly in the global South. Nixon defines his key phrase thus:

> By slow violence I mean a violence that occurs gradually and out of sight, a violence of delayed destruction that is dispersed across time and space, an attritional violence typically not viewed as violence at all.
>
> (2011: 2)

The fire at the Chernobyl nuclear power plant in 1986 involved spectacular violence, though the Soviet regime concealed it from the world. The slow violence of the longer-term effects of radiation, though, is harder to discern and represent. 'Victims' had to prove they deserved their status in a context where science, politics, law and environmental advocacy interacted in unpredictable ways. Their plight became still more complex in 1991 when the state in which the accident occurred, the Soviet Union, broke up. The 'intimate expertise that was both bodily and bureaucratic' (p.49) developed by Chernobyl victims also emerged among the survivors of a horrific release of poison gas from the Union Carbide plant in Bhopal, India, in 1984. Whilst around 8000 people died immediately or soon after the disaster, tens of thousands more were afflicted to some degree. As with Chernobyl, what Nixon calls 'biocitizens' had to prove that their injuries, illnesses and deformities qualified for compensation from the company, Dow Chemical, that bought Union Carbide in 2001.

Indra Sinha's novel, *Animal's People* (2009), based on Bhopal but set in the fictional parallel city of Khaufpur, has become canonical within ecocriticism. 'Animal,' the narrator, is a severely deformed young man who refuses to be defined by the event that poisoned him: 'Ous raat, cette nuit, that night, always that fucking night' (2009: 5). As this quotation suggests, Animal's voice is earthy, demotic, direct and devoid of self-righteousness. Unlike his neighbours, who seek justice, Animal mainly wants to have sex. The novel's plot ensures the 'Kampani' – fictional counterpart to Union Carbide – is subject to comic, if not legal, justice. Nixon's compelling account shows how the adolescent filth and rambunctious 'picaresque' journeying of *Animal's People* aligns surprisingly with *Silent Spring* in terms of the books' unfolding of time:

> Both Carson and Sinha ... strike a complex temporal note, through blended elegy and apocalypse, lamentation and premonition, inducing in us a double gaze backward in time to loss and forward to unrealized threats.
>
> (Nixon 2011: 64)

For Nixon, slow violence challenges us to 'devise arresting stories, images, and symbols adequate to the pervasive but elusive violence of delayed effects' (p.3). As we will see, the most pressing and difficult form of slow violence is climate change.

Where Nixon is indebted to postcolonial theory (ch.2), notably Ramachandra Guha and Joan Martínez Alier's advocacy of 'the environmentalism of the poor', (1998) Stacy Alaimo draws on STS and feminism for her theory of 'trans-corporeality'. Alaimo acknowledges why her feminist forerunners downgraded the biological body to highlight the mutability of gender, but insists that 'the notion of biology as destiny, which has long haunted feminism, depends on a particular – if not peculiar – notion of biology that can certainly be displaced by other models' (2010: 5). Thus reclaimed, the human body can be seen as enmeshed with, not separate from, innumerable Earth Others, from the microbiomes in our guts to the creatures we eat and live with. Alaimo explains that:

> By emphasizing the movement across bodies, trans-corporeality reveals the interchanges and interconnections between various bodily natures. But by underscoring that *trans* indicates movement across different sites, trans-corporeality also opens up a mobile space that acknowledges the often unpredictable and unwanted actions of human bodies, nonhuman creatures, ecological systems, chemical agents, and other actors.
>
> (p.2)

Like Heise, Alaimo explores her novel theoretical construct in relation to a wide range of texts, from Muriel Rukeyser's Modernist poetry to Todd Haynes's disquieting movie about multiple chemical sensitivity, *Safe* (1995). Her perspective, informed by ecofeminism and environmental justice (ch.2), shows that trans-corporeal movements of substances and meanings arise out of, as Lousley puts it, 'socially uneven encounters and entanglements.'

From this summary, we can see that environmental problems require analysis in cultural as well as scientific terms, because the answers to scientific 'problems in ecology' continually interact with cultural systems of value, meaning, beauty and risk that emerge and shift over time. Ecological problems are historical; they come into being through complex processes of **environmentality**, and some, such as acid rain, fade away though the good offices of science, technology, regulation and cultural change. Ecocritics draw on several other disciplines, including sociology of risk, postcolonial theory and STS, in these examples, to help them grapple with phenomena that, as Clark observes, risk proliferating into 'everything'. At the same time, the emergence of canonical literary texts helps the field to maintain coherence: in the case of pollution, these include Don DeLillo's *White Noise* (1984), Richard Powers's *Gain* (1998) and Helon Habila's *Oil on Water* (2010), besides *Animal's People*. By contrast with important strands in literary theory, ecocritics seek to balance the literal and figurative aspects of texts, and see 'culture' and 'nature' not as distinct domains in a hierarchical relationship, but as provisional fictions that are thoroughly interwoven, as in the term '**naturecultures**'. For this reason, ecocritics sometimes refer to phenomena such as the city of New Orleans, Hurricane Katrina, the psychopharmaceutical Prozac, or a Black girl's hair as '**material-semiotic**'; that is, just like Taylor's description of 'smog', as real and symbolic through and through (Alaimo and Hekman 2008). Effective communication is hampered, though, by the way leading ecocritics coin their own neologisms for very similar phenomena: Alaimo's 'trans-corporeality' is a lot like Timothy Morton's '**mesh**', Karen Barad's 'agential realism', Serenella Iovino's 'new materialism' (see ch.2), and STS scholar Andrew Pickering's 'mangle'. Perhaps we should invite some engineers to help us agree on a standard.

This book breaks the monolithic conceptions of 'nature' and 'environment' down into tropes so we can see the thematic, historical and geographical particulars of environmental discourse more clearly. It seeks to analyse critically the tropes brought into play in environmental debate, and, more tentatively, to predict which will have a desired effect on a specific audience at a given historical juncture. We can see from historical examples like acid rain and the thinning of the ozone layer that multidisciplinary research and political action *can* be successful, though climate change is an exceptionally daunting wicked problem that may be insoluble. Regardless, ecocritics feel duty-bound to pitch in. Indeed, the whole project of ecocriticism is motivated by environmentalist concerns, and so my account is, in that sense, biased. However, I strive throughout to represent diverse texts and positions accurately; to judge them by what they say rather than what they leave out; and to be clear and explicit about my own judgements. The difference between this approach, which I call '**multi-partiality**' (as distinct from impartiality), and the activist orientation of most ecocriticism is most obvious in the 'Indigeneity' chapter.

The next chapter outlines the main political and philosophical positions within the broad spectrum of environmentalism, in part to make clear that no single perspective unites all ecocritics. From Chapter 3 onwards, the analysis is arranged under the names of important ecocritical tropes, starting with 'Pastoral', the most deeply entrenched, and concluding with the construction of 'The Earth' as a whole. The internal structure of some chapters is different from previous editions, as explained in the Preface, with earlier ones focusing on historical origins and later ones assuming more dispersed 'rhizomic' or 'fascicular' structures. The chapters follow a rough trajectory from traditional concerns with the local to contemporary concepts of the global: from place to space, from earth to Earth. Chapters 3 to 5 examine a linked series of tropes that are indebted to the Euro-American Judaeo-Christian narrative of a fallen, exiled humanity seeking redemption, but fearing apocalyptic judgement: 'Pastoral', 'Wilderness', 'Apocalypse'. Chapter 6 asks why, and to what effect, we look at domestic and wild animals, and Chapter 7 explores the notion of 'Indigeneity' as the outcome of centuries of interaction, mostly conflictual but sometimes constructive, between European settler conceptions of 'Ecological Indians' and Indigenous traditions and innovations. In the final chapter, I explore the meanings that have clustered around the idea of the whole Earth, first pictured in NASA photographs in the 1960s, especially the suggestion that we are now living in a human-dominated geological epoch, the Anthropocene. The topic of climate change, which takes centre stage at the end, runs through the book just as it increasingly permeates our lives, polities and cultures.

2

POSITIONS

Environmental cultures are best understood with reference to the political and philosophical frames, or 'positions,' we bring to them. Each position understands environmental crisis in its own way, emphasising aspects that are amenable to solution in terms that it supplies or threatening to values it holds dear. Each one, moreover, might provide the basis for a distinct ecocritical approach with specific literary or cultural affinities and aversions.

Although they are presented here as distinct positions represented in ecocriticism by particular writers, the reader may identify with aspects of more than one position. Our own feelings and commitments are more complex and ambivalent than the labels would imply. Moreover, in our politically polarised societies, readers should heed psychologist Jonathan Haidt's advice: 'A good place to look for wisdom ... is where you least expect to find it: in the minds of your opponents' (2006: 242).

CORNUCOPIA

Despite the broad consensus among scientists about the environmental threats posed by modern civilisation, statistician Bjørn Lomborg argues in *The Skeptical Environmentalist* that most, if not all, such dangers are

DOI: 10.4324/9781003174011-2

illusory or exaggerated. He contests what he calls 'the Litany of our ever deteriorating environment' (2001: 3) by focusing on data showing fundamental long-term global trends that tell a different, more complex, story (pp.5–12). Despite Lomborg's title, though, his 'cornucopian' position supports environmental protection only to the minimal extent justified by economic benefit or human preference.

The positive claim of cornucopians such as Lomborg is that human welfare, as measured by long-term trends in literacy, life expectancy or calorie intake per person, has demonstrably increased along with global population, economic growth and technological progress. They argue that, in the long run, the supposed scarcity of natural resources is belied by falling prices of food, minerals and commodities relative to wages; as a specific resource becomes harder to obtain, the price increases, leading entrepreneurs to search for substitute sources, processes or materials. 'Scarcity' is an economic, not an ecological, phenomenon, which will be remedied by capitalism, not the reductions in consumption urged by environmentalists: 'The fact is that the concept of resources itself is a dynamic one; many things become resources over time. Each century has seen new resources emerge' (Beckerman 1995: 60). Wind was an important resource in the age of windmills and sailing ships, and is valuable again in the era of renewable energy. On this view, more people on the planet means more resourceful brains, more productive hands, more consumption and therefore more economic growth. In *The Rational Optimist* (2010), science writer Matt Ridley suggests that a middle-class Western family enjoys luxuries out of reach even to the 'Sun King' Louis XIV of France, the wealthiest man in the eighteenth century. The reason, he says, is that humans' ideas can be shared and conserved through generations: '[J]ust as sex made biological evolution cumulative, so exchange made cultural evolution cumulative and intelligence collective' (p.350). The future, therefore, is most likely rosy:

> So long as human exchange and specialisation are allowed to thrive somewhere, then culture evolves whether leaders help it or hinder it, and the result is that prosperity spreads, technology progresses, poverty declines, disease retreats, fecundity falls, happiness increases, violence atrophies, freedom grows, knowledge flourishes, the environment improves and wilderness expands.
>
> (p.358)

All but the last of these claims are defensible thanks to the astonishing bonanza of 'free' power derived from fossil fuels since the eighteenth century. It is, says Ridley, equivalent to 660 enslaved humans per average American, 360 per French person and 16 per Nigerian, or nearly a trillion for the global population in 2010 (p.236). However, the global environment has definitely not 'improved' by most measures, nor wildlands expanded in recent centuries, as the Worldwatch Institute's *State of the World* reports, for instance, track in grim detail from 1984 to 2017.

This book agrees that 'environmental problems', including resource depletion, are dynamic and historical (or 'socially constructed' (ch.1)), not simply objective facts. In this sense, some environmental problems, such as industrial smog, acid rain and CFC pollution of the ozone layer, have indeed come into being and been resolved, as discussed in the previous chapter. But Ridley's language ('disease retreats') suggests that these improvements happen by themselves, when the historical evidence shows that environmental remediation is usually hard-won in the teeth of strenuous opposition – from cornucopians.

Apart from conservative economists, cornucopian arguments are not generally accepted in universities; indeed, Lomborg's book was sharply critiqued by academics from a range of disciplines. Cornucopian views are more often disseminated by anti-environmentalist corporate lobby groups and 'think-tanks'. Whilst twentieth-century communists also believed in earthly cornucopia, its modern proponents are political conservatives who argue that dynamic capitalist economies spontaneously generate solutions to environmental problems as they arise. Cornucopian culture is both pervasive – especially in the USA – and ignored by ecocritics with the exceptions of Frederick Buell's *From Apocalypse to Way of Life* (2004), Sarah MacFarland Taylor's *Ecopiety* (2019) and Greg Garrard and colleagues' transnational study of *Climate Change Scepticism* (2019). This is unfortunate but not surprising: as persuasive as cornucopians' faith in human progress can be, they take little or no account of the non-human environment, as Lomborg states explicitly: 'the needs and desires of humankind represent the crux of our assessment of the state of the world' (p.11). Environmentalists advocate, by contrast, for value systems that take the intrinsic or inherent worth of non-humans and ecological systems as their starting point. Otherwise, we could end up glorious sovereigns of an impoverished planet.

ECOLOGICAL MODERNIZATION

'The tale of traditional environmentalism is one of sacrifice and struggle', according to Amanda Machin. 'The heroic figure of the ecologically minded citizen faces the daunting trial of ineradicable environmental limits: sustainability can only be won through the hardship of economic loss' (2019: 208). This inherently tragic storyline is deeply unattractive to politicians who wish to be elected, and so Western parties across the political spectrum have endorsed the alternative narrative of ecological modernisation (EM) in which economic growth and environmental protection are complementary:

> Not only does the [EM] discourse suggest that the environment might benefit through the innovation encouraged by market mechanisms, it also asserts that, conversely, the market can benefit from environmental challenges by implementing strategies and tools to protect the environment, [as] industries and businesses enhance their efficiency and the rising demand for green technology drives innovation and development.
>
> (p.211)

While EM advocates share the cornucopians' enthusiasm for capitalism, they also endorse political intervention in the form of incentives and regulations to guide entrepreneurial activity. EM's pro-market, pro-regulation combination appealed to the European Union, in particular, which adopted it in the late 1980s as a cornerstone of its emergent transnational identity and a potential source of market advantage with the USA.

EM's predominance in the political marketplace has invited much criticism. From the right, EM is attacked for imposing unnecessary regulations, which were identified with 'Brussels' (i.e. the European Union) in the UK before Brexit and are inaccurately conflated with socialism in the USA. Political ecologists (see below) argue that EM does not yield real environmental benefits. Richard York and Eugene Rosa state that 'contrary to predictions of [EM Theory], we have consistently found in analyses of a diversity of environmental impacts that the most highly modernized nations ... have the highest environmental impacts' (2003: 276). Whilst modernisation can lead to more efficient resource use, this frequently results in an increase in both production and consumption (p.280) – what is known as 'Jevon's Paradox' (ch.8). Moreover, as Machin points out, the EU's embrace of EM discourse effects a 'double depoliticisation' of environmental issues: 'on the one hand, politics is rendered unnecessary, since market mechanisms can deliver the solution; on the other, politics is made impossible, because the discourse is "common sense"' (p.224).

Academic initiatives from the quantitative disciplines such as Life Cycle Assessment and Environmental Impact Assessment align with EM's assumptions and objectives, but EM theory has found few defenders in the environmental humanities. Martin W. Lewis's *Green Delusions* (1992) combines a vigorous attack on radical environmentalism with a reformist programme that emphasises the role of science, technology and government policy change. Against the 'Arcadian' approach of radicals advocating de-urbanisation, use of non-synthetic products and low-technology solutions, Lewis's 'Promethean' environmentalism promotes the 'decoupling' of human economy and natural ecology, such as urban densification and further intensification of agriculture, in order to protect nature. The anti-interventionist, 'nature knows best' approach that Lewis ascribes to radical ecologists is inadequate: 'Prometheans maintain … that for the foreseeable future we must *actively manage* the planet to ensure the survival of as much biological diversity as possible. No less is necessary if we are to begin atoning for our very real environmental sins' (1992: 251). Lewis is a Senior Fellow at the Breakthrough Institute, a California think-tank that promotes EM. To date, though, no ecocritics have explicitly aligned themselves with EM.

ECOFEMINISM

Deep ecology (see p.33) identifies the anthropocentric dualism, humanity/nature, as the basis of anti-ecological beliefs and practices, but ecofeminism also questions the androcentric dualism, man/woman. Ecofeminism involves the recognition that these two arguments share a common 'logic of domination' (Warren and Wells-Howe 1994: 129) or underlying 'master model,' that 'women have been associated with nature, the material, the emotional, and the particular, while men have been associated with culture, the nonmaterial, the rational, and the abstract,' (Davion 1994: 9) and that this should suggest common cause between feminists and environmentalists.

Ecofeminism has been an important strand in academic and popular environmentalism since the 1960s, though the term was first printed in 1980. 'Radical ecofeminists' in the 80s and 90s attacked the hierarchy by reversing the terms, exalting nature, spirit, emotion and the human or non-human body as against culture, reason and the mind. Thus, Sharon Doubiago asserts that 'ecology consciousness is traditional woman consciousness'; 'Women have always thought like mountains, to allude to Aldo Leopold's paradigm for ecological thinking. (There's nothing like the experience of one's belly growing into a mountain to teach you this.)' (Doubiago 1989: 41, 42). Yet, most feminists argue against the acceptance of a 'feminine essence' grounded in biological sex, arguing instead that gender is culturally constructed. Even a positive valuation of femininity as 'closer to nature' thanks to female biology or social experience neglects the reality that all the gender distinctions we know have been constructed within patriarchal societies. Radical ecofeminism has been criticised by ecofeminists with a philosophical or sociological orientation (Warren and Wells-Howe 1994; Mortimer-Sandilands 1999), who point out that 'a truly feminist perspective cannot embrace either the feminine or the masculine uncritically, [but] requires a critique of gender roles, and this critique must include masculinity *and* femininity' (Davion 1994: 9). Greta Gaard (2017) dubs the new consensus 'critical ecofeminism'.

While Gaard cites numerous sources for critical ecofeminism, the presiding figure is **Val Plumwood** (1939–2008), whose *Feminism and the Mastery of Nature* is a persuasive account of ecofeminist philosophy. Plumwood argues that differentiating men from women, humans from nature, or reason from emotion, does not itself constitute problematic anthropo- or androcentrism. Rather, the underlying model of mastery shared by these forms of oppression is based upon *alienated* differentiation and denied dependency: in the dominant Euro-American culture, humans are not only *distinguished* from nature, but *opposed* to it in ways that make humans radically alienated from and superior to it. This polarisation, or 'hyperseparation', often involves a denial of the dependant relationship of the superior term to the inferior (1993: 47–55). So, for example, Plumwood shows how philosopher **René Descartes** (1596–1650) proposed an influential account of the difference between mind and body that struggled to eliminate all traces of the body from the domain of reason. He had to:

... reinterpret the notion of 'thinking' in such a way that those mental activities which involve the body, such as sense perception, and which appear to bridge the mind/body and human/animal division, become instead, via their reinterpretation in terms of 'consciousness', purely mental operations.

(p.115)

Descartes hyperseparated mind and body, and denied to animals not only the faculty of reason, but the whole range of feelings and sensations that he associated with thought. They were bodies without minds, effectively machines.

Plumwood critiques the gendered reason/nature dualism, which she presents as 'the overarching, most general, basic and connecting form' (p.44) of a historically varied series of dualisms. It serves this general analytical function because 'reason' has so often been called upon to hyperseparate both 'rational' men from 'emotional' women and humans from animals, and so can stand in for both dominant terms. She does not reject either science or reason, but critiques philosophies that polarise reason and nature in opposition: so, whereas scientific 'objectivity' historically decreed that any talk of intention or purpose in nature constitutes unscientific anthropomorphism (ch.6), Plumwood advocates a recognition of both similarity and difference in the human-nature continuum. We can continue to distinguish reason and emotion, man and woman, human and animal, whilst questioning their neurotic estrangement within the mainstream philosophical tradition. In doing so, the mastery model that legitimates anthropo- and androcentrism is undermined.

Reason, once rescued from its idealisation by androcentric philosophy, can acknowledge and respect 'earth others', avoiding both ultra-rationalistic alienation and animistic assimilation: 'We need to understand and affirm both otherness and our community in the earth' (p.137). This position rejects cornucopian dualism, which sees the rational human subject as entitled to dominate nature, along with simplistic monism, which risks submerging the distinctive capacities and needs of the human species in an undifferentiated, apolitical ecosphere. Still, the notion of 'hyperseparation' is clearly relative, and Plumwood does not specify the appropriate degree of separation of reason and nature, male and female, and so on. Moreover, as Damayanti Banerjee and Michael M. Bell argue, 'Patterns of domination of women and nature can be found in more societies than in the West, but Plumwood does not identify the logic of domination outside of the West' (2007: 8): as we see in chapter 7, also in pre-Christian Icelandic society. It is crucial to the ecofeminist case that, as Gaard puts it:

> Euro-Western culture is so permeated by Cartesian rationalism that children are taught at an early age not to receive—and certainly not to trust—the information being sent continuously by the animate world that surrounds us, and the diverse human communities with whom our lives are interwoven.
>
> (Gaard 2017: 23)

This is both a simplification and an exaggeration: **instrumental rationality**, which precludes consideration of Earth Others, takes many forms, most of them unconnected to Descartes, and, conversely, Euro-American culture is anything but wholly rationalistic, as Simon Schama explains: 'The cults which we are told to seek in other native cultures – of the primitive forest, of the river of life, of the sacred mountain – are in fact alive and well and all about us if only we know where to look for them' (1995: 14).

Ecofeminism is increasingly interwoven with other strands of environmental thought: Gaard sees the sustainability, environmental justice and ecofeminist movements as having 'synergistic potential', (p.35) despite their differing emphases, while Plumwood's later work gravitated towards **neo-animism**, a type of new materialism. Catriona Sandilands has pioneered ecofeminist analysis, dubbed 'queer ecology', that takes account of sexuality as well as gender. Its task:

> ... is to probe the intersections of sex and nature with an eye to developing a sexual politics that more clearly includes considerations of the natural world and its biosocial constitution, and an environmental politics that demonstrates an understanding of the ways in which sexual relations organize and influence both the material world of nature and our perceptions, experiences, and constitutions of that world.
>
> (2010: 5)

In concert with discussions in Human-Animal Studies about 'queer animals' (ch.6), queer ecology has generated innovative ecocritical readings, though it has also been criticised for selective use of scientific evidence (Garrard 2010).

POLITICAL ECOLOGY AND ENVIRONMENTAL JUSTICE

Political ecologists believe, with ecofeminists, that environmental problems follow from systems of domination or exploitation by other humans. Political ecology includes two factions traceable to nineteenth-century radical thought: eco-socialists are inspired by the communism of **Karl Marx** (1818–1833) and **Friedrich Engels** (1820–1895), and social ecologists draw on the anarchism of **Mikhail Bakunin** (1814–1876) and **Pyotr Kropotkin** (1842–1921). Social ecology and eco-socialism share the insight with cornucopian economists, whom they diametrically oppose politically, that the notion of ecological 'limits' is a kind of mystification. Radical ecologists (see p.30) fear that societies will 'overshoot' the capacity of natural systems to provide resources and absorb waste, but political ecologists counter that scarcity is actually created by capitalistic forms of production that depend on the manipulation of supply and demand. They claim that apparent 'limits' produced by capital's structural need for perpetual growth will disappear if we change the political organisation of society so that production to meet real needs replaces production for wealth accumulation. It is worth noting that, whilst this argument is persuasive in relation to resources and sinks, it is far less so when applied to non-substitutable and economically invisible resources such as freshwater aquifers or biodiversity. Eco-socialists differ from social ecologists such as **Murray Bookchin** (1921–2006) primarily in their vision of the ideal replacement for capitalist societies: the former seek a classless communist society (Pepper 1993: 207–8), whereas the latter envisage radical decentralisation along anarchist lines (Clark 1990: 9).

Eco-socialists continue to make important contributions to theorisations of the Anthropocene era (see ch.10) and urban political ecology (Walker 2012: 73), but the broader environmental justice (EJ) orientation has largely subsumed political ecology, probably because Americans tend to have an allergic reaction to 'socialism' and prefer to seek redress by judicial ('consequent') rather than political and regulatory ('antecedent') means. EJ started in the USA after the United Church of Christ published a national report in 1987 that claimed to show toxic waste facilities were disproportionately sited near racial minority communities (Walker 2012: 85) and then Robert D. Bullard wrote the provocatively-titled *Dumping in Dixie* (i.e. the former slave-holding American South) in 1990. Bullard explains how numerous social and historical factors combine to bring about environmental racism, including racially-biased enforcement action and White suburbanites' ability to organise to defend their neighbourhoods: 'Public officials and private industry have in many cases responded to the NIMBY [Not In My Back Yard] phenomenon using the Place-In-Blacks'-Back Yard (PIBBY) principle' (2019: 4). Allegations of environmental racism, though, were troubled by methodological difficulties, leading Christopher Foreman Jr to remark in *The Promise and the Peril of Environmental Justice* (1998) that 'Empirical support for claims of disproportionate pollution impacts and discriminatory regulatory enforcement is actually much weaker than environmental justice advocates usually admit' (1998: 3). Nevertheless, Foreman commends EJ advocates for resisting a purely technocratic framing, saying: 'activists and angry community residents are disinclined to allow epidemiologists, toxicologists and statisticians to define the premises of their movement' (p.61). Gordon Walker's balanced critical introduction to EJ is careful to distinguish between evidence of *unequal* exposure, itself contested, and normative claims that such inequality is necessarily *unjust*. Whilst Walker explains why robust quantitative evidence is hard to acquire (p.57), he goes on to describe advances in multi-factor quantitative and qualitative methods centred on 'particular cases, experiences and narratives' (p.61), both of which provide support for EJ advocacy. He concurs with Bullard and colleagues' 2008 finding that 'although the current assessment uses newer methods that better match where people and hazardous waste facilities are located, the conclusions are very much the same as they were in 1987' (pp.406–7).

Ecocritics who reference empirical EJ research seldom foreground either its complexity or its controversies. Nelta Edwards, though, acknowledges the methodological challenges in her study of the Alaskan Native community of Point Hope, where experts considered elevated cancer rates in the 1990s 'statistically insignificant' because of the small size of the population. When it was reported in 1992 that radioactive isotopes had been buried 30 years before at a nearby research site, Edwards states that 'community members in Point Hope, although furious about the deception, felt vindicated, for they had long suspected that buried poisons left by scientists had caused their cancer' (Adamson, Evans and Stein 2002: 108). In Edwards's analysis, scientists sent to investigate employed language 'to distort the "truth"' (p.110) through their 'overemphasis on smoking' (p.111) as a likely cause of the cancers, and by 'minimizing the amounts of radioactive material used in the ... experiment' (p.112). Edwards's ambivalence is instructive as she seeks to recognise local and Indigenous knowledge without completely dismissing the, potentially well-founded, claims of epidemiologists.

The normative element of EJ encompasses distributive justice, which seeks equal access to environmental goods and protection from harms; procedural justice, which mandates fair participation in decision-making processes (what Edward calls 'democratic epidemiology' (p.117)); and justice as recognition, which confronts 'practices of cultural domination and oppression, being rendered invisible through non-recognition, and being routinely maligned or disparaged in stereotypical and stigmatis-ing public and cultural representations' (Walker 2012: 50–1). Since issues of recognition are concerns of contemporary literary studies more broadly, it is easy to see why ecocritics endorse EJ enthusiastically. Whilst EJ emerged in the USA with a national and racial focus, it increasingly aligns with what Joan Martínez-Alier calls the 'envir-onmentalism of the poor', which 'builds on the premise that the fights for human rights and environment [in the Global South] are insepar-able' (2014: 240). In literary studies, ecofeminism and postcolonial ecocriticism are melding with EJ, and, as Gaard points out, incorporating 'intersectional' analyses 'in order to describe the "intra-actions" ... of race, class, gender, sexuality, ethnicity, age, ability, and other forms of human difference' (2017: 206). The result is a compelling synthesis of perspectives on social justice and environmental activism.

EJ and related approaches have rightly challenged the ethnocentrism of ecocriticism and drawn attention to the ways that relationships of power, privilege and oppression drive environmental destruction. EJ is, though, prone to exaggerate the strength of the relationship between social justice and environmentalism, as when T.V. Reed claims that 'environmental problems cannot be solved without addressing the dras-tic political and economic inequalities existing within and between nation states' (2009: 26). In fact, many *have* been solved, usually by political pressure, government regulation and technological change, while inequalities between nations decline because poor countries like

China get richer (at the expense of the environment), not because of global redistribution. Furthermore, EJ advocates often ignore the unpleasant reality that responding to marginalised groups' claims may itself have damaging consequences. Supporting the right of Native Americans in the Columbia River watershed to demand the removal of four hydroelectric dams to encourage salmon to return, Janice Johnson notes that they 'provide less than 5 percent of the region's hydropower' (Adamson, Evans, and Stein 2002: 269). This, though, is in a context where reducing the use of fossil fuels requires a dramatic and sustained *increase* in renewable energy capacity. Social justice and environmental protection are neither inherently opposed nor inevitably aligned.

RADICAL ECOLOGY

The central idea of radical ecology can be captured in one word: 'limits'. Humans have always known about ecological limits, and sought to live within or expand them (by selective burning or irrigation, say), but the formal conceptualisation of limits is credited to **Thomas Robert Malthus** (1766–1834). His 1798 book, *An Essay on the Principle of Population*, observes that:

> ... the power of population is indefinitely greater than the power in the earth to produce subsistence for man. Population, when unchecked, increases in a geometrical ratio. Subsistence increases only in an arithmetical ratio. A slight acquaintance with numbers will shew the immensity of the first power in comparison with the second.
>
> (1998: 4)

Every baby that survives to puberty can engender more babies, whereas a new field under cultivation does not yield yet more fields, so no matter how quickly agricultural production increases, the geometrical or exponential growth of population must outpace it. Contrary to the utopianism of **William Godwin** (1756–1836), Malthus argues that population will naturally increase to the point where some combination of sexual morality ('preventative checks') and 'misery and vice' ('positive checks' (p.4)) halts the growth. As Hannes Bergthaller observes, 'Efforts to circumvent this '"imperious all pervading [sic] law of nature" [p.5], Malthus argued, could only backfire: the English poor laws, for example, by alleviating the pressure of the positive checks, also removed the incentive to apply preventative checks, i.e. they encouraged imprudent reproductive behavior, and would in due course produce more misery' (2018: 41). This 'Malthusian curse' ensures that even egalitarian societies must eventually revert to conflict and competition for scarce resources.

Malthus was the first thinker to insist that social policy be guided by ecological necessity. His *Essay* founded the science of demographics and inspired **Charles Darwin** (1809–1882) and **Alfred Russel Wallace** (1823–1913) to conceive of an evolutionary struggle for survival, which in turn formed the basis of scientific ecology. Though he only appears in a footnote, Malthus is also the guiding spirit behind *The Limits to Growth* (1972), one of the most influential environmentalist books ever published. Subtitled, 'A Report for the Club of Rome's Project on the Predicament of Mankind', the book is the outcome of an international, interdisciplinary project to quantify and model the dynamic interactions between 'the five basic factors that determine, and therefore, ultimately limit, growth on this planet – population, agricultural production, natural resources, industrial production, and pollution' (Meadows et al.: 11–2). Employing a computer model developed at MIT instead of Malthus's 'acquaintance with numbers' (i.e. his mental model), the Club of Rome nevertheless projects 'overshoot' of some critical natural limit – on food production, pollution absorption, resource availability – and 'collapse' (p.125) by the year 2100. Changed assumptions about technological capacity, nuclear energy output, or agricultural efficiency only alter *when* the collapse takes place in the model world, not *whether* it occurs. Crucially, the Club of Rome emphasises that the graphs throughout the book 'are *not* exact predictions' but rather 'indications of the system's behavioral tendencies only' (p.93). Radical ecologists differ in their political responses to ecological limits, but they share the belief that 'the *essential* problem' – however long ingenuity may defer the reckoning – 'is exponential growth in a finite and complex system' (p.145). While specific scenarios of overshoot and collapse, like those in Paul Ehrlich's *The Population Bomb* (1968) (ch.5), have not come to pass, the existence of hard limits cannot be discounted, and we are still well within the hundred-year timespan of *The Limits to Growth*.

Within radical ecology, there are three sub-groups with distinct identities and emphases. *Neo-Malthusians* focus on overpopulation, by contrast with most environmentalists who downplay the role of human numbers (almost 8 billion in 2021) in growing ecological impacts. Dave Foreman, a founder member of the environmental activist organisation Earth First!, refers to a 'Man swarm' that 'swells like the black, living, withering mouth-clouds [of locusts] that have ransacked fields since the first digging stick scratched a line in dirt' (2011: xviii). He conveys our demographic takeover of Planet Earth by claiming that:

> 50000 years ago there were more tigers than *Homo sapiens*. More gorillas, more chimpanzees, more orangutans, more blue whales, more jaguars, more white rhinos. Today, for every wild tiger on Earth, there are *two million* human beings.
>
> (p.8)

Foreman argues against continued immigration to the USA because 'The world cannot afford more [affluent] Americans' (p.155), whilst insisting on the difference between his position and conservative 'immigrant-bashers': 'We need to say that the question is *how many* not *who*' (p.167). Despite their efforts to dissociate themselves from earlier Malthusians who dismissed social safety nets and promoted selective 'breeding' of valued types of humans, or 'eugenics', environmental neo-Malthusians have come to some 'chilling conclusions' (Bergthaller 2018: 42) about how societies should implement ecological limits. Ehrlich argued, for instance, that food aid and medical assistance to countries deemed incapable of self-sufficiency should be replaced by compulsory sterilisation and a 'triage principle' in famine relief (1971: 156). Such triage would categorise 'hopeless' countries and their inhabitants as exceptions (ideally temporary) to the notion of universal human rights, as Bergthaller points out:

> One of the most frequently heard criticisms of neo-Malthusian thinking is that it is inherently misanthropic and denies the dignity of human life. But this is at best a half-truth. Rather, what it implies is that human dignity requires self-limitation .... Because overpopulation threatens to debase all human lives and to make them expendable, the imperative of averting it entails that some of these lives may (or even must) be treated as debased and expendable.
>
> (pp.42–3)

Such rationality, or callousness, is needed because neo-Malthusians think humans cannot permanently escape the Malthusian curse.

In the 1990s, when ecocriticism was emerging as a distinct literary field, it was influenced by *deep ecology*, though the phrase seldom appears in contemporary research. The 'poet laureate' of deep ecology is Gary Snyder (ch.4) and its philosophical guru is **Arne Næss** (1912–2009). Næss sets out eight beliefs of deep ecologists in George Sessions's definitive anthology *Deep Ecology for the Twenty-First Century* (1995). The crucial ones are as follows:

1   The well-being and flourishing of human and non-human life on Earth have value in themselves (synonyms: intrinsic value, inherent worth). These values are independent of the usefulness of the non-human world for human purposes.

2   The flourishing of human life and cultures is compatible with a substantially smaller human population. The flourishing of non-human life *requires* a smaller human population.

(Sessions 1995: 68)

Deep ecologists are also critical of over-consumption in wealthy countries, which multiplies the impact of their populations.

Deep ecologists think that the first principle distinguishes them from mainstream environmentalists: where 'shallow' approaches take an instrumental approach to nature, arguing for preservation of natural resources only for the sake of humans, deep ecology demands recognition of intrinsic value in nature. They identify the dualistic separation of humans from nature promoted by Western philosophy and culture as the origin of environmental crisis, and demand a return to a primal identification of humans and the ecosphere. The shift from a human-centred, or anthropocentric, system of values to a nature-centred, or ecocentric, one is the core of the radicalism attributed to deep ecology, bringing it into opposition with much of Western philosophy and religion. Deep ecology is distinguished from neo-Malthusianism by its emphasis on spirituality and humane (albeit not just human) values. Ecocentrism encompasses belief systems derived from Eastern religions, such as Taoism and Buddhism; from heterodox Christians such as **St Francis of Assisi** (1182–1226) and **Pierre Teilhard de Chardin** (1881–1955); and from modern versions of Native American, pre-Christian Wiccan, shamanistic and other 'primal' religions.

Bioregionalism is the third strand of radical ecology. Kirkpatrick Sale's seminal *Dwellers in the Land* (1985) explains that a bioregion is an eco-political unit that respects the territories of pre-existing Indigenous societies, as well as the natural boundaries and constituencies of mountain range and watershed, ecosystem and biome. Opposing 'giantism' at every level, bioregionalists promote decentralisation of the economy, in the form of regional diversification and self-sufficiency, as well as the anarchistic dismantling of the centralised nation-state in favour of confederated self-governing communities of 1,000 to 10,000 people. Sale asserts that: 'Here, where people know each other and the essentials of the environment they share, where at least the most basic information for problem-solving is known and readily available, here is where governance should begin' (Sale 1985: 94–5). Bioregionalism is a politics of 'reinhabitation' that encourages people to explore the capacities and limits of the socio-ecological landscape in which they already live.

Bioregionalism may help make common cause between Indigenous communities, vernacular opponents of homogenising global culture and transregional environmental organisations working at a local level. Determining the boundaries of bioregions is not always straightforward, though. In North America and Australia, the sovereign state is larger than most bioregions, so there will be fewer collisions with pre-existing jurisdictions, but the same cannot be said of, say, the Jordan River watershed in the Middle East. Although, as Lawrence Buell points out, bioregionalists may not really be able to redraw political boundaries, they can 'provoke within and against ingrained [map-focused] grid-think keener attention to how interaction with topography, climate, and non-human life directs not only how people ought to live but also the way they *do* live without realizing it' (2005: 84).

A further objection is that forced and voluntary migration has changed the world's cultural landscape just as the movement of plant and animal species has transformed the world's biogeography. Mitchell Thomashow therefore argues for a paradoxical 'cosmopolitan bioregionalism':

> In the twenty-first century we face the prospect of multiple ecological and cultural diasporas, millions of migrants attempting to salvage their ecological and cultural integrity .... In the twenty-first century, having a homeland will represent a profound privilege. Living-in-place may become a quaint anachronism, reinhabitation a yuppie utopian vision.
>
> (2002: 123)

Bioregional ecocritics, especially in Western North America, seek to address these criticisms alongside readings of regional literatures that provide greater attunement to specific places (Lynch et al. 2012).

NEW MATERIALISM

The previous positions are influential both within universities and outside. Individual citizens, governments and environmental organisations draw on them to define and describe their viewpoints. New Materialism (NM), by contrast, is hardly known outside the environmental humanities. It has roots in several fields and disciplines, but is principally a philosophical movement inspired by the work of Gilles Deleuze and Félix Guattari, though this is an ironic description in its own right because, as the Preface explains, Deleuze and Guattari themselves disclaimed tree-shaped models of inheritance in favour of non-hierarchical 'rhizomic' networks of interconnection. NM also draws on Bruno Latour's research in Science and Technology Studies (STS), and on two ground breaking books: Karen Barad's *Meeting the Universe Halfway: Quantum Physics and the Entanglement of Matter and Meaning* (2007) and Jane Bennett's *Vibrant Matter: A Political Ecology of Things* (2010). By 'entanglement', Barad means both the uncanny phenomenon in quantum physics of action at a distance and a general condition of inseparability of the knower and what they know. Barad writes that: 'Individuals do not pre-exist their interactions; rather, individuals emerge through and as part of their entangled intra-relating' (2007: ix). Barad uses 'intra-relate' in place of 'inter-related' to dislocate our default assumption that human minds are separate from, and superior to, the things they know. Bennett's playful, overtly-speculative book focuses on agency, which she suggests is distributed throughout the world around (and inside) us, rather than being concentrated exclusively in human subjects. Indeed, *Vibrant Matter* rhetorically challenges the very idea of a 'self' as the author of our actions, including Bennett's own authorship of the book:

> The sentences ... emerged from the confederate agency of many striving macro- and microactants: from "my" memories, intentions, contentions, intestinal bacteria, eyeglasses, and blood sugar, as well as from the plastic computer keyboard, the bird song from the open window, or the air or particulates in the room, to name only a few of

> the participants. What is at work here on the page is an animal-vege-
> table-mineral-sonority [i.e. sound] cluster with a particular degree and
> duration of power. What is at work here is what Deleuze and Guattari
> call an **assemblage**.
>
> (2010: 23)

NM frequently includes such heterogeneous lists, which draw attention
to what Bennett calls 'thing-power', or the 'childhood sense of the world
as filled with all sorts of animate beings, some human, some not, some
organic, some not' (p.20). This resistance to hierarchies of being, such as
consciousness vs life vs lifeless matter, is called a 'flat **ontology**' because
all participants in an assemblage potentially have agency, hence meaning
and value. As Bennett admits, though, NM lacks inherent moral or
political significance (p.84), and since 'the perfect equality of actants'
(p.104) is both impossible and contrary to human self-interest, she merely
advises that readers 'proceed politically, technologically, scientifically, in
everyday life, with careful forbearance, as you might with unruly relatives
to whom you are inextricably bound and with whom you will engage
over a lifetime, like it or not' (p.116).

Like Plumwood's ecofeminism, NM sets itself in opposition to
'mechanical materialism' (p.91), which distinguishes dualistically
between human minds and a 'material world ... considered passive,
inert, unable to convey any independent expression of meaning' (Iovino
and Oppermann 2014: loc.207). While the resemblance is seldom
acknowledged, NM also recalls the monism and ecocentrism of deep
ecology, although Jeffrey Jerome Cohen calls NM 'dis-anthropocentric'
(2014: loc.328), which implies moving away from anthropocentrism
without ever being able to renounce it. In its ecocritical incarnation,
NM is unique in its insistence that, as Serenella Iovino and Serpil
Oppermann explain in their seminal anthology, 'a *material* ecocriticism
examines matter both *in* texts and *as* a text, trying to shed light on the
way bodily natures and discursive forces *express* their interaction whether
in representations or in their concrete reality' (loc.192). (*Italics* do a lot
of *work* in NM writings.) We saw in the Introduction that culture
changes the world and vice versa: defining wildfire as a foe rather than an
ally, and suppressing it on that basis, led to denser forests and, in recent
years, bigger conflagrations. Thus, say Iovino and Oppermann, 'material
forms—bodies, things, elements, toxic substances, chemicals, organic and

inorganic matter, landscapes, and biological entities—intra-act with each other and with the human dimension, producing configurations of meanings and discourses that *we can interpret as* stories' (loc.309, my emphasis). We might say that, taken together, aerial fire-bombers; fire scars on trees and soot deposits in lake sediments; Indigenous fire-keeping stories; heroic fire-fighting movies like *Only the Brave* (dir. Joseph Kosinski, 2017); and colonial fire-suppression legislation intra-act in a history that *can be interpreted* as an entangled, **material-semiotic** (ch.1) 'story' of arid Western landscapes, though none of these phenomena, from fire scars to movies, interpret themselves. In any case, Iovino and Oppermann's relatively cautious claim is soon revised to the stronger assertion that 'every living creature, from humans to fungi, *tells evolutionary stories* of coexistence, interdependence, adaptation and hybridization, extinctions and survivals' (loc.313, my emphasis). This vacillation between less and more controversial, or less and more anthropomorphic, claims is also typical of NM.

When Descartes argued in the seventeenth century that animals were indistinguishable from complex machines, some of his contemporaries disagreed. Today, it would be hard to find a defender of his view, yet NM relies on the universality of Cartesian dualism to motivate its alternative. The suggestion that living beings have the capacity to act autonomously, even unpredictably, is both unoriginal and barely controversial, so NM's distinctive claims are: that *matter* tells stories – Iovino and Oppermann speak of 'storied matter' (loc.184) – and that things ordinarily considered non-living – stones, bicycles, electricity networks and the like – have meaningful agency too. Val Plumwood's 'Journey to the Heart of Stone', for example, is an impassioned rejection of 'bullying concepts … such as anthropomorphism' (Plumwood 2007: 18), and a consequent call to 'reinvest with speech, agency and meaning the silenced ones, including the earth and its very stones, cast as the most lifeless and inconsiderable members of the earth community' (p.19). Oppermann, too, asserts that 'stone, like any other matter, moves, desires, and creates' (loc.876), while Gaard suggests that 'From a Buddhist perspective, … the imputed indifference of rocks and other minerals, might be better understood as equanimity, the ability to be present to life without placing conditions on how life shows up' (2017: 83). The obvious rejoinder is that rocks, unlike, say, humans and black bears, manifest no desire and never lose their equanimity, except when acted upon by an external force. Though Plumwood insists she is advocating for a materialist spirituality, not something supernatural, an 'old materialist' (i.e. geophysical) account of the observed behaviour of stone seems to explain it exhaustively, without the need for additional 'agency'. Hence Timothy Clark criticises some materialist ecocriticism as 'intellectually fragile' (2019: 111) thanks to its dependence on a 'heavily caricatured antagonist' (p.112): the notion that western thought allows only for human subjects and 'dead matter.'

It is to Iovino and Oppermann's credit that they include NM sceptics in *Material Ecocriticism*. Hannes Bergthaller, for instance, commends NM for liberating ecocriticism from the Romantic notion that modernity has estranged us from Nature (ch.3), then goes on to question Bennett's narrative of material co-authorship: '*As a book*, [Vibrant Matter] is composed not of blood sugar or bird-song, but only of a distinct series of letters—and that series of letters is largely indifferent to the particulars of its material instantiation: no matter whether they are printed on paper, displayed by an electronic reading device, or handwritten with a pencil, we still recognize them as versions of the same book' (loc.1066). Regardless of the assistance from caffeine or gut bacteria, Bennett's book is an intentional act of a distinctively human brain. Eco-narratologist Erin James incorporates NM in her theory by acknowledging elemental forms of 'material narrativity' such as 'ice cores, tree rings, and geological strata' (2022: 21), but she disagrees that one can 'read a mushroom, electricity, or plankton *as* a narrative, as those material realities lack the key components of this particular type of text: they do not have a narrator and a narratee, they do not sequence events in a particular timeline, etc.' (p.71) (see also Clark 2019: 108–11).

NM has injected lively prose, as well as lively 'storied matter', into the ecocritical corpus. It has drawn needed attention to the ways in which humans orchestrate technologies and Earth Others to achieve their ends, rather than ever truly *creating* anything, and underscored the reality that we are symbiotic organisms who became human by co-evolving with Earth Others, including dogs, fire-sticks, wheat, smallpox and, yes, gut bacteria (Haraway 2008). Nonetheless, the moment when the climate crisis asks us to take greater responsibility for the fate of the Earth, and to discriminate fairly amongst humans in terms of contributions and vulnerabilities, may not be the ideal time to encourage dispersal of responsibility across an assemblage of actants.

There is a saying: 'to a hammer, everything looks like a nail.' Thus, scholars working from these various positions define 'environmental problems' in ways that their preferred prescription – economic growth, gender equality and so on – can solve, and identify a related *root cause* of socio-environmental disruption, such as Plumwood's reason/nature dualism, which is frequently supposed to have begun at a particular moment of history. Schama criticises such 'penitential' histories, which 'differ [only] as to when the Western fall from grace took place' (p.13). They also necessarily ignore or minimise remarkable achievements of modernity, such as the spread of literacy and the elimination of many infectious diseases, making them just as implausible as cornucopian narratives that pretend modernity is *good* for the environment. Furthermore, a large-scale environmental challenge such as climate change is a vast 'wicked problem' (Hulme 2009: 334) that has neither a single cause nor a 'silver bullet' solution (ch.8). According to Clark, ecocritics, as lovers of books and ideas, are especially prone to the fallacy of 'ascribing most problems and ills of the world to some sort of intellectual mistake or set of false assumptions, as if all of human society were an academic seminar writ large' (p.115). Scholars who remain humbly aware of the limits, as well as the capabilities, of any one position or academic discipline are more likely to contribute constructively to addressing wicked problems.

3

PASTORAL

OLD WORLD PASTORAL

As we have seen (ch.1), Rachel Carson's 'A Fable for Tomorrow' begins
with pastoral imagery that contrasts with the fallen landscape blighted
by pesticide pollution. Just as Carson places the unblemished land in
the past, so the first book of the Christian Bible and Jewish Torah,
Genesis ('Bereshit' or 'in the beginning' in Hebrew), describes a Garden
of Eden created by God for the use and pleasure of Adam and Eve, the
first humans: 'And out of the ground made the LORD God to grow
every tree that is pleasant to the sight, and good for food' (KJV 2:9).
Tempted by a serpent, identified by tradition with God's enemy Satan,
Adam and Eve eat forbidden fruit from the tree of knowledge of good
and evil, and are ejected from the Garden into a mortal existence of woe
and hardship. The first recorded formal gardens were grown at least
2500 years ago in ancient Persia, and were called 'paradise', from the
Persian *pairidaeza* (meaning 'enclosure' or 'park'), by Greek admirers,
who later gave that name to the garden of Eden. Islamic invaders of
Persia in the seventh century CE endowed the existing walled gardens
with the symbolism of Paradise in the Koran (Remington, Goodsir and
Strong 2015: 10). **Hesiod** (c.750–650BCE), a Greek poet, describes a

DOI: 10.4324/9781003174011-3

past age in which 'a golden race of mortal men ... lived like gods without sorrow of heart, remote and free from toil and grief' in his *Works and Days* (ll.109–120), and goes on to tell of ages of silver, bronze, and heroes, each more violent than the last, culminating in the poet's own age, that of iron, of which he says: 'would that I ... had either died before or been born afterwards' (ll.170–201). Many other cultures have origin stories of peace and plenitude, which mankind disrupted. Whereas Adam named the animals after Jehovah created them, though, Indigenous North American stories (ch.7) often depict humans as late arrivals to a world that belonged first to other animals, and 'we learned to be human in large part from the land and our other-than human relatives' (Justice 2018: 76). Hesiod's mythic **declensionist historiography** has its counterparts in some environmentalist metanarratives, in which modernity – whenever it began – is a fallen condition by comparison with a pastoral origin.

Pastoral has a narrower sense, also rooted in the ancient Mediterranean, of poems and stories about retreat from the city to the countryside. It originates in the *Idylls* of the Alexandrian poet **Theocritus** (c.318–260BCE), a collection of 30 poems in which Sicilian shepherds sing songs to woo shepherdesses and win competitions. Theocritus' poems are less idealised than we might imagine, including both hard work and earthy humour. 'Idyll V' includes references to bestiality and hetero- and homosexual lust, whilst 'Reapmaster Milton' of 'Idyll X' counters Boucaeus' lovelorn song with more pragmatic verses of his own: 'let the reapers rise with the rising lark, rest in the heat, and not leave off till dark' (1978: 100). The natural environment is carefully observed too: Chris Fitter commends Theocritus' 'assiduous naturalism' and 'correct natural history' that 'embed a paradisal tonality in the closely mapped familiar world' (1995: 41). Thus, the *Idylls* show that civilised poetic artifice need not be the enemy of 'naturalism'. The pastoral tradition after Theocritus revolves around three terms: 'idyll' or *eidullon*, originally the 'small picture' or poetic vignette, which came to mean the idea of rural escape or repose itself; 'bucolic', deriving from *boukolos* meaning 'cowherd', one of the typical singers of the idyll; and 'pastoral', a term of Latin origin retrospectively applied to Theocritus' work thanks to the shepherds (Latin *pastor*) therein. The later pastoral tradition follows 'Idyll VII' in contrasting the frenetic, corrupt, impersonal city, in which its audiences lived, with the peaceful, abundant countryside.

The Roman poet **Virgil**'s (70–19BCE) *Eclogues* allude to Theocritus frequently, but are set in faraway Arcadia, then a remote region of present-day Greece. As we saw in chapter 2, Martin Lewis distinguishes what he sees as progressive, 'Promethean' environmental modernisation from nostalgic 'Arcadian' types of radical ecology, which suggests that word still has backward-looking connotations. Timothy Saunders's sprightly revisionist reading, though, prefers to call Virgil's poems 'bucolic' rather than pastoral, and sets out to 'place rather less emphasis on the *Eclogues*' intermittent concern with absence, melancholy and loss, and rather more on their range and complexity, as well as on their audacity, novelty, ambition and wit' (2013: 2–3). It was, though, the melancholic Virgil that had an enormous influence on later pastoral poetry, especially English Renaissance verse. The received version of Virgil is also a point of departure for two proto-ecocritical studies of pastoral, **Leo Marx**'s (1919–2022) *The Machine in the Garden* (1964) and *The Country and the City* (1973) by **Raymond Williams** (1921–1988). Whilst Marx is scathing about pastoral as a 'cultural symbol' in American culture, calling it 'the starting point for infantile wish-fulfillment dreams, a diffuse nostalgia, and a naïve, anarchic primitivism', he elevates Virgil as the model of serious American pastoral writing 'that is invaluable for its power to enrich and clarify experience' (2000: 11). He thus distinguishes between popular 'sentimental' pastoral and its 'complex' literary counterparts, which 'qualify, or call into question, or bring irony to bear against the illusion of peace and harmony in a green pasture' (p.25). Williams, a Marxist critic, draws attention to the politics of eviction and dispossession in the *Eclogues*, and even identifies a prophetic moment in 'Eclogue IV' that hints at utopian possibilities. For Williams, pastoral has always been characterised by nostalgia, and so, no matter where we look into its history, we will see what he calls an 'escalator' taking us back further into a supposedly better past. At the same time, he argues, 'what seemed a single escalator, a perpetual recession into history, turns out, on reflection, to be a more complicated movement: Old England, settlement, the rural virtues – all these, in fact, mean different things at different times, and quite different values are being brought into question' (p.12). In an era of ecological change far more rapid than any lamented by Theocritus and Virgil, we may need to reclaim nostalgia rather than dismiss it, as we will see.

Taking our cue from Williams, we can identify three temporal orientations of pastoral: the *elegy* looks back to a vanished past with a sense of nostalgia; the *idyll* celebrates a bountiful present; the *utopia* looks forward to a redeemed future. Once schematised like this, the relationship of pastoral and the Judaeo-Christian conception of time becomes clear: Genesis 3, the story of Man's fall, is essentially an elegy of lost pastoral bounty and innocence. In **John Milton**'s (1608–1674) *Paradise Lost* (1667), an elaboration upon Biblical materials, pastoral Eden is influenced by Graeco-Roman models, and Man's Fall partakes in a shared elegiac mood: 'O unexpected stroke, worse than of death! / Must I leave thee Paradise?' (1992: Book XI. ll.268–9). At the same time, the series of covenants between God and Man offers the possibility of present grace, as for example after the Flood, when God promises that nature will be sustained as part of a renewed covenant, and as chapter 5 explains, the end of the world presaged in the *Revelation* of St John is a utopia – for the chosen few.

As humanistic thought emerged in Europe, starting in the fourteenth century CE, scholars looked to Greek and Roman sources, in addition to or instead of Judaeo-Christian ones, to inspire what came to be known as 'the Renaissance', or 'rebirth'. As such, classical authors not only founded the pastoral genre, but were, as Brooke Holmes explains, intentionally chosen as progenitors (Holmes 2017). In visual art, **Nicolas Poussin** (1594–1665) and **Claude Lorrain** (1600–1682) painted Biblical and classical figures in idealised, yet richly detailed, landscape settings, some explicitly identified as a 'Pastoral Landscape' or 'Arcadia'. Their neo-classical work epitomised the 'picturesque' style, and it made landscape painting into a more credible art form. In the eighteenth century, British aristocrats transferred painted landscapes back onto real ones, remodelling estates like Stowe and Stourhead in the 'British Virgilian' style (Schama 1995: 539), in which temples, obelisks and waterfalls could be glimpsed within carefully planned vistas. At the same time, tourists of the picturesque in places like Britain's Lake District might carry a 'Claude-glass', a pocket mirror (sometimes rose-tinted) with which they could frame appropriate scenery. Just like selfie-seekers, Claude-glass users turned their backs on the physical landscape, sometimes with disastrous effects.

Terry Gifford recounts the literary part of this history in *Pastoral* (2nd edn, 2019), a book in the New Critical Idiom series that gives a fuller account of the topics discussed here, and elsewhere the same author reviews the major ecocritical treatments of pastoral (Gifford 2017). The pastoral genre just described is the first of four senses of the term that

Gifford distinguishes. The second sense is 'any literature that describes the country as providing an implicit or explicit contrast to the urban,' (p.2) which aligns with Marx's description of sentimental pastoral. The third sense, which predominated in Marxist criticism after Williams, is 'pejorative, implying that the pastoral vision is too simplified and thus an idealisation of the reality of life in the country,' (p.2) while the fourth is simply books about sheep and other grazing animals. Gifford goes on to refine his influential notion of 'post-pastoral', an ecologically-attuned revision discussed below.

For Williams and his successors, the complexity of classical pastoral was stripped away as the genre was adopted by poets wishing to flatter their lordly sponsors by praising the beneficence of their country house. Pastoral imagery, says Williams, came to exist 'not in a living but an enamelled world' (p.18). Certainly, if Renaissance pastoral is nothing more than 'political allegory [that] had little to say about the actual environment' (Gifford 2019: 202), the pejorative sense of 'pastoral' would be justified. Ken Hiltner's *What Else Is Pastoral?* (2011), though, persuasively overturns the Marxist view, not by denying the political uses of the genre, but by attending to the environmental history of England in the sixteenth and seventeenth centuries. London, especially, was transformed in this period: its population grew *tenfold* while its infrastructure was barely improved. Poets did need to toady to aristocrats, just as Williams argues, but their aversion to the polluted city and desire for pastoral retreat were more than merely conventional. Indeed, he suggests that we read London itself as an ironical work of pastoral art that revealed the English countryside to artists: 'as early modern London contrasted so strikingly with its surroundings, the endangered environment encircling the city would have been revealed ... in an entirely new manner by this city work' (p.48). Hiltner contends that Renaissance pastoral is characterised by 'a general lack of lavish mimetic images, a sense of the country being opposition to the city, belief in an immanent God, a deep appreciation for plants and animals, and intense feelings for the environment' (p.88), which is a very different picture to the pejorative Marxist one.

Hiltner's revaluation needs to be qualified, in some respects, by another study of the period, Robert N. Watson's *Back to Nature: The Green and the Real in the Late Renaissance* (2006). While Watson, too, presents pastoral poetry (among other artefacts) as more than political allegory, he tends instead to render it as philosophical allegory. He sees Renaissance art as manifesting epistemological anxiety about visual and verbal representations getting between us and reality, and develops a witty, wide-ranging account of art's inevitable failure to assuage the anxiety: 'As the persistent references to the Garden of Eden suggest, the movement back to nature was partly a code for a drive back toward some posited original certainty – a drive baffled by paradox and by history, leaving the pastoralist merely posing with his back to nature' (p.6) – as with a Claude-glass, say. Romantic environmentalists and deep ecologists think that urbanisation and technological comforts alienate us from nature, and prescribe immersive experiences to return us to it. For Watson, though, our supposed estrangement is really just a trick Western culture played on itself: once the anxiety about mediation was aroused, every attempt to circumvent it in art – in the stunning exactitude of **Johannes Vermeer**'s (1632–1675) paintings, for example – only made it worse. After all, the more we try to bridge the gap between mind and matter with words, the more words we have: 'The nostalgia for a world of unmediated things manifested itself as a fabric of language' (p.72). For Watson, late Renaissance pastoral is a stylised literary genre that seeks, impossibly, to circumvent itself.

Pre-ecocritical discussions of pastoral in the Romantic period suggest that it saw a decisive shift towards a more 'ecological' orientation. Keith Thomas's summary of eighteenth century environmental culture in *Man and the Natural World: Changing Attitudes in England 1500–1800* (1983) states that:

> ... there had gradually emerged attitudes to the natural world which were essentially incompatible with the direction in which English society was moving. The growth in towns had led to a new longing for the countryside. The progress of cultivation had fostered a taste for weeds, mountains and unsubdued nature. The new-found security from wild animals had generated an increasing concern to protect birds and preserve wild creatures in their natural state. Economic independence of animal power and urban isolation from animal farming had nourished emotional attitudes which were hard, if not impossible, to reconcile with the exploitation of animals by which most people lived.
>
> (1983: 301)

For Thomas, Romanticism is the high point of a counter-modernising movement that had taken shape in the previous century. His contemporary, Raymond Williams, also took a broadly positive view of Romantic pastoral, as indicated by the shift in *The Country and the City* from mid-eighteenth century 'Pleasing Prospects' to 'The Green Language' of Romanticism. Later Marxist critics in the 1980s were less indulgent, analysing canonical authors such as **William Wordsworth** (1770–1850) as poets of pastoral in Gifford's third, pejorative, sense of the word. It was in this context that Jonathan Bate's *Romantic Ecology* (1991) set out to recover Wordsworthian pastoral as a forerunner of the renewed environmental activism that followed the discovery of a 'hole' in the Earth's ozone layer in 1985 and the 1990 publication of the First Assessment Report (FAR) of the Intergovernmental Panel on Climate Change (IPCC) (chs.5 and 8). In American ecocriticism, Lawrence Buell's *The Environmental Imagination: Thoreau, Nature Writing, the Formation of American Culture* (1996) likewise placed the work of **Henry David Thoreau** (1817–1862) at the head of a newly-relevant tradition of nature writing. Jeremy Davies's review, 'Romantic Ecocriticism: History and Prospects', acknowledges the 'invigorating' effect of Bate and his successors, but warns that what he calls 'idealist ecocriticism' is 'too often … a way of reading that simply imposes upon Romantic writings the assertion that they foreshadow, intuit, or preview the critic's own views about environmental issues' (2018: 6).

The risk of presentism or anachronism is reduced if past and present appear in a dynamic relationship, as in Kate Rigby's *Reclaiming Romanticism: Towards an Ecopoetics of Decolonization* (2020), rather than a linear one of supposed 'influence'. Rigby acknowledges the contribution of European Romantic poets to colonial culture, and yet she elicits their 'potentials for a decolonizing praxis' (p.4) by putting them into conversation with, among others, contemporary Black American and Australian Aboriginal poets. **John Clare** (1793–1864), a poet and agricultural labourer, is a pivotal figure for Williams, Bate and Alan Bewell (see p.47), as well as Rigby, in this instance for his 'attention to empirical detail' (p.96), compared to contemporaries, and for his introduction into the pastoral tradition of 'a whole new attentiveness to the particularities of [his] other-than-human fellow creatures, and the varied perils that they faced' (p.94). Clare's 1820s poem, 'Wild Bees,' for example, names identifiable species and sketches their behaviour – even when it's 'threatening' (p.96). Rigby puts what she calls Clare's 'crea-turely' ecopoetry (p.99) in dialogue with African-American poet Nata-sha Trethewey's 'Carpenter Bee' (Dungy 2009: 143) in order to 'reclaim' him from colonial versions of Romanticism. In seeking to disentangle Romanticism from colonialism, Rigby's account is more ambivalent than Bate's 'wholly affirmative' (p.2) one. Nevertheless, they both assume that apparent continuities of implicit values between the Romantic period and the present matter more than the enormous cultural and ecological discontinuities.

A contrasting historical materialist methodology indebted to Marxist forerunners animates Alan Bewell's fascinating *Natures in Translation: Romanticism and Colonial Natural History* (2017). Bewell focuses on the vital role of natural history, especially botany, in advancing European colonial-ism, and he contradicts Thomas and Bate when he observes that 'The cul-tural preoccupation with nature was thus often just as much a product and expression of modernity as a reaction against it' (p.6). His methodology encompasses 'both the new physical natures that were transferred and resettled across the planet and those that appeared as representations on the pages of philosophical, literary, and scientific texts,' (p.8–9) although by contrast with New Materialists (ch.2), Bewell examines the interaction of 'colonial natures' and British imperial culture rather than collapsing them into a single 'story'. In the case of Tahiti, inhabited by Polynesians for at least 900 years by the time Captain Samuel Wallis arrived in 1767, Bewell compares the historical ecology of the island with written accounts of Eur-opeans such as **Admiral William Bligh** (1754–1817), captain of the mutinous *Bounty*. He notes that 'Although Polynesians had introduced about thirty domestic and fifty accidental species …, the island [in 1767] is estimated to have had about seven hundred indigenous species of plants, of which roughly 60 percent were endemic to French Polynesia' (pp.108–9). Today, 'having lost one-third of its indigenous species, and having gained more than fifteen hundred exotic species, Tahiti is essentially a cosmopolitan nature, with three times as many immigrant as native plants' (p.109). When Bligh visited the island in 1788 it was already populated by Eur-opean pigs, cattle, cats and rats, plus peppers and pineapple from South America, Mexican pumpkins, Persian figs and pomegranates, and oranges from tropical Asia. He took away hundreds of seedlings of the native breadfruit plant, which is now a staple food in Jamaica. In contrast to postcolonial scholars like Beth Tobin in *Colonizing Nature* (2005), Bewell sees both loss and gain in this vast global redistribution of species, depicting British Romanticism as part of a remarkable 'translation culture' that plans, records, celebrates, and sometimes mourns colonial power over plants. Not only is Romantic environmentalism quite different from our own, according to Bewell, the natures it describes are often changed beyond recognition: 'At every point one sees natures that exist no more or that were in the process of becoming traces' (p.51). The empirical and textual evidence in Bewell's book underlines the vital point that 'Nature' is neither monolithic nor ahistorical, and a materialist ecocriticism interested in historical sources must be responsive to ecological as much as cultural discontinuity.

Early ecocritical treatments of pastoral were initially 'affirmative' because they were reacting against the what Kate Soper dubs the 'nature-scepticism' (1995: 34) of Marxist, deconstructionist and postmodernist critics of the 1980s, and they promoted a consensus that the Romantic period saw a revolution in attitudes to nature. Hiltner, though, identifies genuinely 'nature-endorsing' elements (alongside necessary praise of lordly patrons) in much Renaissance poetry, and Bewell shows how Romantic-period writers both participated in and critiqued the colonial re-ordering of global natures. Indeed, as Soper reminds us:

> The societies that have most abused nature have also perennially applauded its ways of those of 'artifice', have long valued its health and integrity over the decadence of human contrivance, and today employ pastoral imagery as the most successful of conventions to enhance the profits on everything from margarine to motor-cars.
>
> (p.150)

The keynote, then, is ambivalence towards pastoral: if it is not inevitably idealising, it is also far from revolutionary, even in seemingly affirmative forms.

COLONIAL AND BLACK PASTORAL IN AMERICA

The following poem by the African-American poet **Lucille Clifton** (1936–2010), which I include in its entirety, stands as an epigraph to two pivotal books on Black Americans and the environment: Camille Dungy's *Black Nature: Four Centuries of African American Nature Poetry*

(2009) and Carolyn Finney's *Black Faces, White Spaces* (2014), a detailed examination and refutation of the widespread 'misperception that non-white people are simply not interested' (p.79) in environmental issues:

> Surely i am able to write poems
> celebrating grass and how the blue
> in the sky can flow green or red
> and the waters lean against the
> chesapeake shore like a familiar,
> poems about nature and landscape
> surely but whenever i begin
> "the trees wave their knotted branches
> and ..." why
> is there under that poem always
> an other poem?
>
> (Dungy 2009: vii)

'Surely' the speaker can write nature poems – indeed, we are reading one – and yet she always senses a duality between 'that poem' of celebration the speaker starts to write and 'an other' poem beneath that threatens to disrupt it. This section explores that duality.

Perhaps the other poem is 'The Haunted Oak' (1901) by **Paul Laurence Dunbar** (1872–1906), a dramatic monologue voiced by a tree used for a lynching:

> I feel the rope against my bark,
> And the weight of him in my grain,
> I feel in the throe of his final woe
> The touch of my own last pain.
>
> (p.160)

Or **Alice Dunbar-Nelson**'s (1875–1935) 'April is on the way', which includes in its painfully ambivalent heraldry of Spring the line: '(Willow trees are kind, Dear God. They will not bear a body on their limbs.)' (p.104). Poems protesting the racial terrorism of lynching, as much as the photographs proudly taken by White participants, helped imbue trees with horrific associations that explain Clifton's inability to celebrate them unequivocally (see Finney: 119).

Pastoral is a myth of natural harmony and plenitude, especially in its 'sentimental' popular form, and so it was frequently evoked by European settlers to make their occupation and 'taming' of colonised places seem natural – even in Australia and South Africa where the climate and landscape were uncongenial (Huggan and Tiffin 2015: 98–126). In eighteenth century America, as Paul Outka explains in *Race and Nature* (2008), 'The beaten wild, aka pastoral, became both a sign of the European settler's power, the corpse of a defeated champion, and the face of nature itself' (p.29). Later, in the nineteenth century, settlers lamented the loss of wilderness, as we'll see in the next chapter, but in the early years of the Republic the dominant view was that America's seeming inexhaustibility made pastoral a practicable reality, not a fantasy as in Europe. Leo Marx's prime example is *Notes on the State of Virginia* (1785) by **Thomas Jefferson** (1743–1826), a slaveholder and America's third president: 'Nowhere in our literature is there a more appealing, vivid, or thorough statement of the case for the pastoral ideal ...' (p.118). Yet, as Sally Smits Masten's analysis shows, 'The exile and genocide of the Native Americans and the stain of continuing enslavement of African Americans haunts Jefferson's *Notes* ... as if these crimes were insuppressible and demand to be countenanced' (2016: 19). While White American men, including abolitionists like Thoreau, were defining wild nature as a space of freedom and rejuvenation, the enslaved Black American remained, as Outka shows, 'part of nature, a "brute" and not a wagon, a domesticated animal and not just capital' (p.55). Like livestock, slaves could be valued for their specific capabilities and, at the same time, treated as wholly dispensable by their owners.

As the northern states industrialised, especially during and after the American Civil War (1861–1865), the South became the default 'pastoral scene' in American literature, popular music and visual art. This 'vision of the South – replete with blooming magnolias, verdant landscapes, white-columned mansions, and a happy African American labor force' (Anderson 2019: 577) – belied wartime deforestation, soils exhausted by cash-cropping, and the brutal imposition of 'Jim Crow' laws that segregated Black and White Americans, extending the social conditions of slavery after its formal abolition. In post-War southern pastoral, 'Negro' characters such as 'Uncle Remus' and the narrators of popular songs like 'Trabling back to Georgia' or 'Alabama Blossoms' (p.592) transition from mere scenery to ventriloquized defenders of the pre-war White supremacist order. Responsive to the market, even a Black writer like **George Marion McClellan** (1860–1934) evokes southern pastoral in his 1916 poem (set in an imagined Mississippi in 1852), 'A September Night':

> Begirt with cotton-fields Anguilla sits
> Half bird-like dreaming on her summer nest
> Amid her spreading figs and roses still
> In bloom with all their spring and summer hues.
>
> (Dungy 2009: 22)

'A Black Man Talks of Reaping' (1926) by **Arna Bontemps** (1902–1973), a poem of dispossession, is much more typical though:

> I scattered seed enough to plant the land
> in rows from Canada to Mexico
> but for my reaping only what the hand
> can hold at once is all that I can show.
>
> (p.95)

It is an example of 'poems written from the perspective of workers of the field', of which Camille Dungy asks rhetorically:

> Though these poems defy the pastoral conventions of Western poetry, are they not pastorals? The poems describe moss, rivers, trees, dirt, caves, dogs, fields: elements of an environment steeped in a legacy of violence, forced labor, torture, and death.
>
> (p.xxi)

If so, they are examples of ambiguous, or complex, pastoral, albeit far more pointed in their exposure of Marx's 'illusion of peace and harmony' than writings by White authors.

Cane (1923) by **Jean Toomer** (1894–1967) is arguably the most remarkable text of the Jim Crow era (1877–1964) to engage poetically with southern pastoral. Toomer was the son of a wealthy mixed-race mother and an emancipated slave who adopted his previous owner's name. He was socially defined as 'colored' growing up and categorised as a 'Negro writer' as an adult, but he eventually rejected all prescribed 'racial positions' and defined himself as 'American', by which he meant a post-racial identity 'of which', according to George Hutchinson, 'he considered himself the first conscious member' (Toomer and Hutchinson 2019: xviii). Toomer acknowledged racism whilst rejecting essentialist definitions of himself.

Cane is deeply inspired by southern Black folk culture, which Toomer experienced during a brief stint as substitute Principal of an agricultural college in Sparta, Georgia, in 1921. The book is not a novel, but rather a disconcerting mélange of unconnected fictional sketches and poems. Masten calls *Cane* a 'collage of lineated and prose poetry' (p.43), while Hutchinson describes the sketches as 'deemphasizing plot and developing instead a "lyric fiction," using repetition and refrain to structure the work' (p.xxii). The book's three parts, which are separated by drawings of arcs rather than chapter numbers, follow the standard pastoral trajectory (from city to country and back again) in reverse: six portraits of Georgian, mostly Black, women are separated by two poems apiece in part one; then six more sketches of urban Black characters in northern cities are jumbled with five more poems; and finally 'Kabnis', a story that reads like a stage play about a northern substitute teacher struggling to get by in Georgia, completes the book. As Hutchinson observes, 'Toomer structured the plot around "slopes," "curves," and "crescendos" of cognition, physical action, and emotion' (p.xxiv).

All three parts are permeated by alienation, disconnection, spiritual hunger and frustrated desire, sometimes across the racial divide, and yet *Cane* fizzes with beauty and vitality. Toomer's idiosyncratic blend of Modernist experimentation with imagery of soil, sound, scent and sensuality is absorbing, not aridly intellectual. Take this lyrical description from the sketch 'Carma':

A girl in the yard of a whitewashed shack not much larger than the stack of worn ties piled before it, sings. Her voice is loud. Echoes, like rain, sweep the valley. Dusk takes the polish from the rails. Lights twinkle in scattered houses. From far away, a sad strong song. Pungent and composite, the smell of farmyards is the fragrance of the woman. She does not sing; her body is a song. She is in the forest, dancing. Torches flare... juju men, greegree, witch-doctors... torches go out ... The Dixie Pike has grown from a goat path in Africa.

(p.13)

Music, a pastoral theme from the earliest times, is in the air as well as flowing through the woman. The visual and olfactory images are exact and unsparing. At the same time, the narrator draws out a subterranean connection between this scene and its inhabitants' African ancestry.

Unlike typical southern pastoral, though, *Cane* encompasses environmental degradation ('November Cotton Flower'), fear of miscegenation ('Becky') and lynching ('Blood-Burning Moon'). 'Portrait in Georgia' is an erotic anatomy, or 'blazon', of a White woman that uses jarring imagery: 'Hair - braided chestnut, / coiled like a lyncher's rope. ... And her slim body, white as the ash / of black flesh after flame' (p.36). Perhaps the narrator's desire is inextricable from fear of violence because lynch mobs often used alleged sexual assaults on White women as their pretext. In 'Box Seat', a narrative of frustrated desire set in a northern city, focaliser Dan Moore imagines himself confronting racist cops with his higher calling:

> "No, I ain't a baboon. I ain't Jack the Ripper. ... Look into my eyes. I am Dan Moore. I was born in a canefield. The hands of Jesus touched me. I am come to a sick world to heal it."
>
> (p.75)

Despite his grandiose, perhaps psychotic, self-perception, he fails to connect erotically to Muriel, who is distracted by the bourgeois sexual mores of her boarding-house landlady Mrs. Pribby. Pursuing her to a theatre, Dan finds that 'The seats are slots. The seats are bolted houses' (p.82). He has to squeeze his large frame into the constrained space next to a 'portly Negress':

> A soil-soaked fragrance comes from her. Through the cement floor her strong roots sink down. They spread under the asphalt streets. Dreaming, the streets roll over on their bellies, and suck their glossy health from them. Her strong roots sink down and spread under the river and disappear in blood-lines that waver south.
>
> (p.83)

Once again, there is the idea that the soil grounds the Negress, connecting her subconsciously to the southern 'homeland'. Angered by his failure to attract Muriel's attention, Dan picks a fight with an audience member, then walks away.

As Lucinda MacKethan explains, 'Part One of *Cane* shows the black southerner in his twilight hour, his strength and beauty still discernible against the complementary background of Georgia pine forest and cane field, but his future jeopardized by the encroachment of the white man's values and oppressive designs' (1980: 17). In the last section, the focaliser, Kabnis, is seen as a deferred 'promise of a soil-soaked beauty; uprooted, thinning out. Suspended a few feet above the soil that would resurrect him' (p.130). Kabnis's inability to draw strength from the redemptive figure of Lewis is counter-balanced, if only a little, by the fact that the book ends at sunrise. Toomer brings an authentically pastoral sense of eroticised nature into jarring contact with the racialised violence that brutally circumscribes it, but *Cane* barely discerns a progressive synthesis. Just like Toomer's dream of being 'American,' it was presumably too soon.

Kimberly Ruffin's *Black on Earth* (2010) captures Clifton's duality of 'that poem' of celebration and 'an other poem' that haunts or disrupts it in what she calls the 'ecological burden-and-beauty paradox' (p.15). On one side, there is the 'burden' of centuries of enslaved labour, followed by Jim Crow laws, migration and, as environmental justice activists have shown (ch.2), disproportionate harm from polluting activities; on the other, Black Americans' embodied enjoyment of nature and rhapsodic responses in poetry and song. Drawing on interviews with former slaves preserved by the Federal Writers Project in the 1930s, Ruffin highlights the knowledge and pleasure they convey. A compelling instance of pastoral voiced by Clara Davis from Alabama, for instance, rejects city conveniences: 'I wants to see de dawn break over de black ridge an' de twilight settle ... spreadin' a sort of orange hue over de place. I wants to walk de paths th'ew de woods an' see de rabbits an' watch de birds an' listen to frogs at night' (p.37). Enslaved people took particular pleasure in the small gardens they were sometimes allowed by plantation owners.

While Ruffin's 'burden-and-beauty paradox' chimes with the views of other scholars and artists, she is careful to emphasise that the burden does not define, let alone limit, Black artists' capacity for ecoliterary response. Somewhat similarly, Finney is ambivalent about the automatic framing of Black environmental experience in terms of victimisation and injustice, asking: 'How is African American participation in a broad array of environmental debates and events *assisted and constrained* by the use of [environmental justice]?' (p.108) The wild and brilliant profusion of African-American nature poetry in Dungy's anthology provides ample evidence that poetic beauty encompasses the burden, and extends well beyond it. In 'mulberry fields', for example, Clifton implies that segregation and slavery have tainted the very soil in a field, and concludes: 'wild / berries warm a field of bones / bloom how you must I say' (p.260). In 'the earth is a living thing', though, she reclaims blackness as a figure of vitality, representing Earth as 'a favorite child / of the universe' that has Afro-American hair (p.6). There is pastoral poetry in Gifford's fourth, most literal, sense, in Sean Hill's prose and poem about being a shepherd, and a superb anti-pastoral by Yusef Komunyakaa, 'Eclogue at Twilight', which graphically depicts a mating jackal being killed by a lioness. Gardens recur, sometimes as sites of simple, or fragile, pleasures, or else, in Major Jackson's 'Urban Renewal XIII' as a redoubt for the speaker's grandfather against violence in a neighbourhood where 'Tidal layers of cement harden men born gentle as the root / crops tended south, the city its own bitter shrine' (p.77). This 'paradise of kale' gives the poet, too, a safe vantage point.

Curated into ten thematic cycles by the editor, *Black Nature* ends with 'Fearless' by Tim Seibles, an invigorating poem about 'the green fire / bounding back every spring' (p.348). It grows to a pitch of enthusiasm for unconstrainable vitality: 'every better / home & garden finally overrun / by the green will, the green greenness / of green things growing greener.' It ends, though, with an image of trees, which are now stalwart, not ominous:

> ... The trees – who
> are they? Their stillness, that
> long silence, the never
> running away.

Despite the burden of the past, including more recent events like Hurricane Katrina (2005) (Ruffin: 158–75) and police shootings of African Americans, Black writers' appropriation and revision of pastoral in the last century is replete with hope, as Ruffin points out: 'African Americans struggle against the burden of societal scripts that make them ecological pariahs, yet they enjoy the beauty of liberating themselves and acting outside of these scripts' (p.16). It is a vital resource for ecocriticism.

This section has focused on African American pastoral, but it is important to recall that more recent Black African migrants to America share the experience of racism without the intergenerational legacy of slavery and Jim Crow. Postcolonial ecocritics, meanwhile, have drawn attention to several distinct versions of settler pastoral, including in sub-Saharan Africa. Byron Caminero-Santangelo criticises White authors, tourists and settlers' representations of 'the "real" Africa as a natural wilderness untouched by culture,' which are complemented, albeit less frequently, by visions of a 'gardenlike order' imposed by colonialism (2014: 24, 28). Caminero-Santangelo's 'postcolonial regional particularism' (p.9) seeks to avoid flattening important differences between African societies even as it employs a critical framework developed in the Western academy. By contrast, Sule Emmanuel Egya suggests that:

> ... Africans, especially those born and raised on the continent, under-stand the connections between physical and spiritual (seen and unseen) entities. They tend to see themselves as part of nature, in that nearly all social life is viewed as starting from the past and cul-minating in the future.
>
> (2020: 68)

As Egya points out, New Materialism (ch.2) involves 'nature being *nego-tiated* back into western civilisation through what appears to be a regime of discourse rather than reality,' (p.68) whereas the interpenetration of human, natural and spiritual agencies is, he argues, a lived reality for Africans. What 'some may see as romantic' (p.69) in Egya's view, we might see as a new twist in the discourse of pastoral.

CONTEMPORARY BRITISH ENVIRONMENTAL LITERATURE

In the Preface to his epic poem *Milton* (1810), **William Blake** (1757–1827) exhorts 'Young Men of the New Age ... Painters! Sculptors! Architects!' to fight for their art in a short lyric that imagines Jesus visiting England 'in ancient time', and exhorts them to build 'Jer-usalem, / in England's green and pleasant Land' (quoted in Whittaker 2018: 384). Set to rousing music by **Hubert Parry** (1848–1918) in 1917, 'Jerusalem' came to stand for 'Englishness' in the course of the twentieth century, despite Blake and Parry's own politics and the varied claims on the hymn of feminists, socialists, imperialists and extreme English nationalists. 'Jerusalem' has been recruited to 'perform a series of often-contradictory ambitions' (p.385), including kicking off Danny Boyle's extraordinary opening ceremony to the 2012 Olympic Games in London, where it serves as shorthand for a sentimental pastoral that remains influential in English, and therefore also British, culture.

Nature is enormously popular in Britain. The BBC produces nature documentaries with a global reach, often presented by Britain's most popular celebrity, David Attenborough (ch.6), and has screened *Spring-watch*, a TV show tracking signs of Spring, from May to June annually since 2005 to audiences in the millions. As Mark Cocker reports in *Our Place*, 'the UK membership [of environmental NGOs] is more than twice the size of the Dutch and more than three times the size of the German. It is an astonishing 25 times greater than that of the French and 87 times more than the Spanish ...' (Cocker 2018: 10). And yet, as the National Biodiversity Network's 2019 'State of Nature' report shows, and Cocker relates in painful detail, actual biodiversity in the UK has been declining disastrously since the mid-1970s. For example, '44 million breeding birds' (p.36) have disappeared since 1966. Pheasants and partridges intensively bred, then released to be shot, 'account for more than half of all the avian biomass in Britain' (p.36). The British have revelled in sentimental pastoral throughout this period.

The popularity and publication of nature writing, by contrast, has come in waves, or freshets: the post-war years, the 1960s, and then a flood since the turn of the millennium. Jos Smith traces the roots of twenty-first-century 'New Nature Writing' to Williams's *The Country and the City* and Richard Mabey's *The Unofficial Countryside*, both published in 1973. The latter 'used the conventions of countryside writing to ... challenge the tidy border between country and city and turned a self-reflexive eye on the ambiguous terrain between the two ...' (Smith 2017: 5). While Mabey is undoubtedly an inspiration to the new generation, though, the paucity of publications in the 80s and 90s suggests that Williams's questioning of 'nature', and the outright hostility of later, less nuanced, Marxists, deterred British nature writers in this period. Still, Smith is right to say that writers like **Roger Deakin** (1943–2006), Robert Macfarlane, Kathleen Jamie, Tim Robinson and Alice Oswald have:

> ... foregrounded socially and politically contested sites, plural meanings and values of place heritage, and new ways of looking and writing that have helped to stimulate a fresh culture of localism. In this tradition the local is not a site of retreat but a vital scale at which we can apprehend the changing world in which we live.
>
> (p.43)

To some ecocritics, though, the entire project is misconceived. Timothy Morton, once a scholar of Romanticism, is now the leading theorist of what he prefers to call 'ecocritique'. In *Ecology without Nature* (2007), he castigates nature writing (and much ecocriticism, too) for its **ecomimeticism**, which he sees as a disingenuous attempt to represent nature transparently:

> The more convincingly I render my surroundings, the more figurative language I end up with. The more I try to show you what lies beyond this page, the more of a page I have.
>
> (p.30)

It is the same irony identified by Watson in Renaissance art and literature.

The problem, according to Morton, is not just that nature writing tries not to be *writing*; it also invokes *nature*, which, 'in its confusing, ideological intensity, ... ironically impedes a proper relationship with the earth and its life-forms' (p.2). And ecocriticism, he says, is 'too enmeshed in the ideology that churns out stereotypical ideas of nature to be any use' (p.13). It is true that ecocriticism can be, to use Kate Soper's terminology, 'nature-endorsing' as well as 'nature-sceptical', (Soper 1995) but the balance tilted towards scepticism long before *Ecology without Nature* was published. Furthermore, Morton's observation that 'nature is history' (p.21) is no surprise either to ecocritics (after Williams) or to nature writers, as Cocker's savage indictment of unequal British land ownership and EU agricultural policy demonstrates. Macfarlane is an innovative and prolific contributor to, and advocate of, the new wave, and he acknowledges that 'nature writing' is an 'unsatisfactory' term for 'this diverse, passionate, pluriform, essential, reviving tradition' (2003). Morton has given ecocriticism some brilliant concepts to play with, but he is prone to exaggeration and factual inaccuracy.

Terry Gifford's notion of 'post-pastoral', by contrast, is more constructive, capacious and sympathetic to the aims of writers themselves. In an extended discussion in *Pastoral* (2019) he emphasises that '"post" … is not after anything, but beyond, outflanking, transcending the pejorative pastoral of false idealisation and retreat from engagement with the complexities of the present' (p.199). Whilst pastoral, anti-pastoral and the related georgic (Edney and Somervell 2022) still exist as distinct forms, post-pastoral is effectively a reconceptualisation of Leo Marx's 'complex pastoral' in the context of environmental crisis. Gifford's criteria range from awe and humility at the complexity of natural processes to the recognition that 'nature' and 'culture' are not opposites but interpenetrating aspects of a unitary reality. His criteria are primarily perceptions, emotions and moral attitudes that post-pastoral might foster, although the sixth is more explicitly political: acceptance of 'ecofeminists' realisation that the exploitation of the planet is of the same mindset as the exploitation of women and minorities' (p.189).

The New Pastoral in Contemporary British Writing (2020) by Deborah Lilley responds that the mode has always been protean and responsive to its cultural and political context, and 'the latest iteration of pastoral to emerge in contemporary British writing is sparked by and shaped – *reformed* – around environmental crisis' (p.29). The characteristics of the prefix-less pastoral she describes include an astute awareness that nature and history are intertwined, not opposed to one another; a pervasive sense of human culpability for environmental harm; and self-consciousness about the intrinsic limitations of human perspectives conveyed in writing. Indeed, several writers relate their own work to that of important predecessors as a way of situating themselves and drawing attention to historical shifts in ideas of nature: Helen Macdonald's *H is for Hawk* (2014) re-reads **T.H. White**'s (1906–1964) anguished falconry book, *The Goshawk* (1951), while **Edward Thomas** (1878–1917) is Macfarlane's guide in *The Old Ways: A Journey on Foot* (2012).

One of Lilley's exhibits is *Edgelands* (2011) by poets Paul Farley and Michael Symmons Roberts, which proclaims its fealty to unloved, disregarded scraps of land from abandoned railways and holiday camps to retail parks. Even as the authors wish to 'break out of the duality of rural and urban landscape writing, [and] explore these unobserved parts of our shared landscape as places of possibility, mystery, beauty,' (loc.202) they recall childhood Lancashire edgelands as 'a kind of Arcadia' (loc.221) where they found freedom precisely because the sites were ugly and unvalued. They remark that, 'At their most unruly and chaotic, edgelands make a great deal of our official wilderness seem like the enshrined, ecologically arrested, controlled garden space it really is' (loc.228). The edgelands' population is a motley bunch: 'boy racers in their newly pimped rides,' (loc.287) waste recyclers and fly-tippers, and bird-watchers clustered around sewage works (loc.1336–54). Farley and Roberts's enthusiasm for landscapes wedged in between the city and 'proper' countryside is engaging, even infectious, if sometimes rather forced:

> Container yards are places of beauty and mystery. Their aesthetic appeal lies partly in their uniformity – hundreds of ribbed steel boxes in a range of colours, emblazoned with Chinese characters or com-pany names – Maersk, Hapag-Lloyd, Hanjin Shipping. They have come a long way, and they bear the scars.
>
> (loc.806)

'Beauty and mystery' – really? Unlike sewage works and weedy old railways, container yards have no ecological value. Lilley accepts this limitation, but concludes that *Edgelands* indicates how nostalgia, long considered a knockdown objection to pastoral, can be recuperated for its 'reflective and reflexive' capabilities, not just its simplifying and regres-sive tendencies. In a context of accelerating environmental change, and widespread cultural amnesia about what has already been lost, pastoral nostalgia undoubtedly has progressive potential (cf. Ladino 2012).

British writers resist pastoral simplifications even when they revisit scenes of natural plenitude from historical periods on the cusp of mod-ernity (wherever that is positioned). Melissa Harrison's novel *All Among the Barley* (2018) is set in Suffolk in the interwar period when the intensification of agriculture is contributing to nationalistic anxieties about 'the English' being 'estranged from their birth-right, from the bonds of blood and soil' (p.91). Edie, the novel's narrator, vividly depicts the riot of birds, mammals and wildflowers on a pre-pesticide English farm, which she takes for granted, but she also conveys the gruelling physical labour (p.132) and vulnerability to the hazards of weather and pests (p.112) of the farming life. The landscape's natural richness is symbolised by an abandoned corncrake chick Edie finds and adopts, and as Dominic Head points out, the reader's knowledge that this species was nearly extirpated in the UK in the 1980s due to chan-ged farming practices gives Harrison's nostalgia 'a purposive diagnostic function' (2020: 363): that of contrasting Edie's heedlessness with our guilty knowledge.

Harrison's novel also reflects implicitly on Williams's pastoral escalator. There are textual allusions to interwar authors of complex pastorals, as Head shows, and then Edie, too, finds herself contemplating her grandparents in nostalgic terms: 'I see now that they were the last of the Victorians, inhabiting a world that had long passed away, and so to be with them was to be granted a temporary reprieve from all the anxieties of the modern age, the sense of things speeding up and going wrong that dogged us all invisibly in those years – even me' (p.61). At the same time, the novel's publication in the aftermath of the 2016 Brexit referendum underlines Williams's observation that 'what seemed a single escalator' is actually 'a more complicated movement', in this case including the decline of biodiversity, material progress for human Britons, and resurgent nationalism in a much-changed form and context. Indeed, the Brexit context may turn out to relate to the corncrake, too, since advocates claim that freedom from the dead hand of the EU Common Agricultural Policy has the potential to yield benefits for biodiversity (Garrard 2020).

The big conservation NGOs may have failed to stem the loss of biodiversity, and yet Britain has also spawned several more radical groups, from the Ramblers Association, which organised trespasses in the 1930s to assert traditional rights of way, through Transition Towns (2006), to climate activist groups such as Extinction Rebellion and the homely-sounding Insulate Britain. Similarly, contemporary British environmental writing overwhelmingly questions sentimental pastoral, including satires such as Jez Butterworth's *Jerusalem* (2009) and the BBC mock-documentary, *This Country* (2017–2020). Thus, James Rebanks's *English Pastoral* (2020) (*Pastoral Song* (2021) in North America) deserves its title in Gifford's fourth, literal sense – the book is an evocative memoir of a sheep-farmer – but derives its impact from its account of the human and ecological cost of agricultural intensification in Cumbria, where Wordsworth found inspiration. Rebanks and his neighbours gradually come to realise that the productive pastoral landscape they inhabit has become a 'green desert' (2020: 201) of depleted biodiversity. By combining the best of traditional farming and modern ecological science, Rebanks argues that 'We can build a new English pastoral: not a utopia, but somewhere decent for us all' (p.209). In other words, exposing the illusions of sentimental pastoral is necessary in order for post-pastoral to be realised on the land.

PASTORAL ECOLOGY

A key characteristic of pastoral is the idea of nature as a stable, enduring counterpoint to the disruptive energy and change of human societies. Both Judaeo-Christian and Graeco-Roman traditions imagine a divinely ordained order of nature, and find proof in the remarkable fitness of the Earth as a habitat for its various species. The Scientific Revolution of the seventeenth and eighteenth centuries accepted this pastoral conception of nature, but refracted it through a new view of the Universe as a great mechanism designed by God. The earlier and later conceptions are brought together in **William Paley**'s (1743–1805) influential *Natural Theology* (1802), in which he compares nature to a pocket watch – the most complex device in Georgian Britain – found on a heath. Such a discovery would surely lead us to conclude 'that there must have existed, at some time, and at some place or other, an artificer or artificers who formed it for the purpose which we find it actually to answer' (Gregory 2009: 604). Even after evolutionary theory supplanted Paley's enthusiastic paean to divine design, the underlying metaphor of Nature as an exquisitely balanced machine remained at the heart of the new science of ecology in the late nineteenth and early twentieth centuries, shaping the rhetoric of emerging environmental movements.

The plant ecologist **Frederick Clements** (1874–1945), for example, proposed that 'associations' of plant species in a particular habitat would necessarily grow together towards a stable 'climax', or equilibrium, stage. Clements developed the idea of 'succession', in which disturbed ecosystems were colonised by fast-growing, hardy 'pioneer' species, then succeeded by slow-growing species with longer life-spans and, sometimes, a tolerance for the conditions produced by the pioneers. He argued that succession progressed from an immature state, with large numbers of a few pioneer species, towards a complex, highly organised 'community' with more diverse species. Later in the twentieth century, though, Clementsian theory was rejected by most ecologists because the plant associations observed during succession turned out to be, as John Kricher puts it in *The Balance of Nature: Ecology's Enduring Myth* (2009), 'accidents of history' (p.90) rather than communities predestined to rise

and fall together. Drawing on numerous ecological studies that underline the role of contingency, or stochasticity, as biologists call it, Kricher comments that:

> The balance of nature paradigm is of little value within evolution and
> ecology. It has never been clearly defined and is basically misleading.
> But the balance of nature is esthetically satisfying, a fact that is largely
> responsible for its continued vigor through the ages.

> (p.23)

Anna Lowenhaupt Tsing explains that ecologists prefer the term 'assemblage' to 'community' because it does not prejudge the nature of the
relationships: 'some thwart (or eat) each other; others work together to
make life possible; still others just happen to find themselves in the same
place' (2015: 22). The pastoral conception of harmonious ecological
communities is more 'esthetically satisfying' than 'it just depends,' and
yet, as Dana Phillips warns, 'ecology is not a slush fund of fact, value, and
metaphor, but a less than fully coherent field with a very checkered past
and a fairly uncertain future' (2003: 45). The next chapter considers how
contemporary writers narrate wild, post-equilibrium assemblages.

The flow of 'fact, value, and metaphor' can, in any case, slosh in more
than one direction, both historically and in present-day criticism.
Whereas early ecocriticism tends to defer to the environmental sciences – or uncritically incorporate received ideas, according to Phillips –
the field today emphasises informed interdisciplinarity. Heidi Scott's
*Chaos and Cosmos: Literary Roots of Modern Ecology in the British Nineteenth
Century* (2014) 'traces the ancestry of ecological science to find lurking
literary forebears' (p.8) such as Mary Shelley's *The Last Man* (1826)
(ch.5), a novel that explores notions of chaos that would revolutionise
ecology in the late-twentieth century. Romantic lyric poems, in Scott's
account, are self-consciously constructed as 'microcosms' of nature that
chime with 'microcosm science', which 'has evolved over 150 years from
nature-based sampled systems to lab-based representative systems, and
finally to computer-based virtual systems' (p.151). Post-equilibrium and
microcosmic ecology are, Scott argues, as much indebted to cultural
precursors as Clements.

One of the distinguishing features of post-pastoral, for Gifford, is its
abandonment of popular ecology, wedded to outmoded models of

harmony and balance, in favour of post-equilibrium ecology (p.199). Post-pastoral is imbued with Daniel Botkin's view that 'nature undisturbed is not constant in form, structure, or proportion, but changes at every scale of time and space' (1990: 62). Clearly, not all changes are desirable, but unlike Clements's climax concept, post-equilibrium ecology looks to human values to decide between them, rather than appealing to the illusory objectivity of a supposedly authentic or pristine state of nature.

4

WILDERNESS

What comes to mind when you think of 'nature'? The answer will depend on both your personal experiences and your cultural context. Comparative landscape aesthetics research is scarce, but I presume White Britons would recall pastoral imagery, whereas Canadians and Americans would reach for stereotypes of wilderness: mountains, rivers and forests, perhaps deserts or swamps. 'This is,' says Kate Soper, 'the nature of immediate experience and aesthetic appreciation; the nature we have destroyed and polluted and are asked to conserve and preserve' (1995: 156). Soper distinguishes nature in this 'lay' or 'surface' sense from two others: the 'metaphysical' sense, in which '"nature" is the concept through which humanity thinks its difference and specificity' (p.155), and the 'realist' sense that defines 'the objects of study of the natural sciences, and conditions the possible forms of human intervention in biology or interaction with the environment' (pp.155–6). These latter two senses are in tension: when nature is conceptualised in opposition to culture, both sides still operate wholly within a physical universe of invariant natural laws. For example, questioning enculturated gender norms misrepresented as 'human nature' is, and must be, wholly in keeping

DOI: 10.4324/9781003174011-4

with acceptance of human biology viewed, as Soper urges, as 'both limiting and empowering':

> Human biology is such that we cannot fly unaided, exist on a diet of grass, survive for more than limited periods without air or water, emit or detect certain sounds or smells, and so on; but it is also such as to have allowed us language, music-making, medicine, the development of a vast array of skills whereby we have evaded or transcended purely biologically imposed limits on our means of transport and communication, enjoyment and survival.

(p.139)

Furthermore, as the last section of the previous chapter explains, the scientific study of ecology in the realist sense can conflict with the aesthetic and ethical assumptions of 'ecology' (i.e. environmentalism) in the lay sense. Many debates in ecocriticism hinge on unnoticed differences in meanings of 'nature'.

This chapter explores the origin and development of wilderness as a sacramental space that promises a renewed, authentic relation of humanity and the Earth. At the same time, it questions how wilderness functions, in North American culture especially, as an ideology that seems the very opposite of anything ideological. For, as **Stuart Hall** (1932–2014) points out, 'the hope of every ideology is to naturalize itself out of History into Nature, and thus to become invisible, to operate unconsciously' (Hall 2021: 9). Just as the *idea of wilderness* has a cultural history (outlined below), so purported *wildernesses* like the Yosemite Valley in California invariably have cultural, as well as natural, histories, which environmental humanities scholars have recovered from the 'invisibility' conferred by categorisation as ahistorical nature. Wilderness, especially as represented in nonfictional nature writing, was central to the emergence of North American environmentalism in the late nineteenth and early twentieth centuries, which in turn inspired ecocriticism in the 1990s. In twenty-first-century ecocriticism, though, both the concept of wilderness and the legacy of advocates like **John Muir** (1838–1914) have been roundly criticised, to the point where scholars routinely disavow wilderness as a 'first wave' (see Preface) concern. After presenting these critiques, the chapter concludes by considering the reintegration of history and nature in 'the new wild'.

OLD WORLD WILDERNESS

Wilderness narratives share the motif of escape and return with pastorals, but the construction of nature they propose and reinforce is fundamentally different. If pastoral is the distinctive European construction of nature, suited to agricultural societies, wilderness fits the settler experience of apparently untamed landscapes in what they called the 'New World', particularly the United States and Canada. Yet settlers crossed the oceans with their preconceptions intact, so the 'nature' they encountered was inevitably shaped by the histories they often wanted to leave behind. Pastoral has both Judaeo-Christian and Graeco-Roman roots, whereas 'wilderness' had primarily theological associations in Europe until the eighteenth century. Wilderness is a threat in *The Epic of Gilgamesh,* written in Mesopotamia around 2100BCE, yet the Judaic scriptures regard it with ambivalence. After the ejection from Eden, the wilderness is both a place of exile and an escape route: Moses led the Israelites into the desert to escape civilised, but enslaving, Egypt. Satan resides in the wilderness: 'Then was Jesus led up of the Spirit into the wilderness to be tempted of the devil' (KJV Matthew 4:1). But so too do early Christian monks whose refuges are situated in deserts to protect them from Roman persecution – and the temptations of the world (i.e. the city). In the Bible, and in later Judaeo-Christian traditions, 'Wilderness manifests both as place of sanctuary and as place of sanction,' as Kylie Crane puts it (2012: 2).

Timothy Morton argues in *Dark Ecology* (2016) that ancient Mesopotamia is the Eurasian origin of what he calls 'agrilogistics':

> ... an agricultural program so successful that it now dominates agricultural techniques planetwide. ... Toxic from the beginning to humans and other lifeforms, it operates blindly like a computer program. The homology is tight since algorithms are now instrumental in increasing the reach of agrilogistics. Big data makes bigger farms.
>
> (pp.42–3)

Although Morton understates the differences between pre-industrial and industrial agriculture, he rightly insists that human survival in cities (the root meaning of 'civilised') 'was a long-term collaboration between humans and wheat, humans and rock, humans and soil, not out of grand visions but out of something like desperation' (p.45). Indigenous cultures do not seem to have forgotten the reality of co-existence and co-dependence: it appears in many of their stories (ch.7). In the Near Eastern and later European context, though, 'Agrilogistics spawns the concept of Nature definitively outside the human' (p.56): nature in Soper's metaphysical sense, but also, visibly, in the lay sense, in that for farming people, wilderness is what lies beyond the cultivated field or pasture. It is not a concept that makes sense either to hunter-gatherers or Amazonian forest-farmers, who 'do not make the distinction between "cultivated" and "wild" landscapes ...; instead, they simply classify landscapes into scores of varieties, depending on the types of species in each' (Mann 2011: 352–3). Indeed, the word 'wilderness' derives from the Anglo-Saxon 'wilddeoren,' where 'deoren,' or beasts, existed beyond the bounds of cultivation. To stray over the fence-line was to risk *bewilderment*.

Superficially, Morton's argument resembles Max Oelschlaeger's claim in *The Idea of Wilderness* (1991): 'Once humans became agriculturalists, the almost paradisiacal character of prehistory was irretrievably lost' (p.28). Oelschlaeger reads a first-wave canon of wilderness writers such as Thoreau (ch.3), Muir, **Aldo Leopold** (1887–1948) and Gary Snyder as deep ecological thinkers (ch.2) who retrieve the premodern sense of a 'sacralized cosmos' (p.28) and confront ecocidal 'modernism'. Morton, though, resists dating the origin of agrilogistics, in common with archaeologists, who emphasise that farming and hunter-gathering are not states of being but modes of survival that can ebb and flow over a given year, as well as over centuries. And he rejects Oelschlaeger's idealisation of an alternative that is lost in the past: the '*arche-lithic*, a primordial relatedness of humans and nonhumans that has never evaporated' (p.63), is for Morton 'a possibility space that flickers continually within, around, beneath, and to the side of the periods we have artificially demar-cated as Neolithic and Paleolithic' (p.80). The arche-lithic seems a fragile alternative to contemporary agrilogistics, though, which has resulted in wild animals making up just 3% of vertebrate biomass while humans make up 32% and livestock 65% (p.44).

THE SUBLIME

Judaeo-Christian ambivalence towards wilderness was resolved in early modern philosophy and literature into something approaching outright hostility. **Thomas Burnet**'s (c.1635–1715) *Sacred Theory of the Earth* (1684) explains mountain ranges as the geological evidence of God's displeasure with mankind, scars inflicted upon a previously unwrinkled globe by the 'Great Flood' that Noah and his family survived. Burnet tells how the crust of the world dried out and collapsed into a watery abyss, releasing a terrible deluge from inside the planet that left the Edenic Earth battered and broken. Some of Burnet's readers found the apocalyptic terror of this ruined world strangely appealing, though, including the philosopher **Edmund Burke** (1729–1797). His *Philosophical Enquiry into the Origin of our Ideas of the Sublime and the Beautiful* represents, as Simon Schama demonstrates, a counter-current in the philosophy of the 'Enlightenment', with Burke setting himself up as 'the priest of obscurity'. For Schama, Burke's sublime was found in 'shadow and darkness and dread and trembling, in cave and chasms, at the edge of the precipice, in the shroud of cloud, in the fissures of the earth' (1995: 450). Whereas the merely beautiful arouses feelings of pleasure, Burke's *Philosophical Enquiry* claims that 'the passion caused by the great and sublime in nature … is Astonishment; and astonishment is that state of the soul, in which all its motions are suspended, with some degree of Horror' (Burke and Phillips 1990: 53). The beautiful is loved for its smallness, softness, delicacy; the sublime admired for its vastness and overwhelming power. These obviously gendered qualities exclude women categorically from sublime experience, as Christine Battersby suggests: 'Via the framework of the Burkean "beautiful", women … found themselves deprived of sisterhood with raw Nature' (2007: 8). Writing back against such constraints, the feminist radical **Mary Wollstonecraft** (1759–1797) includes sublime description in *A Short Residence in Sweden, Norway and Denmark* (1796) as 'a way of countering the newly emergent gender ideals which confined women to the (distinctly inferior) category of the "beautiful"' (p.8):

> The impetuous dashing of the rebounding torrent from the dark cavities which mocked the exploring eye, produced an equal activity in my mind: my thoughts darted from earth to heaven, and I asked myself why I was chained to life and its misery? Still the tumultuous emotions this sublime object excited, were pleasurable …
>
> (Wollstonecraft, Godwin and Holmes 1987: 153)

When Burke's *Enquiry* was published in 1757, it fed a growing movement that sought out untamed mountainous landscapes, rather than spurning and avoiding them. Tourists in search of the picturesque travelled to the European Alps, and later the mountainous regions of Britain, to test their mettle and enjoy elevated vistas. The painter **John Robert Cozens** (1752–1797) produced startlingly gloomy, atmospheric watercolours of sublime European landscapes such as 'A Cavern in the Campagna, Rome' (1786) (Schama 1995: 473–8). *The Prelude* (1805), William Wordsworth's poetic autobiography, extols his hike over the Simplon Pass in the Alps in awe-struck blank verse:

> ... The brook and road
> Were fellow-travellers in this gloomy pass,
> And with them did we journey several hours
> At a slow step. The immeasurable height
> Of woods decaying, never to be decayed,
> The stationary blasts of waterfalls,
> And everywhere along the hollow rent
> Winds thwarting winds, bewildered and forlorn,
> The torrents shooting from the clear blue sky,
> The rocks that muttered close upon our ears—
> Black drizzling crags that spake by the wayside
> As if a voice were in them—the sick sight
> And giddy prospect of the raving stream,
> The unfettered clouds and region of the heavens,
> Tumult and peace, the darkness and the light,
> Were all like workings of one mind, the features
> Of the same face, blossoms upon one tree,
> Characters of the great apocalypse,
> The types and symbols of eternity,
> Of first, and last, and midst, and without end.
>
> (2001 [1805]: lines 556–75)

The unfolding of the experience in a single sentence conveys the speaker's struggle to describe a welter of contradictory, vertiginous sense-impressions. Meliz Ergin sees the overall effect as one of resolution: 'Immersed in the powerful workings of the landscape ... the poet perceives even opposing qualities like dark and light to be in ungraspable harmony, and concludes that they must be the "workings of one mind"' (2017: 16). Crucially, this (implicitly Christian) harmony holds in tension the ideas of cataclysmic disruption of Nature ('Apocalypse ... first and last') and endurance ('Eternity ... without end'). It is also possible, though, to discern rising panic in this passage as the speaker fails to encompass the sublime landscape in language, and is forced to seek refuge in grand abstractions as a way to regain conscious control.

The sublime eventually changed public policy as well as art: Words-worthian Romanticism directly inspired the creation of Britain's National Parks in the 1950s, as Jonathan Bate shows (2013). They were all sublime landscapes, including rugged coastlines and mountainous regions such as Wordsworth's home in the Lake District, until the designation of the New Forest (2005) and the South Downs (2009). Unlike the unpeopled wildernesses designated as National Parks in North America, British National Parks include human settlements and are expected to require ongoing management. Still, the Romantic affection for sublime landscapes means that National Parks seldom protect acutely endangered habitats like hay meadows and wetlands, which partly explains why, as Mark Cocker argues (ch.3), conservation in Britain has been an abysmal failure.

The British countryside would seem to be too long-settled, too obviously a product of history, for wilderness writing to find much purchase. Robert Macfarlane acknowledges as much in *The Wild Places* (2007), and yet his book fights back against 'obituaries for the wild,' well-founded as they are, by seeking out remaining wildernesses where he can 'step outside human history' (p.11, p.9). He finds solace hiking Rannoch Moor in the Scottish Highlands, for instance:

> We woke to a dawn of indigo and bronze, and we walked within that light for hours, passing in and out of the bays along the serried northern shore of Loch Bà. Thin beams of sun were probing down through gaps in the clouds. They looked like searchlights sweeping the Moor's emptiness for fugitives, or lasers measuring its enormous extent.
>
> (p.80)

Macfarlane's simile could be seen as amplifying the drama of the scene, whilst also admitting his contemporary perspective. The structure of a self-educational travelogue shapes and directs his vivid, evocative prose, culminating in an 'understanding of wildness not as something which was hived off from human life, but which existed unexpectedly around and within it: in cities, backyards, roadsides, hedges, field boundaries or spinnies' (p.226). In this respect, Macfarlane's (somewhat contrived) realisation resembles Paul Farley and Michael Symmons Roberts's starting point in *Edgelands* (ch.3). Still, Macfarlane concludes with a plea for the necessity of wildness, especially as embodied in Earth Others:

> The seal's holding gaze, before it flukes to push another tunnel through the sea, the hare's run, the hawk's high gyres: such things are wild. Seeing them, you are briefly made aware of a world at work around and beside our own, a world operating in patterns and purposes you do not share. These are creatures, you realise, that live by voices inaudible to you.
>
> (p.307)

And if *The Wild Places* indulges in something like Romantic marketing, perhaps the 'colourful, abundant style of an advertising copyist' can be seen as a necessary counter to corporate 'greenwashing', as Sally-Ann Mair Jones proposes (2013: 58). Her distinction is yet more important, and shakier, in North America, which has vast thinly-populated lands, most taken by force or treaty from Indigenous peoples, and a deeper, more contested, wilderness tradition.

WILDERNESS IN NORTH AMERICA

According to David R. Williams, the Protestant version of wilderness is a founding myth of America. It is 'the place where the soul goes to experience God' (2021: 1320); a place of 'relinquishment' (p.1313) and terror, but also of cleansing and redemption:

> For the Christians who brought the American Wilderness tradition to these shores, that true sense of the beauty and holiness of the creation, that sense of pure presence, ... comes only after relinquishing our constructions, or contraptions, and entering this wilderness; the resurrection of a true vision comes only after the blood and pain of crucifixion.
>
> (p.1312)

Whilst his argument is eloquently, even defiantly, arborescent and first-wave (Preface), it does draw needed attention to the preponderance of evangelical Protestant upbringings among the 'ecological heroes' (p.1324) of the White male American wilderness tradition. This section introduces a few prominent figures, and the next considers why the wilderness canon has, as Williams puts it, 'received much grief of late and scarce can be found in our graduate schools and journals' (p.1317).

As Charles C. Mann shows in *1491: New Revelations of the Americas before Columbus* (2011, 2nd edn), the wildernesses that caused colonists to marvel and quail were actually at various stages of rebound from Indigenous management, which had been abruptly ended by disease, warfare and population collapse (ch.7):

> Until Columbus, Indians were a keystone species in most of the hemisphere. Annually burning undergrowth, clearing and replanting forests, building canals and raising fields, hunting bison and netting salmon, growing maize, manioc, and the Eastern Agricultural Complex, Native Americans had been managing their environments for thousands of years. ... [They] made mistakes. But by and large they modified their landscapes in stable, supple, resilient ways. ... But all of these efforts required close, continual oversight. In the sixteenth century, epidemics removed the boss.
>
> (p.363)

Both the dense forests of the East and the vast herds of bison on the Prairies are now seen by many environmental historians as, ironically, ecological *consequences* of colonialism: 'Far from destroying pristine wilderness, ... Europeans bloodily *created* it' (p.371). And then they set about destroying it, and soon after lamenting what they had done.

If pastoral is what colonists get when they have conquered the wilderness, a figure like Henry David Thoreau must feature in any consideration of both tropes. His *Maine Woods* (1864) is a foundational example of the wilderness tradition – superficially secularised, according to Williams – that applies the ancient rhetoric of retreat to the endless-seeming miles of sublime landscape in America. After climbing Mount Katahdin, the tallest in the state, Thoreau writes:

It is difficult to conceive of a region uninhabited by man. We habitually presume his presence and influence everywhere. And yet we have not seen pure Nature, unless we have seen her thus vast, and drear, and inhuman ... Nature was here something savage and awful, though beautiful. This was that Earth of which we have heard, made out of Chaos and Old Night.

(1972: 71)

Intriguingly, reaching the physical high point is a disappointment for both Thoreau and Wordsworth: the American feels only disorientation at the summit, and the British poet realises he has scaled the famed Simplon Pass only when he starts to descend. Thoreau's reflections on the way down Katahdin suggest he is either panicked or inspired by materiality:

... this matter to which I am bound has become so strange to me. I fear not spirits, ghosts, of which I am one, – *that* my body might, – but I fear bodies, I tremble to meet them. What is this Titan that has possession of me? Talk of mysteries! Think of our life in nature, – daily to be shown matter, to come into contact with it, – rocks, trees, wind on our cheeks! the *solid* earth! the *actual* world! the *common sense! Contact! Contact! Who* are we? *where* are we?

(p.71)

Thoreau's urgent questioning fails to discover the 'workings of one mind' under the tumult of appearances. Indeed, the sublime bewilderment brought on by the mountain scenery forces Thoreau to question his very being.

John Muir, one of Thoreau's most enthusiastic disciples, contributed more than any other single writer to the establishment of wilderness as a touchstone of American cultural identity and a basis for conservation activities. He is best known for hymning the virtues of California's Sierra Nevada mountains and for his political campaigns on behalf of wilderness preservation. In *My First Summer in the Sierra*, Muir's journal entry for 15 July, 1869 recounts a view of 'sublime domes and canyons, dark upsweeping forests, and glorious array of white peaks deep in the sky, every feature glowing, radiating beauty that pours into our flesh and bones like heat rays from fire' (1992: 232). It was scenes like these that fuelled Muir's environmentalist passion. However, Michael P. Branch explains that the book was written 42 years after the revelations it recounts, and so should be seen (rather like Thoreau's *Walden*) as 'both a first-hand account of an experience and a carefully elaborated retrospective rendering of that experience.' Branch praises Muir's 'lyrical and rhapsodic prose,' and notes, with Williams, that while his 'ecological insights have struck a chord with readers whose sympathies lean toward pantheism, Buddhism, or Taoism, it was nevertheless Christianity that supplied this latter-day wilderness votary with his literary vocabulary' (2004: 145–6). Yosemite Valley, Muir's cathedral, was the first place in America protected by an Act of Congress in 1864. Muir's writings and personal activism would lead to the creation of Yosemite National Park in 1890 and the formation of a wilderness protection organisation in 1892, the Sierra Club, which he served as president for 22 years.

Muir's most famous assertion is that 'when we try to pick out anything by itself, we find it hitched to everything else in the universe. One fancies a heart like our own must be beating in every crystal and cell, and we feel like stopping to speak to the plants and animals as friendly fellow mountaineers' (1992: 248). He is an incisive and sardonic critic of anthropocentrism, as in a diary entry ridiculing the 'numerous class of men' who 'are painfully astonished whenever they find anything, living or dead, in all God's universe, which they cannot eat or render in some way what they call useful to themselves' (p.160). He even proclaims that 'if a war of races should occur between the wild beasts and Lord Man, I would be tempted to sympathize with the bears' (p.155), a radical statement of ecocentric piety that was fortified by thorough scientific knowledge of botany and geology. Branch therefore calls *My First Summer* 'a literary monument to the idea of an extended community within which humans may recognize their kinship with the wider world of nature' (p.152). Muir's plummeting reputation in recent ecocriticism is considered in the next section.

When it comes to depictions of the Sierra Nevada mountains, Muir wrote the book but **Ansel Adams** (1902–1984) took the pictures. He visited Yosemite annually, learning to take and process photographs at the Sierra Club lodge there, and publishing them in the Club's *Bulletin*. After his death, the State of California designated over 100,000 acres of the Sierra the 'Ansel Adams Wilderness Area'. Adams's best-known images are his black and white shots of mountains and valleys, in which wilderness attains an iconic status. They were generally taken in winter or early spring, in only the clearest weather conditions, using red or green filters for enhanced contrast of rock and snow, sky and cloud. The photographs position the viewer decisively outside the scene, an impression accentuated by their epic scale and eerie stillness. In this respect, they are quite different from the examples of Romantic sublimity discussed above: Wordsworth and Thoreau's subjectivity is threatened with obliteration, whereas Adams's photographs are safely serene, epitomising the purity of the wild with their starkly defined regions of sky, rock, water and forest untainted by signs of human presence. Adams's visual language thus emulates Muir's praise of the untouched Sierra Range: 'In general views no mark of man is visible upon it; nor anything to suggest the wonderful depth and grandeur of its sculpture' (Muir 1992: 614). Neil Campbell criticises exactly this tendency in Adams to advocate a 'frozen idealization of place as a myth, as Edenic Promised Land', which ignores an alternative view of 'the West as [a] culturally constructed, social landscape, a zone of contact and encounter where interaction and dialogue takes place at all levels ...' (2008: 184). Indeed, 'Winter Sunrise, Sierra Nevada, from Lone Pine, California', (1942) with its exquisite chiaroscuro, would have looked very different if Adams hadn't erased 'LP', whitewashed onto the hillside by a local high-schooler, from the image (Gallery n.d.).

In truth, Adams was anything but socially disengaged: he took 'Winter Sunrise' whilst undertaking a photojournalism project, *Born Free and Equal: The Story of Loyal Japanese-Americans*, which challenged the US government's racist policy of internment. Jennifer Ladino's nuanced reading of the book commends Adams for 'enlist[ing] mythical nature in order to build a case against a particular social injustice' (2012: 92), but questions the book's representation of internees as an imprisoned 'model minority'. Ecocritical tropes do not come with their ideological significance attached, like a luggage tag. The specifics of text (or image) and context matter every time. Reception matters too: Adams's sublime landscapes are far more popular than his documentary photos, and yet scholars know nothing, empirically, about their psychological and cultural impact, as Adrian Ivakhiv notes: 'The only way to properly assess whether such enframing of nature results in a sense of mastery or in a humbled recognition of natural beauty is to conduct careful, contextual analysis of audience responses' (2008: 18). We return to empirical ecocriticism in the Conclusion.

Representations of wilderness have racial resonances beyond the war-time internment of Japanese Americans. As we saw in the last chapter, Black Americans have an ambivalent relationship with nature that is conditioned by America's history of enslavement and racial violence. *Gloryland* (2009) by African-American park ranger Shelton Johnson – described by Ladino as an 'obscure but one-of-a-kind [historical] novel' (2019: 177) – narrates the path of protagonist Elijah Yancy through that history, from post-Civil War South Carolina to a career in the US 9th Cavalry as a 'buffalo soldier' (as Native Americans called Black troopers due to the texture of their hair). After a White man hurls a racial slur at Elijah in the street, he reflects:

> ... I ain't ever been a nigger. But I'm Seminole and I'm colored, just like the sundown I'm colored, like dirt that's warm and black and red too, like the sun's been shining so long the dirt remembers all that light and holds onto it.
>
> (2009: 17)

Elijah's narrative voice is rich and persuasive, especially in the early chapters when he risks his life rebelling against the naked racism and cruelty of White society in the Deep South. Under threat of lynching, he escapes westwards, living off the land and feeling continually hunted, until he finds refuge in the army. True to the history Shelton Johnson retells and re-enacts as a ranger at Yosemite, Elijah finds solace when he reaches a place where, as Ladino puts it, 'John Muir-caliber awe is possible for people of any skin color. People of color belong here, *Gloryland* affirms, and they have for a long time' (p.178). Near the end of the novel, Elijah reflects that:

> Some folks pray for a sweet hereafter, but it's already everywhere round us, the air we take in, the light that fills us, and the darkness. ... It's the dusty trail winding down to El Capitan, into the cool shadows of black oaks, the wet meadows their roots embrace, and a river, cold and bright, that never stops singing.
>
> (p.269)

Johnson's novel is less believable when Elijah narrates – or rather, refuses to narrate – the 9th Cavalry's participation in the Indian Wars, the Spanish-American War and the US occupation of the Philippines (1898). Whilst it makes sense that Elijah's mixed ancestry would cause him to empathise with the Natives his cavalry troop forces onto reservations, he expresses some suspiciously twenty-first-century attitudes throughout these middle sections. Ladino claims that Elijah is right to refuse personal shame, instead blaming US imperialism, but she doesn't acknowledge the way Johnson's otherwise-observant narrator skims over these painfully ambivalent episodes.

The wilderness canon that features heavily in early ecocriticism includes *Land of Little Rain* (1903) by **Mary Austin** (1868–1934), *A Sand County Almanac* (1949) by **Aldo Leopold** (1887–1948), *Desert Solitaire* by **Edward Abbey** (1927–89) and *Pilgrim at Tinker Creek* (1974) by Annie Dillard. These writers are discussed in detail in Don Scheese's *Nature Writing* (2013); reviewed as part of an increasingly inclusive movement in John Elder's 'American Nature Writing' (2019); and passed over in Christian Hummelsund Voie's energetic, New Materialist (ch.1) defence of 'Nature Writing in the Anthropocene' (Voie 2019). Williams is right, nevertheless, that they 'scarce can be found' on reading lists today.

Canada and Australia are, like the USA, Anglophone settler colonies whose landmasses include vast areas of wilderness – the North and the Outback – and yet neither has an equivalent to American nature writing. Canada's best-known twentieth-century nature writer, **Farley Mowat** (1921–2014), is accused of misrepresenting both wildlife and the Inuit people of the Canadian Arctic. Wilderness is more prominent in fiction, poetry and visual art. Notably, in the 1970s, a period of intense cultural nationalism and unaccustomed global recognition for Canadian writers, Margaret Atwood published a closely related series of books including *Survival: A Thematic Guide to Canadian Literature* (1972); a popular novel, *Surfacing* (1979); and *The Journals of Susanna Moodie* (1970), a superb poetic re-writing of the memoir of a nineteenth-century English immigrant. Canadian national identity has long been defined defensively, first in relation to Britain and France, and later the USA. Indeed, when in 1972 the Canadian Broadcasting Corporation (CBC) asked radio listeners to complete the phrase 'As Canadian as ...' a witty teenager wrote: '... possible under the circumstances' (Manning

2007). Atwood, in her own work of cultural definition, describes a 'map of the territory' of Canadian literature that offers 'shared knowledge' without which 'we will not survive'. The defining symbol of the USA is 'the frontier'; that of England is 'the island' (though the island is actually called Great Britain); and Canada is 'undoubtedly Survival, *la Survivance*' (Bradley and Soper 2013: 15–6). Whilst cultural and even national survival may be at stake, more usually the 'main idea' is 'hanging on, staying alive' (p.16). The Canadian wild, according to Atwood, is more lethal, less pristine and alluring than the American.

Her map points, among other places, towards her own novel *Surfacing* (1972), in which an unnamed narrator takes some friends north from the city to her family cottage in Quebec, ostensibly to try to locate her father. The threats to this environment from logging, hydroelectric projects and commercial tourism are coded as 'American', driving the protagonist into an increasingly alienated and paranoid state. She sees this as 'border country' (1979: 20), and later as 'occupied territory' (p.115): 'In the bay the felled trees and numbered posts showed where the surveyors had been, power company. My country, sold or drowned, a reservoir; the people were sold along with the land and the animals, a bargain, sale, *solde*' (p.126). As her unresolved grief over an enforced abortion 'surfaces', it collides with her discovery of her father's drowned body in a lake. She eventually leaves the cabin and her friends, declaring that she has no name and is 'through pretending' to 'be civilized' (p.162). Ultimately, though, the protagonist decides to return, hoping that 'the Americans' can be 'watched and predicted and stopped without being copied' (p.183). Rosemary Sullivan's 1987 article '*La forêt* or the Wilderness as Myth' explains that 'Atwood's subject is the polarization that results from our compulsion to explain and master nature' (Bradley and Soper 2013: 38), anticipating the ecofeminist reading of *Survival* that later became dominant.

In visual art, the paintings of the Group of Seven and **Thom Thomson** (1877–1917), made in many cases in the first half of the century, were lionised in the 1960s and 70s both for their striking painterly techniques and for their distinctive representation of Canadian wilderness. Thomson's 'Pine Island', (1914) for example, depicts the lakes and forests of Ontario as beautifully pure and defiantly hardy, clinging to the rock of the Canadian Shield. In 'Death by Landscape', a short story from *Wilderness Tips* (1991), Atwood layers memories of a childhood wilderness camp with adult meditations upon Group of Seven paintings: 'They are pictures of convoluted tree trunks on an island of pink, wave-smoothed stone, with more islands behind; of a lake with rough, bright, sparsely wooded cliffs; of a vivid river shore with a tangle of bush and two beached canoes, one red, one grey' (p.110). The adult protagonist Lois feels a strange attraction for these paintings, which derives from her uncanny sense that 'there is something, or someone, looking back out.' It emerges that her friend Lucy inexplicably vanished in her company at Camp Manitou, and that she was blamed. The adult Lois refuses to return to the North, but regards her paintings with a fond obsession:

> ... these paintings are not landscape paintings. Because there aren't any landscapes up there, not in the old, tidy European sense... . Instead there's a tangle, a receding maze, in which you can become lost almost as soon as you step off the path. There are no back-grounds in any of these paintings, no vistas; only a great deal of foreground that goes back and back, endlessly ...
>
> (pp.128–9)

The twist is that 'Every one of [the paintings] is a picture of Lucy': she lives in them, glimpsed only at the edge of vision. Equivocating between the artistic and environmental meanings of 'landscape', and exploring a morbid fascination with the way both paintings and forests recede endlessly, Atwood shows an ironic awareness of the construction of wilderness that was less prominent in the earlier novel.

Canadian critics, writers and artists have been proving Atwood's 'Survival' thesis wrong ever since. Questions of colonisation and ethnic identity like diaspora, hybridity and Indigeneity dominate CanLit, not wilderness, although they are sometimes combined (ch.7). In *Beyond Wilderness: The Group of Seven, Canadian Identity, and Contemporary Art* (2007), Peter White concedes that the Group remains 'inescapable as a point of reference,' both for populist celebration and critique, and re-contextualisation. Gu Xiong and Andrew Hunter's 'Ding Ho/Group of 7,' (2000) for example, sardonically situates two of **Lawren Harris**'s (1885–1970) snowy wilderness paintings within a mosaic of Chinese Communist propaganda (pp.208–9), while Robert Fones's 'Natural Range' series (1983–4) draws attention to the absurdity of, as Benedict

Anderson puts it, 'nationalization' of wilderness by 'human naming' (p.246). Kylie Crane draws on Atwood's 'Survival' thesis in her comparative postcolonial study of Canadian and Australian 'myths of wilderness', but modifies it to emphasise that 'the implicit or explicit threat that wilderness harbors towards individual survival works to uphold the dualism of human versus nonhuman nature within a framework that masks the survival of indigenous people in exactly these spaces' (p.4). The examples she chooses, though, are surprisingly few and, in the case of Atwood's *Oryx and Crake* (ch.6), tenuous. Kate Rigby claims, conversely, that 'wilderness neo-romanticism arrived only very late in Australia, largely via the influence of US environmentalism from the late 1970s, and it swiftly came under fire in the contemporaneous context of the Aboriginal land rights movement ...' (2020: 20–1). Distinct as Canada and Australia are geographically and historically, it seems that consciousness of Indigenous inhabitation (among literary authors and scholars if not more widely) made the wilderness ideal so disreputable that, tourism brochures aside, it is only ever referenced ironically. The shift is reflected in wilderness governance: as recently as 1970 in Canada, Indigenous and other existing residents were deported when new Parks were created, whereas almost all National Parks in Canada established after 1985 involve resolution of Indigenous land claims, or are designated 'Reserves' pending agreement.

THE TROUBLE WITH WILDERNESS

William Cronon's essay 'The Trouble with Wilderness' kicked off a sustained furore when it was published in 1996. It rehearses some of the history presented here, quoting Wordsworth and Thoreau, and supplements it with an account of the myth of frontier in which bourgeois men relinquished their civilised trappings so that their authentic selves could emerge. The upshot of his argument is that wilderness 'quietly expresses and reproduces the very values its devotees seek to reject' (1996: 15). It is, for Cronon, an invention of alienated urbanites who buy the works of Muir and his followers, but seldom attempt to emulate him, which sets up a sacred ideal in which nature is only authentic if we are entirely absent from it. And if humans are already present, like the Miwok Natives and White miners who lived and worked in the Yosemite Valley before it was 'protected', they must be expelled – repeatedly, in the case of the Miwok. Thus wilderness is a space reserved for privileged leisure (although ecological motivations were added later) that denies its own historicity, just like Hall's definition of ideology above. The flipside, says Cronon, is that the places where we actually live and work, and where we earn the money to buy the hiking equipment to sustain us in the wilderness, remain unloved and unprotected.

John Muir's declining esteem among ecocritics goes beyond espousing this troubling conception of wilderness and its characteristic exclusions. Born in Scotland and raised in Wisconsin, Muir avoided fighting in the Civil War by moving to Canada, and then, in its aftermath in 1867, walked from Indiana to Florida. *1,000 Mile Walk to the Gulf,* published posthumously in 1916, records his impressions, which include 'demeaning and stereotypical' portraits of African Americans, according to Paul Outka's *Race and Nature* (2008: 159). The problem, for Outka, is that Muir identifies Black people *with* nature and so he depicts them as incapable of *appreciating* it. After Muir sails to San Francisco in 1868, his 'narrative of discovering the sublime West ... traces the process of forgetting the explicitly racialized geography of the east and south' (p.156). In the Sierras, says Outka, 'whiteness can hide in plain sight' because 'the trauma of race is at once utterly effaced and an ambiguous and threatening other lurking just over the eastern horizon' (p.70). As wilderness, Yosemite seems to exist beyond racial difference – Elijah in *Gloryland* is relieved that in Yosemite 'These red firs don't care who we are or what we are' (p.222) – and yet for Muir, in Outka's account, 'Natural appreciation becomes a supposedly neutral test that determines a subject's character – the sort of neutral test that privileged whites just happen to pass in overwhelming numbers' (p.159). In this century, Shelton Johnson seeks to undo the normative Whiteness of wilderness both through his own efforts as a Yosemite ranger and by depicting the fictional Elijah as comfortable there. Carolyn Finney undertakes similar work when she highlights two pivotal pieces of US legislation: the Wilderness Act and the Civil Rights Act, both passed in 1964. She describes the 'discrete social, cultural, and geographical milieus' (2014: 45) of the lawmakers involved, and argues for their integration in the present day. Former US President Barack Obama, too, challenged what Jennifer C. James calls 'the reification of spatial imaginaries in discussions of blacks and nature' when he vacationed in Montana in 2009 (2011: 176), and more recently he has presented 'Our

Great National Parks' (2022), a Netflix series extolling the beauty and ecological value of what Obama calls 'our shared birth-right' in wild nature.

Even Muir's ecological sainthood is questioned today. He argued against early Park officials who understood the value of Indigenous burning of grassland and understory (ch.1 and 7), and advocated for trees to be protected by preventing and putting out fires. The result was a doubling of the forest density in Yosemite and, eventually, much bigger fires throughout Western North America. As Eric Michael Johnson reports: 'After a century of fire suppression in the Yosemite Valley biodiversity had actually declined, trees were now 20 percent smaller, and the forest was more vulnerable to catastrophic fires than it had been before the US Army and armed vigilantes expelled the native population' (2014). While it seems unfair to blame Muir for not anticipating this outcome, the story does add weight to criticism of the 'fortress conservation' model that he helped to found. Postcolonial ecocritics (Huggan and Tiffin 2015), political ecologists (Hayes and Ostrom 2005) and NGOs like the WWF seem to be converging on the view that systematically excluding local people from wildlands is not only unjust; it can be counter-productive.

Cronon emphasises that his critique is levelled at the wilderness ideal rather than the 'legitimate empirical question in conservation biology of how large a tract of land must be before a given species can reproduce on it' (p.22). As Prerna Singh Bindra argues in *The Vanishing: India's Wildlife Crisis* (2017), for example, the flourishing of wild Asian elephants, Bengal tigers and jaguars is incompatible with almost any human presence. Conversely, we might observe, wilderness writing feeds a flourishing outdoor recreation industry that ironically employs an 'aesthetic of relinquishment' (Buell 1995: 143–79) – going to the woods, as Thoreau writes, 'to live deliberately, to front only the essential facts of life' (1992 [1910]: 72) – to motivate an unsustainable economy of acquisition centred on hiking, camping and 'recreational vehicles' (RVs).

As a result, the books transform the places they describe. Tyra Olstad asks:

> Have you been to Walden Pond? If so, instead of walking through woods where Henry Thoreau lived deliberately, you may have parked

in the paved lot, toured the cabin replica, and bought a few souvenirs at the gift shop – trinkets reading "Simplify! Simplify!" … Countless once-wild corners of the [USA] have changed almost beyond recognition since they were celebrated in beloved works of American nature writing.

(2020: 1)

Her response to this quandary is an engaging work of **narrative scholarship** that reads *Arctic Wilderness* (1956) by **Bob Marshall** (1901–39) as inspiration for, and contrast to, a gruelling hiking trip to the Gates of the Arctic National Reserve (GAAR) in Alaska. The account blends illuminating historical and textual material with descriptions of a punishing, genuinely dangerous, experience (even with a rescue beacon). Olstad concludes with a riposte to Cronon's claim 'that wilderness is "entirely a cultural invention"' (p.17), saying he 'has not been to GAAR.' This widespread reflex among critics of Cronon – that he must not have experienced anywhere *wild enough* – misses the point. He never denies the existence, or value, of wildness, and Olstad's honest, stylish and reflexive narrative rather underscores his argument. What, besides a potent fantasy ideal, could motivate such a hideous journey?

THE NEW WILD?

In American popular culture, the allure of wilderness, complete with normative Whiteness, remains. The masculine form, as in Werner Herzog's *Grizzly Man* (2005) (ch.6) or Sean Penn's exquisitely filmed *Into the Wild* (2007), narrates an idealistic rejection of civilisation that leads to tragedy, whereas in the feminine version centred on the figure of 'Cheryl Strayed' in *Wild* (2014, dir. Jean-Marc Vallée), the wilderness trial culminates in self-acceptance. *Into the Wild* and *Wild* have much in common: they are adapted from non-fictional books; they are structured around inspirational quotations of poetry and song; and their protagonists adopt pseudonyms that suit their 'wild' personas. As Pramod K. Nayar argues, 'The lives of both McCandless and Strayed posit a clear binary: a corrupt and materialist human society and the purer, and purifying, wilds of the American landscape. The wild is the space of self-discovery, healing and escape' (2019: 94). For Strayed, though, there is sexual threat as well as companionship and affirmation on the

Pacific Crest Trail, whereas Chris McCandless (aka Alexander Super-tramp) enjoys a typically masculine freedom of action. Because the Supertramp persona 'identifies an ego-defying sense of wilderness immersion with natural selfhood' (Menrisky 2019: 49), he pushes his relinquishment to the point where he starves to death in an abandoned bus in Alaska. McCandless's realisation, too late, that the binary of wilderness and civilisation is a fatal illusion has not deterred numerous fans from trying to emulate him.

Meanwhile contemporary nature (or, increasingly, 'environmental') writing and ecological art most often depicts wilderness as vulnerable rather than sublime, and emphasises how it can elude our aesthetic responses and categories. Scott Hess's 'Imagining an Everyday Nature' usefully surveys these developments and argues ecocritics should attend to urban, agricultural and other working landscapes as much as 'wild' ones. He rejects Timothy Morton's suggestion that the word 'nature' is too contaminated to use any more (ch.3), saying that everyday nature 'does not just deconstruct but re-inhabits the legacy of "nature"' (2010: 104). The trajectory of American environmental writing parallels the previous chapter's recuperation of pastoral in British nature writing, albeit with greater attention to environmental justice. The remainder of this chapter contrasts the still-popular American wilderness ideal, which lost much of its complexity and ambivalence as it descended from Romanticism, and various treatments of wildness.

Trace: Memory, History, Race, and the American Landscape (2015) by Lauret Savoy epitomises this shift. It is a beautiful, unsparing 'tracing' of Savoy's autobiography and genealogy, all framed within two encounters with deep time: the author's visit, aged seven, to Point Sublime, a viewpoint for the Grand Canyon, and her discovery of a cryptic fossil in the Canadian Rock-ies as a geology graduate student (p.184). Savoy recounts, first, a California childhood in which she 'never knew race', and then, after moving to Washington, DC, distressing experiences of playground racialisation and official prejudice in history books:

> What I couldn't grasp then was that twining roots from different continents could never be crammed into a single box. I descend from Africans who came in chains and Africans who may never have known bondage. From European colonists who tried to make a new start in a world new to them. As well as from Native peoples who were

displaced by those colonists from homelands that defined their essential being.

(p.20)

The adult Savoy turns this baffling complexity to advantage, seeking to 'refrain from dis-integrated thinking and living, from a fragmented understanding of human experience on this continent' (p.47). One of the stories she excavates is that of Fort Huachaca, the army camp in Arizona near the Mexican border where her mother worked as a nurse during the Second World War. If Elijah Yancy had been a real trooper in the 'all Negro' 9th Cavalry, he would have been based there during the Indian Wars (pp.142–3). As the base grew during the twentieth century, every facility was duplicated to ensure racial segregation: 'Two officer's clubs. Two station hospitals. Two sets of chapels, theaters, service clubs, day rooms – even flagpoles' (p.145). Yet every recovery of historical texture and presence, in places that seek mainly to forget it, is shadowed by Savoy's awareness of irredeemable loss. As she observes of the fossil record: 'Millions of years may be lost in the gaps between black shale laminate so thin as to be pages of a book at night' (p.185). *Trace* is a remarkable achievement, even if its historicisation of landscape comes at the expense of ecological attention.

Savoy's narrative structure deftly layers multiple time-periods in a subjective and emotive order, rather than a chronological one. Annie Proulx's *Barkskins* (2016) is an epic novel of equivalent ambition and accomplishment that traverses the period 1693–2013 in historically-ordered sections, and ranges to Holland, China, Brazil and New Zealand whilst remaining centred on the trans-border region of Maine, Vermont, and southern Quebec and Ontario. The title is the regional name for foresters and lumberjacks: two lineages of them descended from French migrants Charles Duquet (later Anglicised to Duke) and René Sel; the first striving to keep itself White and European, the other creating a Métis family by intermarriage with the Mi'kmaq. These family histories are entwined with the environmental history of the forests as much as with each other. At first, the characters are impressed by the capacity of European technologies to fell the illimitable woods:

René felt the power in this ax, its greedy hunger to bite through all that stood in its way, sap spurting, firing out white chips like china shards. With a pointed stone he marked the haft with his initial, R. As he cut, the wildness of the world receded, the vast invisible web of filaments that connected human life to animals, trees to flesh and bones to grass shivered as each tree fell and one by one the web strands snapped.

(p.12)

Sel even experiences the forest as taunting him with its scale and vitality: 'He was powerless to stop chipping at it, but the vigor of multiple sprouts from stumps and still-living roots grew in his face, the rise and fall of his ax almost a continuous circular motion' (p.57). The Mi'kmaq are half-appalled and half-entranced: 'many welcomed the ways of the Acadian French—their clothing, their stout boats, their vegetables and pork roasts, the metal tools, glass ornaments and bolts of fabric, their intoxicating spirits and bright flags and even their hot bare bodies, so pale' (pp.181–2). Over time, they develop increasingly 'double lives, the interior reality warring with the external world in a kind of teetering madness' (p.187). While Mi'kmaw and Métis characters participate in the ever-accelerating annihilation of the forest, they are revolted by the waste, much like Arminius Breitsprecher, a German forester who tries to foster a more regenerative timber industry.

Barkskin's three centuries of forest history forms a kind of bassline to ethnic and family conflict, sexual passion and betrayal, and many sudden deaths: the timber baron Duke murdered by the timber thief Dud McBogle (p.146); Jinot Sel's family wiped out by cholera after a neighbour brings round 'delicious water' from her well (p.413); Achille's Mi'kmaw wife and young children slaughtered by English soldiers (p.194). The novel is startlingly realised, as in this scene where 'choppers' from a dozen nations and tribes await the sunrise to start work: 'They stood in the still and merciless cold, ax heads beneath their jackets thrust up into their armpits to keep the steel from freezing, waiting for the light, so cold they could feel the arcs of their eyebrows, ice-stiffened nostril hairs' (p.298). At the same time, as Stig Abell notes, Proulx's is 'an entirely unforgiving eye' that yields a 'parade of sheer ugliness' as well as hardship (2016: 23). It is true, too, that *Barkskin*'s 'range and pace mean that the lives of major characters can sometimes pass by in little more than a blur' (p.24), though the sense of an inhuman temporality, closer to the lifetimes of trees than people, is ample compensation. Proulx's informed, respectful, un-idealised, depiction of the Mi'kmaq and Métis occasionally hints at a possible future beyond colonial violence and environmental destruction, as when Kuntaw Sel tries to explain the relationship of colonists and Mi'kmaq as akin to water and mackerel oil that keep separating. He concludes:

> 'Sometime I hope for this Canada that the Mi'kmaw oil will blend with the water and oil come to the top. We will hold our country again someday,' he said, 'but we will be a little bit changed—a little bit watery and the white men be a little bit oily.'
>
> (p.601)

Barkskins' braided, discontinuous narrative structure recalls the use of time-lapse photography in nature documentaries to reveal processes too slow for direct observation, such as the melting of Arctic sea-ice or the growth of a bramble, though its characters' perceptions of the forest are equally shaped by cultural difference, especially between the settler colonial and Mi'kmaw/Métis families. Most settlers are lured to America by the image of:

> ... the rich continent with its inexhaustible coverlet of forests, its earth streaked as a moldy cheese with veins of valuable metals, fish and game in numbers too great to be compassed, hundreds of millions of acres of empty land waiting to be taken and a beckoning, generous government too enchanted with its own democratic image to deal with shrewd men whose people had lived by their wits for centuries.
>
> (pp.531–2)

Over the centuries, the Indigenous inhabitants of the 'empty land' participate in, and suffer from, the plundering of that seemingly 'inexhaustible' wealth.

An equally revealing narrative innovation distinguishes Richard Powers's *The Overstory* (2018), another chunky novel about trees, forests and the humans that cherish and exploit them: the major sections are titled 'Roots', 'Trunk', 'Crown', and 'Seeds', which suggests an analogy between the structure of a tree and that of the story. The first section, though, is subdivided by the names of nine major characters, each of them associated with a different species: in the case of Olivia

Vandergriff, for example, the ginkgo is the unnoticed tree outside her student flat (Powers 2018: 146) where she accidentally electrocutes herself in her introductory chapter. Nicholas Hoel inherits a family farm in Iowa together with a stack of photos of a lone chestnut in the yard, which his predecessors took once a month for 75 years. Its time lapse record of the tree 'spiralling up into the air like a corkscrew fountain' (p.408) contrasts painfully with the elliptical narration of the annihilation of the American chestnut, once 'the most harvested tree in the country' (p.12), by chestnut blight in the first decades of the twentieth century.

Tree-centred contingencies lead most of the characters to converge (in the 'Trunk' section) on a protest against the logging of old-growth redwoods in California. A stunning episode depicts Olivia and Nicholas occupying a platform 200 feet up in a 'mother' redwood tree named Mimas, a tree so vast and old it is its own ecosystem. Nicholas is overwhelmed: 'Cloud, mountain, World Tree, and mist – all the tangled, rich stability of creation that gave rise to words to begin with – leave him stupid and speechless' (p.264). Yet this moment of Romantic sublimity is subordinated within the design of the novel to subterranean interconnections that aim, according to Monica Manolescu, at 'displacement of the center of gravity of [the socio-ecological] community towards trees rather than at an inclusion of non-human beings in a community dominated by humans' (2021: 9). Paul Quinn contrasts *Barkskins*, 'a brilliant long novel', with *The Overstory*, which he describes as an 'encyclopedic' novel in which 'scale is not just a question of word count or historical sweep but of multiscalar patterning' (2018: 22). The events and preoccupations that draw the characters together are repeatedly compared with the fungal mycorrhizae and rhizomic root systems that interconnect trees underground, as we learn from Dr Patricia Westerford, a biochemist who discovers that sugar maples warn each another of impending insect attacks. Her book *The Secret Forest,* a fictional counterpart to Peter Wohlleben's popular, and controversial (Moor 2021), *The Hidden Life of Trees* (2015), supplies the novel's conceptual and empirical 'overstory.' Studying a copse of aspen she reflects that:

... these fifty thousand baby trees have sprouted from a rhizome mass too old to date even to the nearest hundred millennia. Underground,

> the eighty-year old trunks are a hundred thousand, if they're a day. She wouldn't be surprised if this great, joined, single clonal creature that looks like a forest has been around for the better part of a million years. ... The thing is outlandish, beyond her ability to wrap her head around. But then, as Dr Westerford knows, the world's outlands are everywhere, and trees like to toy with human thought like boys toy with beetles.
>
> (p.131)

This 'outlandish' wildness, which is far bigger, and less perceptible, than popular conceptions of wilderness, is revealed to each character in turn, and the force of the experience is enhanced by metafictional critiques of the scalar limitations of conventional novels (cf. ch.8). For example, Olivia is moved by a nineteenth century novel she reads high up in the redwood, but laments the characters are:

> "... all imprisoned in a shoe box, and they have no idea. I just want to shake them and yell, *Get out of yourselves, damn it! Look around!* But they can't, Nicky. Everything alive is just outside their field of view."
>
> (p.293)

Frequently the human characters are represented, and even think of themselves, as conduits rather than authors of this wild knowledge. Thus, Manolescu identifies a 'surprising complementarity of scientific and animist discourses about trees' (p.11) in *The Overstory,* which aligns it with pioneering ecofeminist Val Plumwood's advocacy of relating to '*nature as powerful, agentic and creative, making space in our culture for an animating sensibility and vocabulary*' (2009 it.orig.; cf. ch.2 'New Materialism'). Marco Caracciolo argues that 'Seeds', the last section, narrates a still-more radical decentring in which, 'aided by machine-learning algorithms [or "learners"], life organizes itself to survive anthropogenic catastrophe and thrive after humanity's extinction or radical transformation' (2019: 53). For Powers, there seems no categorical distinction between three kinds of wildness: that of 'nature'; of frail, dependent, unpredictable human animals; and of emergent artificial intelligences. At the same time, his bravura performance as *author* only underscores the unique responsibility of humans, who are 'chosen by creation to *know*' (p.282).

Scholarly writing seldom warrants direct comparison to literary fiction, but Anna Lowenhaupt Tsing's *The Mushroom at the End of the World* (2015) is an exception. It is an extraordinary work of **multispecies ethnography** that tracks the *matsutake* mushroom, much sought-after in Japan, through several cultural, economic and ecological contexts. Tsing describes the structure as a 'riot of short chapters' and 'an open-ended assemblage, not a logical machine' (p.viii), underselling the intense curiosity with which she pursues the mushroom to Finland, Japan, China, Canada and Oregon, USA, integrating knowledge we might classify as anthropological, economic and ecological. She rejects both progressive and **declensionist** metanarratives, pointing out astutely that 'Progress still controls us even in tales of ruination' (p.21). Instead, she looks to the mushroom (*Tricholoma matsutake* in Linnaean taxonomy) for stories of human and biological flourishing in the least promising environments. *Matsutake* is a mycorrhizal fungus that lives entangled with the roots of several species of tree, and it proliferates, unpredictably, in disturbed or 'degraded' patches of forest. Its cultural and monetary value in Japan, moreover, gives rise to a startling variety of socio-ecological adaptations in the human communities that hope to gather it. This fungus is stubbornly wild – it cannot be cultivated intentionally, and so resists the capitalist logic of 'scalability', or 'the ability of a project to change scales smoothly without any change in project frames' (p.38) – and yet it mainly thrives, in North America anyhow, in 'the ruins of scalable forestry' (p.42). Tsing's book embeds post-equilibrium ecology (ch.3, 'Pastoral Ecology') at both a thematic and structural level, much as *The Overstory* does with arboreal rhizomes, and it, too, celebrates wildness even as it is distanced from the popular ideal of wilderness. It could also be considered an exemplary 'eco-cosmopolitan' narrative (ch.8).

Perhaps the biggest problem with wilderness is that the human aesthetic sense yields few ecological insights, and our assumptions about what is 'pristine' or 'degraded' tell us more about our enculturated prejudices than biodiversity. Non-fictional works including Emma Marris's *Rambunctious Garden* (2011) and Fred Pearce's *The New Wild* (2015) back up their sharp criticism of the wilderness ideal with empirical evidence that 'A historically faithful ecosystem is necessarily a heavily managed ecosystem' (Marris 2011: 12), and that, contrary to the 'green xenophobia' (Pearce 2016: xi) of invasion ecologists, 'Most alien species add to local diversity and enrich species-poor environments' (p.18). There are clear examples of alien species causing extinctions, especially when novel predators (such as the brown tree snake *Boiga irregularis*) are introduced onto islands (e.g. Guam), yet most introductions, according to Pearce, are harmless or beneficial.

Both authors focus on Hawai'i, often mentioned as a site of island extinctions, where Marris describes arduous efforts to restore habitats to an undegraded (i.e. pre-colonial) state:

> But restoring the islands' ecosystems to the way they were in 1777 would be restoring them to a state very much shaped by the Polynesians who had been living there for at least one thousand years: a semi-domesticated landscape filled with species the Polynesians brought with them, including taro, sugarcane, pigs, chickens, and rats, and missing others, including at least fifty species of birds, who were hunted out by the first arrivals.
>
> (p.4)

Pearce notes that although 71 species of endemic flowering plants are now extinct, 'more than a thousand new plants have arrived' (p.12) to add to the 1500 Hawai'ian species remaining, and yet this cosmopolitan nature (ch.3) is seldom acknowledged, let alone celebrated. Likewise, cities are seen 'as hotbeds of alien invasions, disreputable ecosystems, and species that just shouldn't be there' (p.173), rather than biodiversity hotspots. Pearce is interested in novel ecosystems (or assemblages) such as the wholly anthropogenic cloud forest on Ascension Island that boasts 300 introduced species of plants (p.7). If we consider wildness to imply the absence or minimisation of intentional management, wildness is increasingly the *opposite* of pristine wilderness, not the value it incarnates. Ascension Island and *matsutake*-rich forests are wild, but not wildernesses, whereas the purity of wildernesses that conform to historical baselines (precolonial or pre-human) can only be maintained by sustained, expensive programs of eradication and maintenance.

In Europe, the contradiction between these two conflated concepts was starkly illustrated by the fate of a 'rewilding' experiment carried out in a Dutch polder (reclaimed land below sea-level) called the *Oostvaardersplassen* (OVP) between the 1980s and its termination in 2018. Ecologists wanted to see if populations of wild herbivores would recreate a Paleolithic savannah-type habitat if left unmanaged, and so they introduced red deer, Konik horses and Heck cattle, which seemed analogous to the wild species of the past. The OVP was represented as a wilderness, and yet it was fenced and had a railway line running through it, so when animals starved in 2005, 2010 and again 2018 there was public outcry. As Bert Theunissen explains, the 'fiasco' was caused, first, by the fact that the OVP was obviously an *artificial* wilderness, in which the Darwinian law of the wild should not apply, and second, by Dutch citizens' expectations, reinforced by ecologists' statements, that the 'natural balance (*natuurlijk evenwicht*) of the grazer populations' (2019: 344) ought to have happened without either human or other predation, when that was never likely to occur. Future rewilding projects will only succeed, Theunissen suggests, if these assumptions are challenged.

The histories of the tropes of pastoral and wilderness are interdependent in Anglophone history, especially in their recent developments. They are equally susceptible to appropriation in any number of political and commercial causes (say, yoghurt pastoral or pickup truck wilderness), and yet these populist forms diverge more and more from the reflective and ecologically-inflected versions I have mainly considered here. Historicisation and evaluation in terms of environmental justice have countered idealisation, challenging comfortable myths like southern pastoral and western American wilderness. Technical innovations, such as Powers's mycorrhizal narrative, have overturned the assumption that environmental writing is naively 'ecomimetic' (ch.3). Given the intense politicisation of sites like the OVP, to say nothing of federally controlled American wildlands, the next phase for environmental writing may be to acknowledge, and address, our polarised societies.

5

APOCALYPSE

MYTHS OF ANNIHILATION AND REDEMPTION

Stories about the end of the world are widespread across historical and present-day societies, though not universal, and they feed into a contemporary apocalyptic trope that is complex and often contradictory. Evangelical Christians draw on the Biblical books of *Genesis, Daniel* and *Revelation* to dismiss environmentalist concerns about climate change, reassuring us that, 'While the earth remaineth, seedtime and harvest, and cold and heat, and summer and winter, and day and night shall not cease' (KJV Genesis 8:22), while climate scientists dance anxiously around apocalyptic projections, desperate both to convey urgency and to avoid 'doomsaying'. **Millennial** movements have suffered embarrassments such as the Great Disappointment of the Christian Millerites, who were not Raptured as expected on April 23, 1843, nor on the revised dates of March 21 or October 22, 1844 (Newman 2010: ch.28), to the amusement of their fellow Americans. The descendants of the Millerites, the Seventh-day Adventist Church, have awaited the millennium peaceably since 1863, advocating vegetarianism and building hospitals, whereas an Adventist splinter group, the Branch Davidians, provoked a lethal standoff with US authorities at Waco, Texas in 1993

DOI: 10.4324/9781003174011-5

in which 80 people died (ch.37). Communism, the most widespread form of secular millennialism (Slezkine 2017: 73–118), was responsible for tens of millions of deaths in China, Cambodia, North Korea, the Soviet Union and elsewhere in the twentieth century. Jessica Hurley and Dan Sinykin conclude that:

> For communities all over the world and for thousands of years, historical expectations, political commitments, social organizations, and affective relationships to the present and future have been shaped by an innumerable and constantly shifting set of apocalyptic visions.
>
> (2018: 455)

The contradictions within the apocalyptic trope follow from its multiple, tangled mythological roots and the unpredictable consequences of people's beliefs. The Biblical Book of Revelation, though, has had an outsized impact thanks to European colonialism and Christian proselytizing. Zakes Mda exemplifies this in his *Heart of Redness* (2000), based on the true story of an 1856 prophecy by Nongqawuse, a young Xhosa woman, which foresaw the White settlers being destroyed and the ancestors returning to life if the amaXhosa killed all their cattle. Whilst the millennial movement in the novel is explicitly anti-colonial, it blends Xhosa ancestor-worship with Christian apocalypticism. The Xhosa Believers suffer a series of 'disappointments', like the Millerites, that culminate in the starvation of around 40,000 people and British colonisation of their land. However, the Believers blame the Unbelievers, who did not kill their cattle, for preventing the fulfilment of the prophecy. Mda's sardonic, erotically-charged novel weaves this internecine dispute among the amaXhosa into present-day debates about development in post-apartheid South Africa. It is, as Roman Bartosch shows, 'a story about *not* understanding the other' (2013: 164) in which an indeterminate blend of colonial Christianity and animism undermines any possibility of a homogenous 'indigenous' amaXhosa identity.

The Judaeo-Christian strand itself emerges from dozens of Jewish and early Christian apocalypses written between 200BCE and 200CE, including *Daniel* in the Jewish Tanakh and Christian Old Testament, *Revelation* in the New Testament, and the apocryphal *Book of Enoch*. According to Damian Thompson, this version of the End:

> ... was mapped out in a new literary genre called apocalypse, from the Greek *Apo-calyptein*, meaning 'to un-veil'. Apocalyptic literature takes the form of a revelation of the end of history. Violent and grotesque images are juxtaposed with glimpses of a world transformed; the underlying theme is usually a titanic struggle between good and evil ... Apocalypticism has been described as a genre born out of crisis, designed to stiffen the resolve of an embattled community by dangling in front of it the vision of a sudden and permanent release from its captivity. It is underground literature, the consolation of the persecuted.
>
> (1997: 13–4)

Apocalypse may have been a new *literary genre*, but apocalyptic *myths* emerged independently in Mayan societies in Mesoamerica (Leeming 2019: 65–7), in the Indian Hindu story of the *kali yuga* (pp.77–80), and in the pre-Christian Germanic myths that were later recorded in the Norse myth of *Ragnarǫk* (pp.81–3). Acknowledging these, though, we can distinguish between the distinctive linear view of time that Judaism and Christianity inherited from Zoroastrianism (Newman 2010: loc.382) and the cyclical temporality of Hindu and Norse tales: the Kali Age concludes with a titanic battle at the end of a Day of Brahma that lasts 4,320,000 years, which precipitates a renewal of the universe for another cosmic Day. The apocalyptic battle of *Ragnarǫk* is discussed in Christopher Abram's *Evergreen Ash*, an ecocritical study of Icelandic sagas in the context of animistic Viking beliefs. Contrary to the assumption that pre-Christian sagas would supply a mythic alternative to modern Western narratives, he finds that 'the Æsir's [Norse gods'] actions can only teach a negative lesson' (2019: 222) because *Ragnarǫk* is precipitated by divine actions that embody just the kind of dualism criticised by Val Plumwood (ch.2). For Abram, the Æsir's failure prefigures (with conscious anachronism) our collective failure to avert climate catastrophe:

> The Norse gods—who had a hand in creating the universe, who are immortal (up to a point), and who have supernatural dominion over all things—cannot prevent Ragnarǫk; *they cannot prevent themselves from causing Ragnarǫk*, even when preventing Ragnarǫk is the only way they can save themselves.
>
> (p.167)

The images of rebirth found in some versions merely underline, for Abram, the failure of both gods and men to imagine a different world to the one destroyed by Ragnarǫk.

The linear/cyclical distinction indicates that time and temporality are crucial to the meaning of various modes of apocalyptic narration. The rupture is often depicted in the past, either in mythic time, as in the similar flood myths found in ancient Mesopotamia, China, India and Mesoamerica, or in traumatic events such as the Black Death pandemic of the late 1340s, the mass enslavement of Africans, the Nazi genocide, or the colonisation of the Americas (ch.7). The Hebrew and Christian flood myth has been adapted into *Noah* (2014, dir. Darren Aronofsky), a sophisticated environmental allegory drawing on Apocryphal and other Jewish sources. The movie represents mankind's sinfulness, which was always the focus of the Noah story, in terms of ecological destruction, while the origins of life are represented by an animation of biological evolution accompanying Noah's narration of *Genesis*. The contrast between the ecocentric vegetarian Noah and his violent nemesis Tubal-Cain is, as George Handley points out, 'not the result of an imposition of modern environmental ethics but is rather drawn from Genesis itself and from Apocryphal literature' (2018: 626). The movie departs from its sources in showing Noah as willing to murder his grandchild to save the Earth *from* humanity, though our kind ultimately gets another chance to prove its worth.

The familiar conception of apocalypse, though, is not a past trauma but 'a future event involving both ending and revelation' (Hurley and Sinykin 2018: 454). Within this definition, we can distinguish, following Kate Rigby's *Dancing with Disaster* (2015), between jeremiad and **millennialism**. Rigby reads Jeremiah, of the Tanakh and Old Testament, as 'arguably the first in a long line of Jewish eco-prophets [for whom] the callous disregard for the plight of animals, birds, and the drought-stricken land is interlinked with the neglect of justice for the poor and marginalized: eco-catastrophe, in [Jeremiah's] reading, is symptomatic of a nation in breach of the covenant in its godless pursuit of power and profit' (loc.481). Jeremiah *warns* of the divine judgement such a breach will yield, rather than making predictions. In this way, the jeremiad, a crucial environmentalist genre, is distinct from millennial narratives that anticipate with grim pleasure a phase of 'redemptive violence' (loc.1524) following the cataclysm. 'Millennial' refers to the thousand years of bliss enjoyed by the saved before 'the final grand reckoning' (Newman 2010: loc.139) of the Second Coming of Jesus Christ, although *Revelation* has more scenes of torture and destruction than bliss. These spectacles appear in medieval artworks such as the Apocalypse Tapestry at Angers, France, and more recently in the popular *Left Behind* series of novels and movies. 'The righteous' will enjoy the millennium while the wicked suffer punishment, a stark moral dualism captured in *Matthew* 25: 31 in the metaphor of a shepherd separating (good) sheep from (evil) goats. It is millennial belief, not apocalypse as such, that glorifies violence and encourages believers to welcome or even to hasten the End Times.

Another relevant aspect of the Christian *Revelation* is its narration by its purported author, 'John'. In the Angers tapestry, this figure is the disciple John, though scholars agree he could not have been the author. Where the John of *Revelation* is a first-person narrator, the figure of John at Angers appears in each of the six panels, responding to triumphs and disasters and witnessing its graphic novel-like series of apocalyptic scenes. We can therefore add questions of narrativity to those of apocalyptic temporality and morality. An apocalyptic narrative must have at least one survivor who witnesses the story, which must be understood, or not, by readers in the pre-apocalyptic present. Russell Hoban's superb postnuclear *Riddley Walker* (1980) is narrated in a strange, altered English, in a recognisable Kentish accent, that marks the rupture between our world and Walker's, and Paul Kingsnorth's *The Wake* (2015), set in the aftermath of the apocalyptic Norman invasion of Anglo-Saxon England in 1066, is written in an imaginary 'shadow tongue' that splices together Old and modern English (p.353). Ecocritical readings of apocalyptic narrative ask who tells the story, and how, and what assumptions are made about communication across historical and cultural discontinuities.

THE SECULAR APOCALYPSE

Apocalyptic themes were secularised in the late eighteenth century. The Romantic poetry of **Percy Bysshe Shelley** (1792–1822) and **William Blake** (1757–1827) appropriated apocalyptic rhetoric for politically revolutionary purposes, and **Lord (George Gordon) Byron** (1788–1824) wrote a poem, 'Darkness' (1816), that envisions the extinction of the sun and the horrific unravelling of the social and natural order that ensues. However, **Mary Wollstonecraft Shelley** (1797–1851) is credited as author of the first apocalyptic novel, *The Last Man* (1826), which describes the destruction of Western civilisation (i.e. Great Britain) by plague in the then-distant 2090s. Narrated by the last man on Earth, Lionel Verney, Shelley's novel is florid, overlong, baggy and disjointed (at one point England is inexplicably invaded by a 'locust visitation' (2020: 296) of Irish and American refugees), but seminal for apocalyptic fiction after its re-publication in the 1960s. In the Romantic period, dramatic ruins were so fashionable that some aristocrats had them specially built on their estates. Shelley, though, represents future ruins as monuments to the disappearance of humanity: 'Our empty habitations remained, but the dwellers were gathered to the shades of the tomb' (p.316). Pramod K. Nayar sees these 'spectral landscapes', which exemplify the 'architectural uncanny', as integral to the secular apocalypse because they suggest that 'The boundary between human civilization, the contemporary and the ancient wilderness ... is accidental, and could be reversed at any time' (2019: 53). Rigby suggests that Shelley's bleak vision was probably inspired by the deaths of three children and many friends from disease; by a host of earthquakes, volcanoes and disrupted weather patterns in the previous years; and by the emergence in her own time of geological evidence that catastrophic 'revolutions' might have shaped life on Earth in the distant past. Shelley's secularisation of apocalypse dispenses with 'the biblical script of redemptive violence' (loc.1524) and, crucially, distinguishes between the fate of mankind and that of nature. Even though he addresses us from a climatically-altered future, Verney indulges in this wry reflection:

> Feel you not the earth quake and open with agonizing groans, while the air is pregnant with shrieks and wailings,— all announcing the last days of man? No! none of these things accompanied our fall! The balmy air of spring, breathed from nature's ambrosial home, invested the lovely earth, which wakened as a young mother about to lead forth in pride her beauteous offspring to meet their sire who had been long absent.
>
> (p.314)

Rigby's reading is illuminating but overly generous, as well as anachronistic, in its conclusion that *The Last Man* 'points ... to the necessity of a process of ecological enlightenment, in which the nonhuman is resituated as agentic, communicative, and ethically considerable' (loc.1752). While Rigby acknowledges the stereotyped depiction of marauding Irishmen and the 'distinctly racist overtones' (loc.1648) of the scene in which Verney is infected with plague by a dying 'negro' (p.335), she does not discuss Verney's view that nature's enduring beauty is wholly pointless without human subjects to enjoy it (p.328). Verney's ecological enlightenment seems intermittent at best.

In the twentieth century, Modernist writers such as **Wyndham Lewis** (1882–1957) and **T.S. Eliot** (1888–1965) incorporated apocalyptic themes in their work, though Lewis's reflected his excitement at the disruptive power of technology and Eliot's conveyed cultural pessimism following the carnage of the First World War (1914–1918). **D.H. Lawrence** (1885–1930), though, combined apocalyptic rhetoric with environmental themes, which influenced the American poet **Robinson Jeffers** (1887–1962), whose philosophy of 'inhumanism' put him at odds with the anthropocentric assumptions of readers and literary critics in his lifetime. Inhumanism, or the 'shifting of emphasis from man to not man' ('Robinson Jeffers'), epitomises apocalyptic ecocentrism as a poetic creed, and it implies a Stoic perspective on the part of the poet. Geneva M. Gano describes Jeffers's work as a 'poetry of ecological witness' (2021: 3), which unflinchingly conveys the shameful truth of human depredations, while David R. Williams suggests that the poet's Calvinist upbringing (alongside many other American wilderness advocates) accounts for his moral austerity and apocalyptic framing in terms of a 'thematic continuity of Protestant thought' (2021: 12). Jeffers frequently asserts the beauty of nature, but lacks Lawrence's descriptive powers, and his ecological relationality is combined with estrangement from humanity, as Gano observes: 'While Jeffers imagined and articulated his relation to all else in the world, from sardines to rocks to stardust in outer space, his relationship with other humans caused him great shame and anguish' (p.17). Jeffers's 'The Purse-Seine' (1937) admits the struggle to describe the terrible beauty of night-fishing a phosphorescent shoal: 'I cannot tell you / How beautiful the scene is'. But then the trapped fish:

... wildly beat from one wall to the other of their closing destiny the phosphorescent
Water to a pool of flame, each beautiful slender body sheeted with flame, like a live rocket

(2002: loc.6398)

The analogy between trapped fish and civilised humans emerges as the poet looks over the lights of 'a wide city' and cannot 'help but recall the seine-net / Gathering the luminous fish'. Far from mourning the 'inevitable mass disasters' that will afflict us as the net of Progress tightens, Jeffers expresses grim satisfaction at the working-out of an inexorable natural law that applies equally to fish and to humans viewed zoomorphically (ch.6). Jeffers's poetry is in fact full of apocalyptic imagery: 'the dance of the / Dream-led masses down the dark mountain' ('Rearmament'), 'man ... blotted out' ('To the Stone-Cutters'), and the meteoric 'mortal splendor' of a doomed America ('Shine, Perishing Republic'). At times there is a qualified compassion for humanity, as when the Earth itself dreams of a heavily symbolic cleansing storm in 'November Surf' and imagines how 'the two-footed / Mammal' might regain 'The dignity of room, the value of rareness' (p.39). More often, though, Jeffers's shame and misanthropic rage win out.

The gradual, still-incomplete secularisation of apocalypse began, according to Rigby, in the aftermath of the 1755 Lisbon earthquake. Prior to this, the 'punishment paradigm' attributed disastrous events to 'divine displeasure toward sinful humanity ... presaging the Final Judgment' (loc.1384). Rigby acknowledges that the punishment paradigm had brutal consequences, as when Jews were made scapegoats for the Black Death, and she agrees that the modern secular framing of 'natural disasters' mostly refrains from blaming victims for their fate, as well as justifying rational preventive measures that save countless lives (loc.123–7). However, she also laments the diminishing of a perspective in which 'social relations and natural phenomena were understood to be interrelated: how people comported themselves with one another, and with other others [sic], had environmental consequences; and environmental disturbances, especially big ones, had moral, religious, and political reverberations' (loc.106). She suggests that the 'modern myth' (loc.170) of 'natural disaster' no longer fits the socioecological entanglement of life on Earth today, where 'natural' causes, such as violent weather events, are accelerated by anthropogenic climate change, and human vulnerability to them is exacerbated by social injustice. Rigby proposes that we revalue the term 'catastrophe', recovering the ancient sense of the word in the *Poetics* of **Aristotle** (384–322BCE):

A true catastrophe, then, is not only a *terminus* but a turning point. In the *Poetics*, the *katastrophē* is intimately associated with *anagnorisis*: the moment of realization, when the tragic hero or heroine is faced with the collapse of their underlying assumptions about themselves and/or others and is brought, painfully and sometimes fatally, to the recognition of the damage that has been wrought by their ignorance.

(loc.447)

It is an attractive proposition, especially as the injustice of climatic disruption becomes more obvious, but it is unclear how supplanting the myth of natural disaster would avoid a return to the scapegoating cruelty of the punishment paradigm.

Heather Hicks, like Rigby, links a shift in apocalyptic narratives to Western cultural and intellectual history:

... with the emergence of modernity in the eighteenth century, apocalypse shifted from its origins as the story of the annihilation of a sinful human world to become, in novel form, the story of the collapse of modernity itself.

(2016: 2)

For Hicks, the questions posed by contemporary post-apocalyptic fiction are: what can be salvaged from modernity, and what is worth salvaging? Given that environmentalism is characterised by ambivalence, if not hostility, towards the modern world, it is not surprising that apocalyptic environmentalism is increasingly open to the notion that a *catastrophe* could be a turning point, not an ending, as well as ambivalent about the trope's core ideas of rupture, revelation and redemption.

ENVIRONMENTAL APOCALYPSE

Apocalyptic rhetoric has been part of environmentalist discourse from the beginning. Lawrence Buell suggests it is:

... the single most powerful master metaphor that the contemporary environmental imagination has at its disposal. Of no other dimension of contemporary environmentalism ... can it be so unequivocally said that the role of the imagination is central to the project; for the rhetoric of apocalypticism implies that the fate of the world hinges on the arousal of the imagination to a sense of crisis.

(1995: 285).

It has also been widely criticised, for example by climate sceptic Christopher Booker, who insists that the 'vision of the coming [climate] apocalypse' (2009: loc.6682; cf. Garrard et al. 2019) is a subconscious cultural narrative that biases both activists and scientists. From a very different perspective, Donna Haraway invites us to think '*without* the self-indulgent and self-fulfilling myths of apocalypse' (2016: 35); to 'stay with the trouble' (p.2) rather than fantasising about 'wiping the world clean' (p.150).

The emergence of modern environmentalism in the 1960s took place in the aftermath of the atomic bombings of Hiroshima and Nagasaki in 1945, and in the midst of the Cold War between the West and the Soviet bloc. It is therefore unsurprising that apocalyptic rhetoric is prominent in Rachel Carson's *Silent Spring* (1962), Paul Ehrlich's *The Population Bomb* (1968) and the Club of Rome's *The Limits to Growth* (1972). The apocalypticism of *Silent Spring* goes beyond the 'strange blight' that falls upon the pastoral scene in 'A Fable for Tomorrow': the use of radioactive fallout as a metaphorical source for descriptions of pesticide pollution, discussed in the Introduction, is potent because the imagery of nuclear detonation defined popular conceptions of the end of the world at the time. Moreover, the fear of lethal fission products such as Strontium-90, undetectable to the senses, provided Carson with a perfect model for the miasma of 'biocides' such as DDT, lindane and dieldrin:

> The most alarming of all man's assaults upon the environment is the contamination of air, earth, rivers, and sea with dangerous and even lethal materials. This pollution is for the most part irrecoverable; the chain of evil it initiates not only in the world that must support life but in living tissues is for the most part irreversible. In this now universal contamination of the environment, chemicals are the sinister and little-recognized partners of radiation in changing the very nature of the world – the very nature of its life.
>
> (1999: 23)

In this apocalyptic scenario, a 'chain of evil' has begun that is 'irreversible', leading Frederick Buell to describe *Silent Spring* as 'anything but understated in its pictures of environmental catastrophe' (2003: loc.119), and to conclude that its author saw ecological catastrophe as inevitable. Whilst Graham Huggan acknowledges *Silent Spring* '*is* relentless and repetitive, with death appearing on almost every page', he argues that 'it also suggests ways of *preventing* [catastrophe] from happening ... by using natural means of pest and disease control' (2016: 78). Cheryl Lousley, moreover, shows how Carson addresses a mature, informed audience that her own writing seeks to create: 'Although *Silent Spring* presents a crash course in organic chemistry, and Carson bases her judgments on a review of empirical research, she mobilizes science by speaking in the voice of the citizen, the "we" who have rights, including the right to know, and with that knowledge have a responsibility to make judgments based on our weighing of the evidence before us' (2018: 419–20). Most ecocritics therefore assess *Silent Spring* as a jeremiad that seeks, unlike Jeffers, to avert disaster.

The same can be said for Ehrlich's *The Population Bomb*, a neo-Malthusian (ch.2, 'Deep Ecology') classic that relies on horrific apocalyptic projections for its persuasive force:

> The battle to feed all of humanity is over. In the 1970s and 1980s hundreds of millions of people will starve to death in spite of any crash programmes embarked upon now. At this late date nothing can prevent a substantial increase in the world death rate.
>
> (1971: xi)

In the first of two 'scenarios', Ehrlich imagines that overpopulation would bring about environmental collapse, international instability and nuclear war in the mid-1980s. In the second, overpopulation facilitates an epidemic of Lassa fever. Failure to regulate birth rates results, according to Ehrlich's remorseless Malthusian logic, in the reign of 'three of the four apocalyptic horsemen – war, pestilence, and famine' (p.48). Ehrlich sees the human species as a teeming, burgeoning, eco-pathological threat, which he compares to a cancer, with its 'uncontrolled multiplication of cells' (p.152). 'Treating only the symptoms of cancer may make the victim more comfortable at first', but 'radical surgery', including compulsory sterilization and withholding of food aid, is the only real hope for the 'patient'.

Ursula Heise shows that treatments of over-population in literature and popular science (including later works by Ehrlich) avoid apocalyptic rhetoric and 'combine more cautious and complex forecasts with a greater emphasis on how population growth is related to such factors as economic conditions, social inequality, women's reproductive health, and access to education' (2008: 80). Paul Morland's *The Human Tide: How Population Shaped the Modern World* (2019) tracks the geopolitical impact of successive pulses of population growth that started in Great Britain in the eighteenth century and are still unfolding in parts of sub-Saharan Africa. Rapid growth in the number of Europeans in the nineteenth century provided troops, colonists and industrial workers that made temporary global dominance possible, which in turn allowed for mass emigration from overcrowded nations. Escape from the Malthusian trap (ch.2) was possible because agricultural and transport technologies greatly increased the size and mobility of harvests, and reproductive technologies 'proved population growth ... could be cheaply and easily tamed by people's choices without their having to restrain their natural appetites' (2019: loc.5077–88). Though Morland briefly discusses the environmental impact of enormous human populations, he expresses cornucopian pride in our escape from Malthusian limits, and suggests that if global population growth stops or reverses in the coming century 'land can be returned to nature and it will be possible to live in a greener planet' (loc.5029).

Frederick Buell's landmark study *From Apocalypse to Way of Life* (2003) concurs with Heise's assessment that environmentalists since the 1970s have shied away from apocalyptic rhetoric. Buell provides 'A history of crisis thought that fully incorporates both the apparent failure of previously forecasted apocalypses and the continuance and even deepening of alarm' (2003: loc.115), though he is at pains to challenge the cornucopians' claims of unwarranted 'doomsaying' (ch.2). He anatomises the abuse they heap on environmentalists, and points to instances where they, too, made inaccurate predictions. As long as environmentalism has existed, corporate interests have claimed that regulation will annihilate their industry, or worse: a chemical industry spokesman alleged in 1963 that 'if man were to faithfully follow the prescriptions of Miss Carson, we would return to the Dark Ages' (cited in Nixon 2011: 146). Not only have corporate 'doomsters' been wrong on numerous occasions, but environmental 'Doomsters ... can turn out to be absolutely correct and vital to humanity's safety' (loc.1576). Nevertheless, Buell argues that 'environmental crisis discourse has left apocalyptic ecologism and doomsterism behind and moved beyond apocalypse into a variety of new conceptual spaces and rhetorics' (loc.924). While the evidence in this chapter confirms the second claim, it rejects the first: there is, ironically, plenty of life in apocalyptic ecologism to this day.

An influential counter-example is Cormac McCarthy's devastating novel *The Road* (2006), which follows a father and son as they struggle to survive in a grey, ashy world devoid of Earth Others. The many interpretations of the novel come in three classes, the first exemplified by George Monbiot's assertion that *The Road* is 'the most important environmental book ever written' (2007). Though Monbiot accepts that McCarthy's portrayal of nuclear winter, a probable cause of collapse in the novel, is exaggerated, he praises *The Road*'s savage honesty about 'the one terrible fact to which our technological hubris blinds us: our dependence on biological production remains absolute.' In other words, Monbiot thinks McCarthy has written a particularly bleak and powerful jeremiad. The second class of reading sees *The Road* as an allegory, in keeping with the long-standing tradition of figuring life and its choices as a journey. Sarah E. McFarland, for instance, criticises apocalyptic fictions that allow us to continue to believe, however tenuously, that 'human exceptionalism' will ensure our species survives, and turns instead to 'the few realistic ecocollapse fictions that do not ratify the generic conventions of species survival [e.g. ending with pregnancy or birth]: the hopeless endings are the point' (2021: 9–10). The unnamed father and son in *The Road* are preoccupied with 'the dual fears of cannibalism ...: both the fear of being cannibalised and the fear of becoming cannibal' (p.67), and indeed the novel includes numerous gut-churning scenes of dismembered bodies and enslaved humans awaiting death. McFarland's reading, though, criticises the father's incoherent, impossible struggle to protect his son – in the name, presumably, of a vanished civilization or in vain hope of a future one – and praises McCarthy for his unillusioned depiction of cannibals who 'have abandoned the pretense of human exceptionalism' (p.68). The cannibals' human captives, says McFarland, are 'treated no worse or better than a chained veal calf or a raped sheep or any one of the millions of enslaved people and animals in the world today' (p.72). On this view, *The Road* functions as a horrifying, if instructive, allegory that demolishes human supremacism by showing our species consuming itself 'in a caloric pyramid scheme' (p.69).

The apocalyptic character of *The Road* might seem beyond question. Certainly, the narration of entropic dissolution is relentless, punctuated only by episodes of appalling suffering and cruelty. McCarthy's prose, though, is exquisite:

> [The father] lay listening to the water drip in the woods. Bedrock, this. The cold and the silence. The ashes of the late world carried on the bleak and temporal winds to and fro in the void. Carried forth and scattered and carried forth again. Everything uncoupled from its shoring. Unsupported in the ashen air. Sustained by a breath, trembling and brief. If only my heart were stone.
>
> (p.10)

At once spare and lyrical, the narrator observes the father and son with, in Dana Phillips's words, 'considerable objectivity' (2011: 180). Such impassivity is the clue to the third class of readings, which argue that 'while in *The Road* the world may have come to an end, the world is also the same as it ever was: filled with mortal peril, because it is shaped by causes the advent of which is pure chance, while the effects of these causes seem more or less deterministic' (p.173). Phillips reinterprets the passage that is taken to imply a nuclear war as a possible meteor strike (McCarthy 2007: 54), which lacks the morally reproving qualities of human conflict, and draws attention to the 'almost documentary flavor' (pp.178–9) of the father's practical activities in the novel. *The Road*, in Phillips's sceptical reading, cannot be apocalyptic because nothing is ultimately revealed: '*the end of the world is simply the end of the world, and McCarthy describes the scene as if he were a policeman dispatched by who knows what agency*' (p.188, italics original). Michael Chabon's review, too, denies that *The Road* is either redemptive or apocalyptic. He calls it a 'lyrical epic of horror' that becomes 'a testament to the abyss of a parent's greatest fears' (2007). If Chabon and Phillips are correct, ecocritics' recruitment of *The Road* into the canon of environmental, or even 'climate', fiction runs athwart the author's intentions and betrays their continued investment in apocalyptic tropes.

The continuing allure of apocalypse is also evident from 'Uncivilisation: The Dark Mountain Manifesto', which takes its name from the last line of Robinson Jeffers's 1935 poem 'Rearmament':

> ... The beauty of modern
> Man is not in the persons but in the

> Disastrous rhythm, the heavy and mobile masses, the dance of the
> Dream-led masses down the dark mountain.
>
> (Kingsnorth and Hine 2009)

Paul Kingsnorth and Dougald Hine, writing 'Uncivilisation' in 2009 during the global financial crisis, dispassionately observe successive social and ecological disasters that give the lie to the 'myth of progress', which 'is to us what the myth of god-given warrior prowess was to the Romans, or the myth of eternal salvation was to the conquistadors: without it, our efforts cannot be sustained.' They claim that 'We are the first generations to grow up surrounded by evidence that our attempt to separate ourselves from "nature" has been a grim failure, proof not of our genius but our hubris.' They consider civilisation overdue for an apocalyptic conclusion, and contradict the obligatory optimism bias of modernity:

> We do not believe everything will be fine. We are not even sure, based on current definitions of progress and improvement, that we want it to be.

The project of 'uncivilisation' (which closely resembles Jeffers's inhumanism) can only be accomplished by artists, they think, because scientists, engineers, politicians and techies are too enamoured of the myth of progress to confront apocalypse honestly. Such art:

> ... sets out to paint a picture of homo sapiens which a being from another world or, better, a being from our own—a blue whale, an albatross, a mountain hare—might recognise as something approaching a truth. It sets out to tug our attention away from ourselves and turn it outwards; to uncentre our minds.

The potted history of 'civilisation' presented by Kingsnorth and Hine is a brutally simplistic, if eloquent, narrative of decline that ends with 'our whole way of living ... passing into history.' John Gray's review of the *Manifesto* approves of its demolition of anthropocentric arrogance, but disputes the implication that 'uncivilisation' would in practice be congenial for poets and storytellers. Historic examples of societal breakdown suggest that the notion of a 'cleansing catastrophe' itself represents delusional 'apocalyptic thinking'. Gray asks: 'How can anyone imagine that the dream-driven human animal will suddenly become sane when its environment starts disintegrating?' (Gray 2009) Certainly, *The Road* suggests otherwise. Naomi Klein agrees with Kingsnorth and Hine that the possibility of failure and collapse should be acknowledged honestly, but asserts, with specific reference to climate change, that:

> ... we don't have to accept failure. There are degrees to how bad this thing can get. Literally, there are degrees.
>
> (Smith 2014)

If Buell's assertion that environmentalism, or at least environmental art, has abjured apocalypse now seems premature, it is primarily because the continuing failure of national and global governance to address climate change has given new plausibility to catastrophic outcomes.

CLIMATE APOCALYPSE

The remainder of this chapter is about climate change, which belatedly emerged as a central concern of ecocriticism in the 2010s. Climate change fiction, dubbed 'cli-fi' by freelance writer Dan Bloom, presents a burgeoning, varied archive that is surveyed in Adam Trexler's *Anthropocene Fictions* (2015) and Adeline Johns-Putra and Axel Goodbody's *Cli Fi: A Companion* (2019). Here, selected examples of *apocalyptic* cli-fi – a large chunk of the archive, one way or another – are discussed, with examples that avoid or refuse this framing held over for chapter 8.

At the time of writing, the United Nations-mandated Intergovernmental Panel on Climate Change (IPCC) has produced five authoritative consensus reports, starting in 1990, on the scale and impacts of anthropogenic climate change, or global heating. Despite the overwhelming accumulation of scientific evidence from numerous distinct disciplines, public opinion in developed countries has only recently moved significantly in favour of decisive political responses. The seeming failure of scientific evidence to motivate action has led, as Trexler explains, to:

> ... desperation for art to bring home the risks of greenhouse gas emissions. Fictionalizing climate change is not about falsifying it, or making it imaginary, but rather about using narrative to heighten its

> reality. The vast majority of novelists have responded to this challenge
> by rendering climate change as an immediate, local disaster.
>
> (2015: 75)

The IPCC anticipates many different climate impacts, from the death of coral reefs to the release of methane clathrate from Arctic tundra, some of which are already unfolding. However, 'only a handful of transformations cover the vast majority' of the hundreds of climate change novels: 'direct heat, catastrophic storms, arctic switches, and floods' (p.78). As Trexler argues, climate fiction suffers from the pressure to deliver cultural change *without* departing too much from constraining narrative templates and expectations.

One of the earliest novels to be explicitly informed by the IPCC's projections is *Parable of the Sower* (1993) by the pioneering Black science fiction writer **Octavia E. Butler** (1947–2006). Though Butler set most of her novels in space, protagonist Lauren Olamina starts writing her diary whilst living in a walled community in Robledo, California in 2024. Climate change has caused prolonged drought, extreme temperatures and near-total social collapse. Rich communities protect themselves from the chaos, while, as Christa Grewe-Volpp points out, 'the majority of the poor, mostly non-white, ... have no possibilities to escape, but suffer from disease, crime, drugs, and violence' (2013: 223). Such sharp socio-geographical divides in cli-fi highlight issues of climate justice, i.e. inequalities in both contributions to, and risks from, global heating.

Lauren's father, a Baptist minister, rules over the community, where sexist and other social hierarchies are tolerated as the price of security. Halfway through the novel, in July 2027, though, the compound is over-run by murderous 'Pyros', thugs whose drug of choice inspires them to arson. Lauren sets off on a trek north, reminiscent of the Biblical Exodus and the Underground Railroad that enabled Black slaves to escape from the American South, with two other refugees from Robledo.

The apocalyptic scenario and survivalist road trip in *Sower* are much like many others. Butler's young, Black, female protagonist, though, shifts the group dynamic from the familiar masculine hero-leader towards a more cooperative, if still clearly messianic, role. Lauren is also endowed with 'hyperempathy', of which she writes:

I feel what I see others feeling or what I believe they feel. Hyperem-pathy is what the doctors call an "organic delusional syndrome." Big shit. It hurts, that's all I know.

(2019: 12)

Lauren's hyperempathy makes fighting off assailants almost as painful for her as it is for them, but it is also the foundation of a new religion, called Earthseed, that she develops in the course of the novel. She sum-marises its creed as follows:

God is Power –
Infinite,
Irresistible,
Inexorable,
Indifferent,
And yet, God is Pliable –
Trickster,
Teacher,
Chaos,
Clay.
God exists to be shaped.
God is Change.

(p.25)

Earthseed's tenets, communicated throughout *Sower* in selections from *The Book of the Living*, present a clear, if corny, alternative to the static, hierarchical, patriarchal Christian faith of Lauren's father. In *Black on Earth* (2010), Kimberly N. Ruffin says Butler creates 'not only an extrabiblical religion but also a theology and religious culture that is compatible with the continuation of a species that constantly endangers itself' (2010: 96). What Ruffin calls Butler's 'religious and scientific syncretism' blends elements of Christianity, Buddhism, evolutionary biology and animism, resulting in a faith that resembles the then-popular deep ecology (ch.2). At the end of *Sower*, Lauren and her followers found a fragile utopian community in Northern California, well short of Canada, their original destination.

Kate Rigby does not consider *Sower* in *Dancing with Disaster*, so it is unclear whether it would qualify as a *catastrophe* in her revised sense.

Lauren repeatedly states that '*The Destiny of Earthseed / Is to take root among the stars*' (p.84), and indeed Butler's second novel, *Parable of the Talents* (1998), though it questions Lauren's messianic role, ends with an Earthseed spaceship leaving our planet. Butler never completed the planned extra-terrestrial *Parable of the Trickster*, so we cannot evaluate whether Earthseed qualifies as a millennial sect, which anticipates apocalypse as prelude to utopia, or is rather anti-millennial, in that Earthseed is a philosophy of perpetual change. Still, reading *Sower* now that we inhabit Butler's middle-distance future, the 2020s, we cannot avoid the question of its 'prescience'. N.K. Jemisin's Foreword to the 2019 edition describes the book as 'powerfully prescient' because it envisages 'A powerful coalition of white-supremacist, homophobic, Christian zealots taking over the country' (p.ix), led by a President who, like Donald J. Trump, promises in *Talents* to 'make America great again'. While it is an arresting coincidence, it seems unlikely that (on present trends) *Sower* will prove broadly prescient. Expecting predictive accuracy invites selective interpretation, and fundamentally mistakes the real purpose of climate fiction.

Switching media to narrative cinema, scientific plausibility barely constrained the makers of *The Day After Tomorrow* (*TDAT*, 2004, dir. Roland Emmerich), an apocalyptic movie in which climate change causes a global superstorm that envelopes the world in snow and ice in a matter of days. The movie grossed $652 million, though, and its wide circulation has attracted the attention of environmental communications and media studies scholars, as well as ecocritics. Alexa Weik von Mossner draws on international audience studies that indicate the movie was 'moderately successful, at least in the short run, in raising awareness for climate change risks among its audiences (across cultures)' (2012: 135). She notes that the heroic narrative of paleoclimatologist Jack Hall (Dennis Quaid) anchors the movie's affective dimension, first as he strives to convince politicians of climatic risk and later as he treks through a blizzard to save his son Sam (Jake Gyllenhaal), who is trapped in New York. The movie also shames the movie's fictional Vice President, who resembles then-Vice President Dick Cheney, into admitting he 'was wrong' not to believe Hall's warnings. Ron Von Burg, reviewing *TDAT*'s role in 'global warming debate' when it was released, considers the views of scientists and activists who worried the movie would discredit real climate science alongside cornucopians' claims (ch.2) that scientists' cautious endorsement of it showed they were untrustworthy 'alarmists'. Burg finds that most scientific organisations reminded audiences that although the spectacle was 'just Hollywood', the scientific aspects were 'not untrue' (2012: 9). The National Snow and Ice Data Centre, for example, said that 'The kind of disaster portrayed in the movie is impossible, but the patterns described by the movie have a distant basis in real concepts being discussed by climate scientists, oceanographers and glaciologists' (cited Burg 2012: 16). *TDAT* seems a blatantly silly, melodramatic movie, and yet, as Mossner explains, it 'stands out as the first Hollywood mega-blockbuster that self-consciously was *about* climate change rather than just using a climatically changed environment as narrative setting and background' (2012: 133). Examples of the latter include *Waterworld* (1995, dir. Kevin Reynold), *Snowpiercer* (2013, dir. Bong Joon-Ho), *Interstellar* (2014, dir. Christopher Nolan), and *Mad Max: Fury Road* (2015, dir. George Miller).

Margaret Atwood's *Oryx and Crake* (2003) is perhaps the most successful apocalyptic climate fiction to date. The two narrative strands of the novel, focalised through Jimmy and his alter ego Snowman, describe a near-future, climatically-altered, hypercapitalist dystopia and a post-pandemic apocalyptic landscape respectively. Here the narrator describes consumers' declining resistance to eating meat from 'pigoons,' genetic hybrids of humans and pigs (ch.6):

> ... as time went on and the coastal aquifers turned salty and the northern permafrost melted and the vast tundra bubbled with methane, and the drought in the midcontinental plains regions went on and on, and the Asian steppes turned to sand dunes, and meat became harder to come by, some people had their doubts.
>
> (2003: 24)

The string of catastrophic climate impacts registers as little more than a nudge to consumers' dietary choices.

Jimmy's world is awash with genetically modified organisms, internet pornography and violence, and promises of limitless pleasure and eternal youth, and it is run by major corporations and their Corporate Security Corps (punningly shortened to CorpSeCorps) unconstrained by governments, national borders or civil society. The annihilation of wild nature is signalled by players of a game called 'Extinctathon' taking the names of extinct species – the list is 'a couple of hundred pages of fine print' (p.81) –

such as 'Crake', Jimmy's childhood friend Glenn, and 'Oryx', a mysterious woman sex-trafficked from Asia. The self-indulgent destructiveness of humanity inspires Crake to engineer a new humanoid species with religious and sexually competitive impulses deleted, and additional survival functions spliced in such as 'UV-resistant skin, … built-in insect repellent, [and] unprecedented ability to digest unrefined plant material' (p.304). Then he releases a lethal haemorrhagic super virus, disguised as a combined aphrodisiac and birth control pill called BlyssPluss, to annihilate the old *Homo sapiens*. Jimmy, saved from the pandemic so he can become the humanoids' leader, mischievously tells the creatures, whom he dubs the 'Crakers,' he is the abominable snowman ('apelike man or manlike ape, stealthy, elusive' (p.8)), or 'Snowman' for short.

The 'Jimmy' and 'Snowman' strands run through the novel in a double-plotted form, creating thematic juxtapositions alongside temporal dislocations. Still, as Gerry Canavan points out, dystopia and post-apocalypse are equally awful:

> Whereas the pre-apocalyptic status quo is generally figured as a lost Golden Age to be mourned, in *Oryx and Crake* its deprivations are quickly revealed to be easily the match of Snowman's wasteland.
>
> (2012: 141)

Moreover, J. Brooks Bouson suggests that 'Crake … seeks to bring about the radical environmentalist post-apocalyptic vision of humanity's return to a utopian Pleistocene world inhabited by small tribes of pre-technological humans' (2016: 349), though environmentalists would condemn his heinous methods. The pessimism of Atwood's jeremiad is evident in that both Crake's rationalised misanthropy and Jimmy's threadbare humanism contribute to the disaster.

Atwood's darkly comic novel underlines the decadence of Jimmy's world, as well as Snowman's desperate efforts to cling on to the vestiges of the past, by contrasting the wild proliferation of trademarks, including ChickieNobs, Happicuppachino, NooSkins, and spliced words for new, spliced organisms such as pigoon, rakunk and wolvog, with the useless old words that Jimmy memorises and Snowman recalls:

> "Hang on to the words," he tells himself. The odd words, the old words, the rare ones. *Valance. Norn. Serendipity. Pibroch. Lubricious.*

When they're gone out of his head, these words, they'll be gone everywhere, forever. As if they'd never been.

(p.68)

Snowman, believing he is the last human on Earth, tries to answer the Crakers' questions, such as 'What is toast?', to little avail:

"What is toast?" says Snowman to himself ... *Toast is when you take a piece of bread – What is bread? Bread is when you take some flour – What is flour? We'll skip that part, it's too complicated. Bread is something you can eat, made from a ground-up plant and shaped like a stone. You cook it ... Please, why do you cook it? Why don't you just eat the plant? Never mind that part – Pay attention.*

(p.98, it. orig.)

Snowman is, like the author of *Revelation*, the witness to catastrophe, though he struggles to communicate with the post-human Craker survivors. Moreover, despite Crake's determination to engineer a naïve replacement for humans that could never become violent or ecologically destructive, the Crakers eventually start to idolise Snowman, thereby threatening to start the cycle of destruction all over again.

Although *Oryx and Crake* was published as a standalone novel, Atwood later decided to write two more set in the same story world. *The Year of the Flood* (*YoF*, 2009) revisits both dystopia and apocalypse from the perspective of two sexually abused women, Ren and Toby, while *MaddAddam* (2013) concludes the trilogy with the last few human women pregnant by Craker men. Canavan calls *YoF* 'an attempt on Atwood's part to clarify (or even rewrite) her earlier book and prevent any possible misinterpretation of it' (p.154), in large part by developing the God's Gardeners, a laughable sect from *Oryx and Crake*, into a credible group of 'ecologically minded religious separatists'. The Gardeners' hymns and sermons, which punctuate *YoF*, recall Butler's Earthseed in their implicit authorial endorsement and awkward blend of scientific and Christian elements. The movement therefore imbues Crake's apocalypse with millennial promise since, as Hannes Bergthaller observes, 'the Gardeners who survive do so because of their apocalyptic beliefs, whereas their efforts to minimize their own ecological footprint are utterly insufficient to ward off the larger environmental collapse' (2010: 738). The later books lack the wild originality of *Oryx and*

Crake, and are less satirical and more moralistic, in keeping with Atwood's millennial turn.

A prevalent motif in climate fiction is what might be called 'present-shaming'. Naomi Oreskes and Erick M. Conway's *The Collapse of Western Civilization* (2014) employs, as its subtitle suggests, 'A View from the Future', to question our failure to act quickly to prevent catastrophe. The scenario in *Collapse* is only a little more plausible than *The Day After Tomorrow*: a 3.9°C global temperature increase by the 2040s (p.24), 5 meters of sea level rise by 2093 (p.30). The apocalypse is narrated by an imaginary Chinese historian in 2393 who superciliously recounts the Western failings that led to collapse, evidently with the intention of embarrassing readers in the present, though Ursula Heise perceptively objects that 'the 24th-century Chinese historian sounds very much like a left-wing American historian of the early 21st century' (2015). Oreskes and Conway have done important work as historians of climate change and denial, but *Collapse* is unsuccessful both as fiction and, presumably, prediction.

Emmi Itäranta's haunting, finely-honed young adult novel *Memory of Water* (2014) is a more interesting, if superficially similar, example. Teenaged protagonist Noria Kaitio lives in the far north of the Scandinavian Union, which has been occupied by the New Qian (i.e. Chinese) state in the aftermath of the collapse of the Western powers. Hundreds of years hence, Noria subsists in a parched, horsefly-ridden landscape fundamentally altered by climate change: 'Drowned islands, coastal plains, river deltas turned salt-bitten; and large cities, now silent ghosts of lives past in their shroud of sea, everywhere, everywhere' (2014: 64). Noria and her friend (perhaps her lover) Sanja dig around in the 'plastic grave' – a rubbish dump of the 'past-world', our present – looking for functional items to recover. As they undertake this blend of mining and archaeology, Noria conjures a woman in the past-world who might somehow become conscious of her struggle, and goes on to hope that this woman 'goes home and does one thing differently that day because of what she has imagined' (p.26). This emotional connection for Noria functions for its present-day Finnish author as a shaming of the reader, who is asked to act on this fictive foreknowledge of apocalypse.

Beyond the breakdown of modernity, represented here as the collapse of the West, *Memory of Water* conveys anxiety about Chinese hegemony, as Sharae Deckard explains:

The Qian Empire is founded in hydrological monopoly, sending water patrols across the hemisphere to police the metered consumption and rediversion of freshwater to Asia. The water-impoverished denizens of former Europe are driven to drinking salt-water and committing forms of "water theft" punishable by death.

(2019: 122)

At the same time, though, the fascistic New Qian army includes blond recruits with Finnish names, and the sacred tea ceremony Noria learns from her father is clearly East Asian in origin. The operative contrast in the novel, then, is between a brutally instrumental use of water for social control and an appreciation of water that recalls Zen Buddhism and Taoism. Noria's father tells her:

"Tea masters believe there are times when water doesn't wish to be found because it knows it will be chained in ways that are against its nature. Therefore the drying of a spring may have its own purpose that must not be fought. Not everything in the world belongs to people. Tea and water do not belong to tea masters, but tea masters belong to tea and water."

(p.91)

Though Noria is ultimately starved to death by the army for keeping a spring hidden from them, she is able to convey secret knowledge of regions of Scandinavia that have recovered their verdancy to her mother before she dies, with the implication that this will break the army's control.

Writing climate fiction involves, as we'll see in the final chapter, many challenges. If the writer chooses an apocalyptic frame, it implies they feel the need to frighten the reader into action. Ecological modernisers (ch.2) Nordhaus and Shellenberger, by contrast, criticise 'a resentful narrative of tragedy' (i.e. climate apocalypse) and recommend a more 'grateful narrative of overcoming' (2007: 18), although both potential frames effectively treat global heating as a challenge for *communication of risk* (Hulme 2009: ch.7). The IPCC does it like this:

Coral reefs ... are projected to decline by a further 70–90% at 1.5°C (*high confidence*) with larger losses (>99%) at 2°C (*very high confidence*). The risk of irreversible loss of many marine and coastal ecosystems increases with global warming, especially at 2°C or more (*high confidence*).

(Masson-Delmotte et al. 2022: B.4.2.)

This statement is from its 'Special Report: Global Warming of 1.5°C' (SR1.5), commissioned to quantify the difference between a 1.5°C increase in Global Mean Surface Temperature (GMST) and the 2°C target agreed in Paris in 2015. In the absence of dramatic, concerted action to reduce greenhouse gas emissions and keep heating well below 2°C by 2100, it is *very likely* (90–100% probability) that almost all coral reefs will be wiped out in that time. The uncertainties are greater elsewhere, from the physical science of cloud formation and the reliability of climate models to the predicted capacity of societies to adapt to climate change, and the IPCC tells you that too.

Or take a popular non-fictional account such as David Wallace-Wells's chilling, impassioned *The Uninhabitable Earth: Life After Warming* (2019), which begins with this statement of risk:

It is worse, much worse, than you think. The slowness of climate change is a fairy tale, perhaps as pernicious as the one that says it isn't happening at all, and comes to us bundled with several others in an anthology of comforting delusions: that global warming is an Arctic saga, unfolding remotely; that it is strictly a matter of sea level and coastlines, not an enveloping crisis sparing no place and leaving no life undeformed; that it is a crisis of the "natural" world, not the human one; that those two are distinct, and that we live today some-how outside or beyond or at the very least defended against nature, not inescapably within and literally overwhelmed by it; that wealth can be a shield against the ravages of warming; that the burning of fossil fuels is the price of continued economic growth; that growth, and the technology it produces, will inevitably engineer a way out of environ-mental disaster; that there is any analogue to the scale or scope of this threat, in the long span of human history, that might give us confidence in staring it down. None of this is true.

(p.3)

Instead of carefully calibrating the risk in the context of a precisely-worded question, such as 'what's the differential impact of 1.5°C and 2°C

GMST increase?', Wallace-Wells intentionally punctures our pluriform complacency by describing plausible consequences of the trajectory of emissions and temperatures in 2019: 2-4°C GWST increase by 2100. He reminds us that many people in history have had to live 'in the ruins of a much wealthier and more peaceful world', but this apocalypse would be far faster: 'in this case, the dark ages would arrive within one generation of the light – close enough to touch, and share stories, and blame' (p.223). Where Oreskes and Conway pile worst case on worst case to the point of absurdity, Wallace-Wells aggregates scientifically-validated scenarios into a tsunami of horror. In the process, he is explicit about timescales – the book is littered with dates – but seldom mentions uncertainty, leaving readers to follow up his citations. *The Uninhabitable Earth* is the most compelling climate jeremiad to date.

Climate fictions, though, have no citations, cannot easily convey uncertainty, and are hamstrung if they provide exact dates, so what *can* they do? Lydia Millet's *A Children's Bible* (2020) is a bleakly sardonic allegory in which a group of families rents a large house near the coast, and the adults leave the children to roam around while they indulge themselves. The teen narrator Evie tells us:

> My mother taught feminist theory and my father sculpted enormous busty women, lips, breasts, and private parts garishly painted. Often with scenes of war-torn or famine-struck locations. The labia might be Mogadishu.
> He was quite successful.
>
> (p.15)

It is not clear whether this searing satire is intentional on Evie's part, although she does remark repeatedly on the apocalyptic scenario as it unfolds:

> At that time in my personal life, I was coming to grips with the end of the world. The familiar world anyway. Many of us were. ... Historians said there'd been dark ages before. It all came out in the wash, because eventually, if you were patient, enlightenment arrived and then a wide array of Apple devices. ... We knew who was responsible, of course: it had been a done deal before we were born.
>
> (p.27)

Disgusted by their parents, the children play a game in which the object is to avoid being identified with them. Evie's main concern is to protect her younger brother Jack, who discovers a Children's Bible – he has never seen one before – which he 'decodes' for clues to their predicament.

The idyllic house and grounds are overwhelmed by a huge storm and biblical flood, prompting the adults to start taking Ecstasy and having affairs, and the children to pack up and leave. Struggling to survive in a post-apocalyptic Eastern USA, the children turn away from their screens:

> We had the corners of buildings and the slope of the hills, the line of the treetops. The more time passed, the more any flat image began to seem odd and less than real. Uncanny delicate surfaces. Had we always had them?
> We'd had so many pictures. Pictures just everywhere. Every hour, minute, or second.
> But now they were foreign. Now we saw everything in three dimensions.
> (p.134)

When the parents do reappear, they remain useless because of their dependence on vanished certainties: 'The parents still believed in Emergency Services' (p.189). On the whole, Evie describes them with a little pity and a good deal of contempt. The survivors retreat to a mansion and fortify it against the mounting chaos outside, which points to the grotesque injustice of climate change: 'The parents' agenda was basically what ours had been: the shelter of wealth' (p.196). Global heating is caused primarily by emissions from wealthy people and countries, whilst its worst impacts will fall on the poor. In 2020, the United Kingdom, with the longest record of historical emissions, was 11th *least vulnerable* to climate change in the world, whilst the most vulnerable was Chad, a country that has and is making a negligible contribution to the crisis (https://gain-new.crc.nd.edu/ranking).

Finally, the children take over their small society, and the parents disappear. The novel concludes with a sickly Jack asking Evie: 'What happens at the end? ... You know. The *story*. After the chaos time' (pp.222–3). Jack's Bible does not include *Revelation*, and so Evie has to decide 'what happens *after* the end':

"OK. Slowness, I bet. New kinds of animals evolve. Some other creatures come and live here, like we did. And all the old beautiful things will
still be in the air. Invisible but there. Like, I don't know. An expectation
that sort of hovers. Even when we're all gone."

(p.223)

The only hope is for a world without us, albeit with some benign consciousness, for which 'art is the Holy Ghost', that lurks in 'The dirt the
rocks the water and the wind' (p.224).

Millet can only depict a thin slice, in spatial and temporal terms, of
the probable future set out by the IPCC and Wallace-Wells, but the
grim humour and allegorical scenario of *A Children's Bible* effectively
skewers the protests of adults, now and in the future, that they didn't
know and couldn't help it:

"Listen. We know we let you down," said a mother. "But what could
we have *done*, really?"
"Fight," said Rafe. "Did you ever fight?"

(p.194)

Characters in apocalyptic fictions seldom seem to notice how *apocalyptic*
they are, but Evie and her young friends know too well what they are
living through, and why – just as we will.

Frederick Buell may be right that environmental organisations avoid
apocalyptic framing, and yet the emotional and aesthetic appeal of
apocalypse is undimmed, as we have seen. Whilst cornucopians accuse
environmentalists of 'doomsaying', it must be said that they too have an
abysmal record of prophecy. In the face of irreducible uncertainty, the
IPCC produces reports that are the most remarkable documents of
multidisciplinary research, synthesis, evaluation, and expert consensus in
the history of science, so climate fictions that are guided by them are
highly likely to prove prescient, in broad terms, if not in specifics. If they
are not, that means the warning was heeded. Just as there is no 'silver
bullet' policy or technology, there is no perfect climate fiction, and we
ought to be suspicious of environmental millenarians wherever they
show up; such movements rarely turn out well. Jeremiad remains an
indispensable environmental genre, though, and is all the more effective
when, like Carson and Wallace-Wells, it recognises the achievements of

modernity rather than floundering in **declensionism** and cultural pessimism. Finally, we should look forward to fictions that, in Rigby's words, refuse to delight in annihilation and instead 'dance with disaster' in a constructive, unillusioned way. Only if we believe human life on Earth *has* a future, after all, will we strive to secure it.

6

ANIMALS

WHY ANIMALS MATTER

Humans have always been fascinated with animals. Our own species hardly appears in Paleolithic cave paintings in modern-day Europe, the earliest known figurative art, whereas they teem with horses, aurochs, felines and other animals. When scholars in the Humanities look at animals, they categorise their research either as a branch of philosophical ethics or as Animal Studies, which is the analysis of the representation of animals in history and culture. Animal Studies is sometimes called Human-Animal Studies, Animality Studies, or Critical Animal Studies; the last of these implies a thoroughgoing vegan critique of vivisection, livestock farming and hunting that seeks abolition of human dominance over animals. Whilst much of this chapter will focus on Animal Studies, which is close kin to ecocriticism proper, it will begin with the long-standing ethical debates that were given renewed impetus by Peter Singer's revolutionary *Animal Liberation* (1975). Singer draws upon arguments first put forward by Utilitarian philosopher **Jeremy Bentham** (1748–1832), who suggested that cruelty to animals was analogous to slavery and claimed that the capacity to feel pain, not the power of reason, entitled a being to moral consideration. Singer gives the label 'speciesism' to the irrational

DOI: 10.4324/9781003174011-6

prejudice that Bentham identified as the basis of our different treatment of animals and humans. Just as women or Africans have been mistreated on the grounds of morally irrelevant physiological differences, so animals suffer because they fall on the wrong side of what Bentham called, with conscious irony, an 'insuperable line' (cited Singer 1995: 8) dividing beings that count from those that do not. Yet it turns out to be impossible to draw that line in such a way that all animals are excluded and all humans are included, even if we turn, as many have done, to the faculties of 'reason' or 'discourse': for Bentham, 'a full-grown horse or dog is beyond comparison a more rational, as well as a more conversable animal, than an infant of a day or a week or even a month old.' The boundary between human and animal is arbitrary and, moreover, irrelevant, since we share with animals a capacity for suffering that only 'the hand of tyranny' could ignore.

The Utilitarian 'principle of equality' states that everyone is entitled to equal moral consideration, irrespective of family, race, nation or species, and for Singer, 'If a being suffers there can be no moral justification for refusing to take that suffering into consideration' (1995: 9). Differences between the objects of our concern will make a difference to what, exactly, we do, so it would be senseless to campaign for votes for animals, but Singer agrees with Bentham that the suffering of a human should not *automatically* count for more than the suffering of an animal. His argument derives from the Utilitarian tradition in ethics, which holds that actions are not right or wrong in themselves, but only insofar as they bring happiness or cause pain.

Mary Midgley (1919–2018) espouses a less radical position in her book *Animals and Why They Matter* (1983), an excellent introduction to animal 'welfarism'. She qualifies the principle of equality, arguing that we are sometimes right to prefer the interests of our human kin, and criticises Singer's analogy of racism and speciesism:

> Overlooking somebody's race is entirely sensible. Overlooking their species is a supercilious insult. It is no privilege, but a misfortune, for a gorilla or a chimpanzee to be removed from its forest and its relatives and brought up alone among humans to be given what those humans regard as an education.

> (p.99)

Bentham, Singer and Midgley stand together in opposition to Descartes, who 'hyperseparated' reason from emotion and mind from body (ch.2,

'Ecofeminism'), and claimed that animals were effectively complex machines. His 'Cartesian rationalism' encouraged scientific physiologists to discount the distressing sounds made by animals during vivisection as equivalent to the ringing of a mechanical alarm clock. The cries and laughter of human emotion, too, were seen as merely automatic responses, as distinct from the rational speech that epitomised the human soul. Female, non-White, disabled or very young people who were considered less rational were also therefore less than human.

Jeremy Bentham was not the only eighteenth-century intellectual to contradict Descartes, however. As Philip Armstrong suggests, 'the greater part of English writing on the subject scrutinized it sceptically and, more often than not, rejected it' (2008: 7). For many, Cartesian rationalism contradicted their daily experience with working and wild animals, as well as running counter to the celebration of cultivated 'sensibility': an attitude of refined emotionality popularised in the early years of the century. For the Swedish scientist **Carl Linnaeus** (1707–1778), though, the abyss posited by Descartes between humans and animals – most obviously, the apes – was refuted by the enormous weight of evidence available, even then, of our underlying similarities to them. Our anatomical 'homology', as it was later called, led Linnaeus to categorise humans at first among the *Antropomorpha* (or 'man-like') apes, in his *Systema Naturae* (1735, first edn). He anticipated outrage, writing to a colleague: 'It does not please [you] that I've placed Man among the *Antropomorpha*, but man learns to know himself [*nosce te ipsum*]' (Linnaeus 1747). In the first nine editions of *Systema,* Linnaeus subdivided humans into four 'varieties' according to skin colour and geographical origin, plus 'wild' (*ferus*) and 'monstrous' (*monstrosus*) kinds. The human capacity 'to know himself' led Linnaeus to add the epithet *sapiens* ('wise') to the genus *Homo* in the 1758 Tenth Edition of *Systema* (Charmantier 2020), in which his binomial system of classification appears consistently for the first time. It is possible that humans were reclassified as the only surviving member of the genus *Homo* due to pressure from theologians. Indeed, some scholars believe that, but for anthropocentric prejudice, we would today be classified in the genus *Pan* alongside the (other) two species of chimpanzee (Diamond 1991), which might provide scientific support for the effort to eliminate the 'insuperable line' in ethics.

While environmentalism and animal liberation are united in opposition to anthropocentric morality, they sometimes conflict in both theory and practice. Animal liberationists generally draw the line of moral consideration at the boundary of sentience or feeling, which, for Singer, falls between crustaceans and molluscs. Environmental ethics, on the other hand, places far less emphasis on the individual organism, but demands moral consideration for inanimate things such as rivers and mountains, assuming pain and suffering to be a necessary part of nature (Curry 2011). These ethical conflicts have practical consequences, in that liberationists are generally opposed to hunting, whereas ecophilosophers argue that exploding populations of a certain species must be culled if they threaten a particular environment. Such disagreements are especially pressing in cases where non-native predators or destructive herbivores threaten fragile ecologies, a scenario T.C. Boyle dramatises to excellent effect in his novel *When the Killing's Done* (2011) (Heise 2016: 151–8). However, since intensive livestock farming is objectionable on both environmental and welfare grounds, Animal Studies may be seen as an important ally of ecocriticism if not strictly a branch of it.

Animal Studies scholars might agree with either Singer or Midgley on questions of practical morality, but they dispute the liberationist conceptual model in which rights are extended to particular animals from a position of superiority that remains unquestioned. Singer is right, in other words, to challenge the 'insuperable line' on ethical grounds, but in seeking to move it so as to exclude mussels and include prawns he leaves the imaginary evolutionary 'ladder' in place. The central claim of Animal Studies, in its productive encounter with the biological sciences, is not that there are no differences between humans and other animals, but that differences are everywhere: humans and animals are different from each other, and all other species are different from each other as well. *Uniqueness is not unique* because differentiation is one of the things evolution does. Even so, Frans de Waal's wry observation that claims of human uniqueness are as predictably unreliable as 'advertisements for squirrel-proof bird feeders' (2001: loc.2939) is well founded: very often a human activity or ability, such as opposable thumbs or lying, is proposed as the defining characteristic of humanity, then turns out to be shared with at least one other species (pandas have opposable thumbs, and vervet monkeys give deliberately deceptive alarm calls).

The philosopher **Jacques Derrida** (1930–2004) made a crucial contribution to contemporary Animal Studies in an essay whose title deliberately plays with Descartes' assertion, 'I think, therefore I am': 'The animal that therefore I am.' Derrida accepts the ethical significance of Bentham's argument: he acknowledges the *unprecedented* proportions of [the] subjection of the animal' (Derrida 2008: 25) and explores more deeply the significance of his central question:

> "Can they suffer?" amounts to asking "Can they *not be able*?" And what of this inability [*impouvoir*]? What of the vulnerability felt on the basis of this inability? What is this nonpower at the heart of power? ... 'Being able to suffer is no longer a power; it is a possibility without power, a possibility of the impossible.
>
> (p.28)

At the same time, Derrida goes beyond the Utilitarian position in challenging the very notion of 'The Animal', a word humans have 'given to themselves, ... at the same time according themselves, reserving for them ... the right to the word, ... to a language of words, in short to the very thing that the others in question would be deprived of' (p.32). With his genius for coining words that encapsulate entire philosophical arguments, Derrida invents '*l'animot*', which includes in a singular term the sound of the French plural for animals, '*animaux*', while at the same time drawing attention to the way in which the word ('*mot*') itself implies the symbolic language of which animals are thought to be deprived, and which defines them, in Descartes and elsewhere, as inferior (see Wolfe 2003). We must therefore think, not (or not only) in terms of the elimination or repositioning of the 'insuperable line', but of the proliferation of differences within a schema of relative hierarchies. In both evolutionary and moral terms, 'better' must always be 'better *at something*'.

In *Animals in Translation*, the autistic animal scientist Temple Grandin, writing with researcher Catherine Johnson, explains why her disability enables her to see the world from a farm animal's point of view more easily than a neurotypical person: 'I think many or even most autistic people experience the world a lot the way animals experience the world: as a swirling mass of tiny details' (Grandin and Johnson 2005: 67). In certain contexts, such hypersensitivity can be a problem, but, as she points out, it can make autistic people exceptionally good at, for instance, quality control on production lines. The hypersensitivity of dogs has allowed some to sense the epileptic seizures of their human companions before they happen, and warn them, yet remarkably, 'the dogs acquired their skills without human help' (p.290). The intimate coevolution of humans and dogs provided the cognitive infrastructure for mutual understanding, and then the individual dogs used their sensory acuity and intelligence to develop this skill. Grandin's examples suggest the common work of Animal and Disability Studies: to challenge the deficit model according to which animals and people are judged according to what they cannot (in some context) do, as in the term *dis*ability and even, as Derrida suggests, in the *word* 'Animal' (Wolfe 2013). Both encourage us to dismantle imaginary, pernicious and simplistic hierarchies, much as Darwinian evolution does, if rightly understood: as de Waal points out, 'Every organism fits on the phylogenetic tree without being above or below anything else' (loc.675).

Donna Haraway's *When Species Meet* (2007) epitomises this radical revision of anthropocentrism and the conventional duality of culture and nature. Whereas Derrida recounts being observed naked by his cat as an experience that accentuates the difference between them, Haraway argues that:

> ... those who are to be in the world are constituted in intra- and interaction. The partners do not precede the meeting; species of all kinds, living and not, are consequent on a subject- and object-shaping dance of encounters.
>
> (loc.177)

Animals, in other words, make us human in a continual process of reshaping, just as we affect the evolution of both domesticated and wild species. As Haraway asserts, 'To be one is always to become with many' (loc.162). She does not underestimate the asymmetry of power that often pertains between humans and other animals, but the love and deep knowledge of dogs that pervades her understanding of species encounters leads her to emphasise the pleasure and freedom that the mutual discipline of animal companionship can engender. A particularly emotive example is the Animal Planet documentary *Cell Dogs* (2004–7) which depicts 'difficult' shelter dogs being trained for release by human prison inmates. Both species act as teacher and student, as 'dogs and people model nonviolent, nonoptional, and self-rewarding obedience to an authority that each must earn in relation to the other' (loc.1130).

Recognising, with Derrida, the limitations of our ordinary ways of talking about animals, and still determined to generate a positive vocabulary that embraces our intimate technologies as well as companion species, Haraway prefers the term 'critter' to encompass the 'machinic, human, and animal beings whose historically situated infoldings are the flesh of contemporary **naturecultures**' (loc.4286). For Haraway, both the threat and the promise of modernity lie in the intimacy or 'infolding' – sometimes marvellous, sometimes appalling – of our bodies and selves and what we misleadingly call 'the environment', critters included. The nature/culture duality is not only harmful, in her view, it is also redundant, because we dwell today among interpenetrating naturecultures.

LOOKING AT ANIMALS: A TYPOLOGY

Much work in Animal Studies is devoted to historicising animals in two ways: it simultaneously traces historical shifts in human representations of animals and recalls the agency of animals in shaping 'human history' (Kean and Howell 2018). The examination of the animal question as an aesthetic issue originates in John Berger's 1980 essay, 'Why Look at Animals?', which claims that, when we look at animals, they may return our gaze, and in that moment, we are aware of both likeness and difference. Hence the peasant 'becomes fond of his pig and is glad to salt away his pork' (2009: 5); for the pre-modern sensibility, the fondness and the slaughter are not contradictory. It is only through industrialisation that most animals are removed from everyday life, and the meat production process hidden away. Once marginalised in this way, the few animals still visible to us can be only 'human puppets' as family pets or Disney characters, or else the objects of spectacle, most often in wildlife books and films, where:

> ... animals are always the observed. The fact that they can observe us has lost all significance. They are the objects of our ever-extending knowledge. What we know about them is an index of our power, and thus an index of what separates us from them. The more we know, the further away they are.
>
> (p.14)

If the pet is just a mirror, reflecting our gaze with no autonomy, TV wildlife is powerless to make its gaze register at all against our imperial eye. To the morality of liberation, which he might regard as a further symptom of our alienated distance from animals, Berger adds a rather different, decidedly gloomy, politics of representation.

We have seen how 'pastoral' and 'wilderness' function as tropes, but 'animal' too has important functions as a trope. At the simplest level, we are familiar with animal similes of the form 'as stubborn as a mule'. The play of likeness and difference in the relationship of humans and animals in general may be analysed in terms of the distinction of metonymy and metaphor:

> The distinctive peculiarity of animals is that, being at once close to man and strange to him, both akin to him and unalterably not-man, they are able to alternate, as objects of human thought, between the contiguity of the metonymic mode and the distanced, analogical mode of the metaphor.
>
> (Willis 1974: 128)

Humans can both be, and be compared to, animals. There is, therefore, an extensive 'rhetoric of animality', as Steve Baker calls it, which is as functional in descriptions of human social and political relations as it is in describing actual animals: 'Culture shapes our reading of animals just as much as animals shape our reading of culture' (Baker 1993: 4).

Animal Studies is a diverse and rapidly growing field, much like ecocriticism. Nevertheless, it is possible to identify some key concepts, which can usefully be schematised into a typology. Attention to the various ways in which people represent animals – in films and books, on YouTube, in policy formulations and scientific experiments, for example – was originally inspired by ethics, but in fact may be considered logically prior to it. After all, a philosophical discussion about animals will inevitably have to work with the 'animals' a culture has proposed to it, even if it should critique them too. For example, animals may be conceived as fundamentally like or unlike humans. Once contiguity (metonymy) is granted, animals may be understood in human terms (anthropomorphism) or humans in animal terms (zoomorphism), and each of these may appear in both crude and sophisticated, critical forms. Even if animals are represented as different to humans, that difference can be construed as a deficit (**mechanomorphism**) or, rarely, as a kind of superiority (allomorphism, a term coined for this book). Thus, while acknowledging that any typology is a risky generalisation, we can set it out in this simplified form, with alternative terms in brackets:

Likeness (metonymy)	Otherness (metaphor)
Animals-to-humans	Denigrating/reductive otherness
Crude anthropomorphism (aka disnification)	*Mechanomorphism* (aka Cartesianism,
Critical anthropomorphism	Anthropodenial)
Critical zoomorphism	*Allomorphism* (aka therioprimitivism)
Crude zoomorphism (aka theriomorphism)	Numinous otherness
Humans-to-animals	

The most familiar term is anthropomorphism, which is most often used as a pejorative implying sentimental projection of human emotions onto animals. In fact, the term was initially applied to the false attribution of human shape and qualities to gods, a critique that left sceptical theologians with a problem: if it is anthropomorphic to represent the Christian God with a beard, is it also wrong to think of Him as loving or just or, indeed, male? Similarly, the sceptical attack on sentimental views of animals risks making it impossible to describe animal behaviour at all, so the problem is to distinguish between kinds of anthropomorphism.

Anxieties about anthropomorphism are justified. While the other types of animal representation may well be culturally contingent, the tendency to perceive mind-like intentionality beyond our own species is universal in neurotypical humans: thus, we plead pointlessly with cars that won't start and computers that crash. Netflix cartoons include talking trains and airplanes, as well as animals. Unless trained to be sceptical, humans infer human agency everywhere; probably dogs are canomorphic and bears ursomorphic. A compelling example of crude anthropomorphism is the dolphin's smile, which has helped to propel the animal to the status of culture hero despite scientific evidence that, in Grandin's words, 'dolphins are big-brained animals who commit gang rape, brutal killings of dolphin "children," and the mass murder of porpoises' (Grandin 2005: 152). On reflection, we know bottlenose dolphins are not smiling; the 'smile' is actually the permanent shape of their mouth, which we have misrecognised based upon human experience. Our projection has had terrible consequences for real dolphins, as former trainer Ric O'Barry acknowledges in the activist documentary *The Cove* (2009), in that 'hundreds of thousands of "happy" cetaceans … have been put to work in … marine shows around the world' (von Mossner 2018). Grandin's own language of 'rape' and 'murder' could also be seen as dangerously anthropomorphic, in that it ignores the social factors in their human originals, such as the legitimation of rape some feminists see in pornography. However, as we shall see, there can be value in such descriptions if handled with caution.

Perhaps the most popular form of crude anthropomorphism is found in children's books and films. Baker has captured one version in the term 'disnification', of which he says: 'the basic procedure of disnification is to render it stupid by rendering it visual' (p.174). Anthropomorphic animal narratives are generally denigrated as 'childish', thereby associating a dispassionate, even alienated perspective with maturity. Disnification exacerbates this existing association, as reflected in the colloquial use of 'Mickey Mouse' to describe something as trivial or worthless. The visual cue of disnification is 'neoteny', or the set of characteristics we instinctively associate with infant humans and animals: large eyes, a big head relative to the body, short limbs and a generally rounded configuration. Both the real panda and the WWF logo in which it appears exemplify neoteny, and also the disnified 'cutesy' relation to nature that it implies. Baker claims that 'there is little point in complaining about this: it is simply how disnification seems currently to operate' (p.182), although his final chapter suggests how non-disnified images of animals might be promoted. David Whitley's study of Disney animations (2016), while it acknowledges disnification, also identifies some surprising counter-currents, such as the obsessively detailed reef backdrop to the thoroughly anthropomorphic and patriarchal narrative of *Finding Nemo* (2003). Although mainstream audiences were probably not ready for Nemo's clownfish father to change sex after his mate's death, as he would in reality, we were treated to Mr Ray's biologically accurate song extolling reef ecology.

Werner Herzog's *Grizzly Man* (2005) provides an illuminating example of the complexity of judgments concerning anthropomorphism. It is a remarkable documentary made up of footage shot by Timothy Treadwell, killed by a bear after 13 summers living illegally in Katmai National Park in Alaska, intercut with Herzog's interviews with

Treadwell's family and friends. In the video clips chosen by Herzog, Treadwell refers to himself as a 'kind warrior' and protector of the grizzly bears. He frequently indulges in Romantic dramatisation of the danger of living among dangerous animals, as well as displaying a crudely anthropomorphic sentimentality distraught by evidence of predation and death. Yet, still, Treadwell's extraordinary understanding of grizzlies is obvious from the thousands of hours he lived unprotected among them. Werner Herzog, despite expressing admiration for his subject as a filmmaker, seems to intend his bleakly existentialist voiceover to be a sharp rebuke to Treadwell's camp theatricality, even though it incorporates contradictions of its own. In the main, Herzog's rhetoric of animality is mechanomorphic, reducing the bears to instinctive machines: commenting on a close-up of the face of the bear that may have killed Treadwell, he argues that 'there is no such thing as a secret world of the bears, and this blank stare speaks only of a half-bored interest in food.' But then he criticises Treadwell's grief over the death of a baby fox: 'I believe the common denominator of the universe is not harmony, but chaos, hostility, and murder.' Clearly terms such as 'murder' and, elsewhere, 'fornication' are every bit as crudely anthropomorphic as Treadwell's rhetoric of 'love' between species, except the human qualities Herzog projects are exclusively the supposedly 'bestial qualities' of uncontrolled sexuality and violence. The footage of the bears matters too: Adrian Ivakhiv's detailed discussion of *Grizzly Man* notes that the gaze of the 'killer' grizzly provides a third perspective that 'reaches deeper into the affective reception of viewers than does its textual accompaniment [i.e. the words of characters], especially when that accompaniment is as contested and multi-voiced as it is in the film' (Ivakhiv 2013: 234). Ivakhiv proposes his own typology (p.247) that, like the one presented here, aims to highlight and clarify the various modes of representation, rather simplifying and moralising them.

Thanks to the influence of Cartesian and later versions of mechanomorphism, as well as a broader preference for 'rational' as opposed to 'emotive' language, the biological sciences have tended to be extremely suspicious of anthropomorphism until quite recently. Ethologists, however, who study animal behaviour in the field, today argue that the accumulated evidence for behavioural as well as anatomical homology between humans and the social mammals means that *critically* anthropomorphic explanation of, for example, cultural transmission of knowledge should be the default position henceforth. According to de Waal and Marc

Bekoff, among others, using anthropomorphic assumptions to frame hypotheses for testing in field observation has proven scientific value. In de Waal's case, use of a term like 'politics' has helped illuminate 'the "demoniacal *Urkraft*" [elemental power] of the [common] chimpanzee, its stormy temperament, its brutal competitiveness, but also its male bonding and unique political complexity' (loc.1233), all of which distinguish the species from the pacific, bisexual bonobo. Without minimising the evident differences from human cultures, ethologists are content to use the term 'culture' to describe non-genetically transmitted behaviour, such as the varied hunting practices of the orca or regional differences in primate tool-making and social interaction. Nevertheless, Bekoff is on dangerous ground when he uses the language of justice and morality to describe the rituals of play in canid species, such as the 'bow' given by the initiator which signals the intention to 'play fair':

> Social play is thus based on a 'foundation of fairness.' Play occurs only if animals agree to cooperate, if they have no other agenda but to play, and if, for the time they are playing, they put aside or neutralize any inequalities in physical size and social rank.
>
> (2007: loc.1438)

Critical anthropomorphism in ethology means employing the language and concepts of human behaviour 'carefully, consciously, empathetically, and biocentrically' (loc.1948). In this way, ethologists align themselves with the views of animals that are commonplace outside science, whilst emphasising the necessity of caution. Moreover, unlike Treadwell and Herzog, critical anthropomorphism is prepared to consider homology of both the valued and the despised tendencies of our species with those of dogs and primates. As Eileen Crist asserts:

> ... there exists no inventory of concepts, or classes of concepts, for which the categorical case could be made that they should never be applied to animals. The only feature of its application that is constant and consistent is the disparaging function of the word *anthropomorphism*. Its meaning, therefore, is strictly its performative function, which is to cast aspersion, in an *ad hominem* fashion, upon any linguistic usage that lifts a mirror between animals and humans.
>
> (Crist 2000: loc.2077)

If there can be no categorical refusal to consider anthropomorphic representations, the same must, as we shall see, be true of zoomorphic ones too. If culture goes, so to speak, all the way 'down' into nature, nature must likewise come all the way 'up' into human existence.

Two novels of elephants demonstrate the implications of this analysis for literature. Barbara Gowdy's *The White Bone* (1999) takes the bold step of employing a third-person narrator who continually uses wild African elephants as **focalisers**. Carefully incorporating zoological knowledge of the matriarchal structure of elephant groups, their prodigious memories, fascination with the bones of their own species and ability to communicate over long distances subsonically, Gowdy also gives some individuals psychic abilities and imagines a religion that binds the elephants together. Moreover, the elephants converse in English dialogue studded with their own terms such as 'Big fly' (ostrich) and 'She-ones' (elephants), which is, as Graham Huggan and Helen Tiffin note, at once 'necessary in humanising the animals, yet dangerous in inviting infantilisation or ridicule' (2015: 174). The animals are individualised in ways that seem plausible for elephants specifically, and this anthropomorphism 'paradoxically liberate[s] the elephants from metonymic, metaphorical or fabular enclosure in the text' (p.171). In other words, Gowdy's elephants are not made to stand for anything else, but endure drought and the depredations of 'hindleggers' (humans) with solidarity, wit and dignity. However, their millennial religion (ch.5) and the New Age overtones of Gowdy's psychic 'mindtalkers' smacks of crude anthropomorphism, detracting from the seriousness of her purpose.

Christopher Nicholson's historical novel *The Elephant Keeper* (2009) is presented as the narrative of Tom Page, an eighteenth-century stable boy charged with the care of two elephants. Once the male, Timothy, is sold on after a bout of musth, Tom's relationship with Jenny, the female, grows from baffled bemusement to deep knowledge and loving intimacy. While aristocrats and scholars debate the animal's capabilities over his head, Tom attempts to teach Jenny skills that will 'demonstrate that the differences between human beings and animals are not so great as some folk believe' (p.132), such as counting. He narrates his frustrated efforts in the form of conversations between himself and the elephant:

Thus I hold a carrot before her eyes. – Jenny, can you see this – you know what it is, do you not? She blinks slowly. – What is it? It is a carrot, Tom. – That is right, it is a carrot, how many carrots is it? – How many? – Yes. It is one carrot, is it not, Jenny?

(p.132)

Jenny's apparent responses can be understood, at this stage, as Tom's inferences from her behaviour, especially the look in her eyes and the motion of her trunk. His habit of speaking for her, in his own mental conversations, at least, resembles the way that people speak on behalf of their companion animals 'as if they could talk, a common form of anthropomorphism that makes sense in a context of sustained cohabitation. However, as the novel progresses, Jenny's words first separate out from Tom's on the page, and then take the form of ordinary dialogue. Indeed, at the conclusion of his narrative, Jenny reveals that she has been writing Tom's story even as he has been writing hers:

'Writing? Jenny, you cannot write!'
'I write in my head,' she replied. 'Surely, is it not true that all writing begins in the head?'

(p.268)

Much as the reader may identify with Tom's devotion to Jenny, it is hard not to judge that he has sacrificed his human relationships for her, and to reach a personal limit beyond which their conversations begin to seem crudely anthropomorphic. As such, the novel may be read as a sophisticated narrative experiment with our own assumptions about our kinship and difference from elephants.

The visual symmetry in the typology above between anthropomorphism and zoomorphism (dubbed 'theriomorphism' in Baker's account (1993)), is apt, in that both the crude forms are interdependent, as, to a lesser extent, are the critical forms. The most vicious kind of crude zoomorphism – racist representation of, for instance, Jews as rats or Africans as apes – depends in turn upon a prior, crudely anthropomorphic projection of despised human qualities onto these animals. The idea of a 'Beast Within' is a precondition for the racialised 'beast' without. It is clear, then, that revaluation of the meaning of human animality, represented zoomorphically, must proceed in tandem with a transformation in our rhetoric of '*l'animot*', because as Timothy Morton puts it, 'Humans are like "animals," but "animals" are not "animals"' (2010: 41). Certainly, humans should not be treated 'like animals', but why should animals be treated 'like animals'? Given how frequently we damn other people with zoomorphic terminology, stigmatising 'feral' working-class children or condemning violent men as 'brutal' (meaning: 'like an animal'), there is much cultural work to be done.

Crude zoomorphism is selective in the mammalian traits it represents as 'animalistic': child-care is ignored in favour of violence and sexuality. It is ironic, then, that homosexual activity amongst animals was for so long reclassified as dominance behaviour, mistaken identity, or necessitated by the absence of the 'opposite' sex – 'almost anything', as Bruce Bagemihl explains, 'besides *pleasurable sexual behavior*' (1999: 106). At the same time, homosexuality in humans has long been condemned as 'unnatural' because other animals supposedly do not do it. If homo- and bisexuality turns out to be quite common in other species, biologists will be obliged to take it seriously and the conservative argument against human sexual diversity will be undermined. Fortunately, 'queer' animals seem to be everywhere.

The most systematic study to date is Joan Roughgarden's *Evolution's Rainbow* (first published 2004), which surveys both animal sexual diversity and species in which intersexuality and multiple genders are normal. For instance, the bluegill sunfish of North America appears in one female gender but three male genders (biologists call them 'morphotypes'), with dramatically different physiologies and behaviours (2013: 78–85). Male bighorn sheep, whose image adorns pickup trucks and American football teams, form groups in which 'almost all males participate in homosexual courting and copulation' (p.138). Domestic rams, given the choice of sex with captive ewes or rams, preferred homosexual copulation at a rate around four times the usual incidence of homosexuality in human societies (p.140). One of our closest relatives, the bonobo or pygmy chimp, is predominantly bisexual (pp.147–50), although common chimps are not. Stacy Alaimo's comment, 'Who knew?' (Mortimer-Sandilands and Erickson 2010: loc.771) captures the amused astonishment that must be a common first response to Bagemihl and Roughgarden. She goes on to comment more seriously that:

> Rather than continuing to pose nature/culture dualisms that closet queer animals as well as animal cultures, and rather than attempting to locate the truth of human sexuality within the already written book

of nature, we can think of queer desire as part of an emergent universe of a multitude of naturecultures.

(loc.820)

Alaimo warns us not to seize on queer animals to legitimise human sexuality, but rather to critically assess it within in the broader context of Earth Others' sexualities. Isabella Rossellini explores a range of those in her engaging *Green Porno* short films (2008–2011).

Scholars like Alaimo have adopted critical anthropomorphism enthusiastically, but are less willing to think of humans as animals if it entails seeing our behaviour as 'already written' in our nature. While crude zoomorphism no longer appears in mainstream culture in racialised forms, it continues to influence popular conceptions of an imaginary 'Beast Within' human beings. It is clear, as Midgley points out, that the Beast Within is a 'scapegoat for human wickedness' (Midgley and Midgley 2005: loc.1170) when we consider that its 'beastly' qualities of violence or unconstrained sexuality bear little relationship to the behaviour of actual animals. The pejorative associations that cluster around zoomorphism help explain the extraordinary furore that greeted the final chapter of E.O. Wilson's *Sociobiology* (first published 1975), where he proposed a Darwinian account of human societies according to which 'history, biography, and fiction are the research protocols of human ethology; and anthropology and sociology together constitute the sociobiology of a single primate species' (2000: 547). While many in the humanities and social sciences continue to reject sociobiology, as well as its offspring, evolutionary anthropology and psychology, it is worth pointing out that, unlike crude zoomorphism, critical zoomorphism involves the rejection of simplistic biological determinism (or essentialism), and attempts to go beyond the sex and violence that predominate in traditional zoomorphism (Buss 2019): scholars have proposed compelling evolutionary accounts of language (Pinker 2007a), morality (Haidt 2012) and even our species' peculiar preoccupation with stories of violent retribution (Flesch 2007). This last example aside, though, Darwinian literary criticism has so far proven sadly unpersuasive (Gottschall and Wilson 2005; Pinker 2007b).

Darwinism dealt a decisive blow to the assumption that humans are **ontologically** distinct from other animals. Before that, the 'insuperable line' was the target of satirists. The fourth and final voyage in *Gulliver's Travels* (1726) by **Jonathan Swift** (1667–1745) takes the narrator to a land of anthropomorphised, ultra-rational Houyhnhnms (horses, to Gulliver's eyes) and zoomorphised human-like Yahoos, who are at once savage and oppressed. Swift's fable not only disentangles reason from humanity, as Armstrong observes, it adds a further anti-Cartesian gesture: the Houyhnhnms' 'reason' allows them to discuss exterminating the Yahoos dispassionately. The 'primitive', degraded yet pitiable 'inhumanity' of the latter is thereby contrasted with the far worse 'inhumanity' of the former, which is systematic and thoroughly rationalised. For Armstrong, Swift's brilliant combination of anthropomorphism and zoomorphism is a radical challenge to the humanism of Descartes and others:

> In keeping with their satirical function, then, the Yahoos and Houynhnhnms ... do not function to support, define, give shape to or bear the human as a concept or category. Rather, they demolish, unfasten, annul, delegitimize or subvert it. ... The modern notion of *homo* as *animal rationale* evaporates under Swift's scorching gaze, and leaves nothing behind.
>
> (p.11)

The price of Swift's insight, though, is a deeply pessimistic view of the possibilities of human nature. Indeed, when Gulliver returns from his last voyage, he remains alienated from his family and other humans, who cannot now appear to him but zoomorphically, as Yahoos.

It is not surprising that *Gulliver's Travels* provides one of the epigrams to Margaret Atwood's *Oryx and Crake* (2003). The chapters alternate between a dystopian future, where protagonist Jimmy lives in an ultra-consumerist society, and a post-apocalyptic, post-human environment in which most of humanity is dead and Jimmy has become 'Snowman', guardian of a race of genetically-modified humanoid 'Crakers' (cf. ch.5). Jimmy's world throngs with genetically-spliced organisms such as 'pigoons': pigs literally anthropomorphised with human genes to make them suitable for organ donation. Both moral and biological distinctions are swept away by the confluence of biotechnology and consumerist desire, leading Jimmy to ask himself: 'Why is it he feels some line has been crossed, some boundary transgressed? How much is too much, how far is too far?' (p.206).

Oryx and Crake is Atwood's only novel with a male protagonist through-out, which may account for the novel's darkly satirical representation of

Jimmy, his Frankensteinian friend Crake and the debauched, narcissistic society that surrounds them. The frenetic, heedless pursuit of youth, beauty, sex and wealth is depicted as primarily driven by men's desires, and by their lack of self-knowledge and responsibility about those desires. Crake, for example, views humans dispassionately, like a Houyhnhnm, but screams when he dreams, while Jimmy's appearance of sensitivity is largely a ploy to persuade women to sleep with him. The rational animal of Enlightenment thought is, in this story-world, a distant memory haloed in vague nostalgia:

> When did the body first set out on its own adventures? Snowman thinks; after having ditched its old travelling companions, the mind and the soul ... It must have got tired of the soul's constant nagging and whining and the anxiety-driven intellectual web-spinning of the mind, distracting it whenever it was getting its teeth into something good.
>
> (p.85)

The mind and the soul have been supplanted by the body of the 'consumer', which is, in Raymond Williams's memorable words, 'a very specialized variety of human being with no brain, no eyes, no senses, but who can gulp' (1989: 216). The narrative momentum of the novel towards disaster, and the resistless correspondence between Jimmy's male desires and those propelling consumerism, ensure Atwood's satire is a bleak prognosis for the survival of our species. Atwood's sequel *MaddAddam* (2013) envisages eventual hybridisation of humans and Crakers, which could be considered an optimistic ending.

Ethologists increasingly accept the value of anthropomorphic hypotheses. Until the 1970s, as Crist's study shows, anxiety about anthropomorphism was embedded in the very language of ethology, in that 'presentation of subjectivity emerges through, and rests upon, lexical elements, grammatical constructs, and patterns of reasoning that are prior to the ascription of mentality' (p.110). For example, employing the preferred mechanomorphic protocols, pioneering ethologists such as **Konrad Lorenz** (1903–1989) and 'Niko' Tinbergen (1907–1988) described animals as objects, and their behaviour in abstract, rather than individual, terms. The **agency** of an animal subject, as animal advocates would see it, was represented instead as the response of an 'instinct' or 'fixed action pattern' to an environmental 'stimulus'. Since we tend to associate automatic reaction and lack of variation with machines, their language strongly corroborated a mechan-omorphic perspective. Moreover, as Crist points out, 'the neglect of indivi-dual variation of behaviors and the disparagement of anecdotal evidence, coupled with generic description as a method of writing, contributed to the impression that the ethological theoretical construct of fixed action patterns was an ontological property of animal behavior in general' (loc.596). The austere, impersonal idiom of scientific description made it seem as though animals were merely the site at which stimuli met responses, with no mediating subjectivity or individual variation at all. Intriguingly, though, Crist also contradicts the argument of ecofeminists such as Val Plumwood and Greta Gaard (ch.2) that mechanomorphic representation necessarily has baleful moral implications. She maintains that Lorenz and Tinbergen were not committed to mechanistic philosophies and did not seek 'to "desubjectify" animals' (loc.1233). Conversely, while it seems plausible that anthropomorphism would make us kinder and more respectful towards animals, in its crude form it is really a way of *not seeing* animals in their own right at all. Smiling pigs in the windows of butcher's shops are one instance; another is the unethical breeding of bulldogs, pugs and Pekinese ('brachycephalic' dogs) to look cute to anthropomorphic eyes despite the misery and severe disability it imposes (Serpell 2005). Thus, although Cartesian and other mechanomorphic constructs may be used to *rationalise* cruel or indifferent treatment of animals, there is no necessary or even predictable relationship between representational forms and moral valuations.

Mechanomorphism outside science is quite rare. Narratives in film and literature are conventionally built around 'characters', whose agency is at once assumed and affirmed, whilst plot implies purposeful actions, rather than automatic responses to stimuli. As a result, popular cultural forms have a strong anthropomorphic bias that even affects stories that were built to resist it, such as Henry Williamson's *Tarka the Otter* (1927): Tarka's behaviour is believably naturalistic, and yet his life story is constructed as a maudlin morality tale. Where mechanomorphism does feature in literature, it delivers a jolt of estrangement, often con-joined with an overtly masculine determination to reject sentimentality. In 'Thrushes', an early poem by **Ted Hughes** (1930–1998) the birds are described as 'Terrifying' and 'attent', 'More coiled steel than living' (Hughes 1995: 39). There is no mention of their mellifluous song, nor any other aspect of their existence beyond predation. Yet even this mechanomorphic image is qualified by the speaker's range of explanations, some of them reductive and others admiring:

> Is it their single-mind-sized skulls, or a trained
> Body, or genius, or a nestful of brats
> Gives their days this bullet and automatic
> Purpose? ...

Mozart is said to have had the same intensity of purpose as the thrushes. For an ordinary man, though, whose 'act worships itself', mindfulness is distracting or painfully alienating. 'Humanity' is, in this sense, a liability.

So it is, too, in the work of **D.H. Lawrence** (1885–1930), but because he dismissed 'mechanistic' accounts of natural vitality, another term is required for Lawrence's animals and their ilk. Anthropomorphism was hateful to him because it typified the inability of a petty, grasping human consciousness to accept anything truly different from itself. Much of Lawrence's animal poetry dramatises the perpetual tension between the reach of our over-celebrated human minds and the numinous otherness of animals. In his poem 'Fish', Lawrence employs human analogies to help us visualise:

> A slim young pike, with smart fins
> And grey-striped suit, a young cub of a pike
> Slouching along away below, half out of sight,
> Like a lout on an obscure pavement ....
>   (Lawrence 1993: 50)

But then the speaker rebukes himself for compromising the otherness, or alterity, of the fish:

> I had made a mistake, I didn't know him,
> This grey, monotonous soul in the water,
> This intense individual in shadow,
> Fish-alive.
>
> I didn't know his God.
> I didn't know his God.

I suggest the term 'allomorphism' ('allo' meaning 'other') for this kind of acknowledgement of the wondrous strangeness of animals, which often involves an overtly sacred language: for Lawrence, the encounter with fish leads to the realisation: *'I am not the measure of creation, / ... His God stands outside my God.'* In the context of his work as a whole, allomorphic representation serves what Armstrong calls Lawrence's 'redemptive therio-primitivism' for which 'Animality, at its most wild and untamed, was not the enemy of humanity, but its possible, perhaps its only, salvation' (p.143). Cut off from animality by his own 'civilised' consciousness, Lawrence continually sought places and people whom he could imagine had a more authentic, 'primal' relationship to animal Others.

One of the most remarkable examples of allomorphic literature is *Translations from the Natural World* (1992) by **Les Murray** (1938–2019), the central section of which, subtitled 'Presence', is a series of poems representing a striking range of other-than-human beings: 'Stone Fruit', 'Shellback Tick', 'Cell DNA' and 'The Snake's Heat Organ' gives some indication of their variety. A poem called 'Migratory', jarringly aligned with the right margin of the page, evokes a migrating bird's instinctual desire for movement, rather than its subjective experience, while 'Two Dogs' is a smelly canine encounter rendered into words. Ambitious as Murray's sequence is, every poem is a vivid testament to the difficulty, if not impossibility, of the representational work it undertakes. As Jonathan Bate observes, even its title embodies a productive tension: '"Translations" is a recognition that the poet's home in the *logos* [language or word] is a different place from the natural world itself, but "presence" proclaims poetry's capacity to reveal the being of things' (2000: 240). For Murray, a Catholic poet, such being is the immanence of his God's grace throughout the natural world, which includes the material, biological processes but also exceeds them. Just as D.H. Lawrence extolled a vision of evolution not as competition and scarcity, but proliferation and 'singling out', Murray explains that *'Presence is why we love what we cannot eat or mate with'* (1998: 385).

A translation between human languages aims to preserve the denotative meaning of the original, whilst addressing the difficulty that connotations can be culturally-specific and untranslatable. In Murray's interspecies translations, the phonemic, syntactic and lexical density and strangeness of the poems pay tribute to the quite different ways in which poems, DNA, flowers and whale songs *communicate*, whilst also rendering the unfamiliar **biosemiotic** worlds of '*l'animot*' stunningly immediate. Whereas Lawrence drew back from anthropomorphic characterisation of the fish, Murray charges through and beyond it in his poem 'Shoal':

> Eye-and-eye eye an eye
> Each. What blinks is I, -
> unison of the whole shoal.
> (p.372)

The being of the fish is in some sense located in the constant distance it maintains from the rest of the shoal. Each animal is only an 'eye-and-eye', but together they make 'I'. Indeed, although the fish remains alive when it leaves the shoal – 'gill-pulse drinks / and nervy fins space-walk' – it loses its 'self'. In other poems, the estranging use of pronouns to suggest radically non-human kinds of selves includes the pigs who say 'Us all on sore cement was we' (p.381) and the cows who refer to themselves as 'All me'.

For Lawrence, the disjunction between his own element and that of the fish emphasised its alterity; for Murray, it is an invitation to explore a sensory lifeworld dominated by varying concentrations of substances dissolved in water, making 'each being a tongue' attentive to 'vague umbrations of chemical'. While their eyes form the basis of their social organisation, which is also their selfhood, the 'earblades' of the fish are acutely attuned to the pressure waves of the 'bird-dive boom' and 'red-fin's gaped gong'. It is striking that in this poem, as in 'Migratory', the rich characterisation of an alien mode of being takes priority over the identity of either species or individual: we never find out which species of fish it is. In that respect, Murray's allomorphism differs from that of foxhunting, bullfighting and fly-fishing devotees, which combines cruelty to individual animals (e.g. the living fox) with reverence for a mystified conception of the species pursued or fought (e.g. 'Reynard') (Scruton 1998; Kennedy 1999). Here and throughout Murray's sequence, neomodernist experimentation with language and poetic form combines with reverential attention to animal Others in a form of allomorphism that recalls Kate Rigby's idea of 'negative ecopoetics': rather than imagining some ultimate form of ecopoetry that would comprehend or adequately represent the 'more-than-human world', she suggests that 'the literary text saves the earth by disclosing the nonequation of word and thing, poem and place' (2004: 437). From that perspective, *Translations from the Natural World* is a collection of necessarily, magnificently failed poems that gesture towards a numinous unity underlying the breathtaking diversity of life.

The typology above provides a simplified schema with which complex and often contradictory ways of looking at animals may be understood. Distinguishing the crude from the critical forms of anthropomorphism and zoomorphism, in particular, is at once difficult and important. Moreover, the examples given here suggest that representing animals is related in sometimes surprising ways to moral and political practices: scientists who conceptualise animals as machines don't necessarily treat them as such, while the bloodshed of the bullring is sublimated by the mythology of *el toro*.

WHY LOOK AT WILD ANIMALS?

For most readers, companion animals are beloved and familiar, their otherness all but invisible, whereas wild animals are more peripheral. Urban foxes in Europe and raccoons and coyotes in North American cities tend to be outshone by the astonishing variety and fascinating behaviour captured by wildlife documentaries and movies. Scholars of film theory and history, Animal Studies and ecocriticism have therefore paid sustained attention to what Gregg Mitman punningly calls 'Reel Nature' (2009) ever since the publication of Alexander Wilson's *The Culture of Nature* in 1992. Their assessments focus on one or more of three aspects of wildlife documentaries: questions of misrepresentation; historical development and cultural context; and 'biocultural' readings of the affective and cognitive impact of wildlife programming. While some films have clearly had a positive impact – *Flipper* (1963) created a constituency of young dolphin admirers who demanded 'dolphin friendly tuna' as adults – those concerned with misrepresentation claim that wildlife documentaries are prone to substitute error for ignorance. In particular, scholars claim that viewers' capacity for full sensory, intellectual and political engagement with nature is narrowed to a purely visual relation, which is further distorted by overemphasis on violence and sex. Nature programming, in other words, may be little better than 'ecoporn' (Welling 2009).

The early Disney documentaries, for instance, are rife with misrepresentation, crude anthropomorphism and outright fakery, as in *White Wilderness* (1958) when captured brown lemmings were forced over the edge of a cliff by a film crew to illustrate their 'suicidal' mass migrations. Wilson charts a shift 'from pastoralism to scientism' from these early efforts to the 1980s, as audiences came to demand scientific accuracy and conservationist advocacy from wildlife programming. The desire to inform as well as entertain is a longstanding tension, as Wilson observes of the National Geographic production *White Wolf* (1989). He points out that the overt, verbal message and the implicit meaning of the action sequences are far from complementary: 'the biologists speculate about wolf language and child rearing, play, security and feeding', but 'the tension of the show is a *dramatic* tension, organized around an edited hunting episode rather than the ideas set out by the biologists'. For Wilson, 'The structure of the movie undercuts the script' (Wilson 2019 [1992]: 141). A similar conundrum affects David Attenborough's narration of *Our Planet* (2019), which explains that caribou populations in North America are plummeting even as the screen is filled with thousands of animals. Absent animals do not make for exciting viewing.

Karla Armbruster's survey of criticisms of TV nature documentaries observes that an hour-long documentary compresses weeks of waiting and hours of filming into a brief, enthralling spectacle. Far from connecting us with nature, this is likely to contrast strikingly with direct experience, as 'a fulfilling experience with the natural world involves more than passively sitting back to be informed and entertained' (Armbruster 1998: 224). This rather fundamental objection aside, Armbruster's essay criticises specific techniques and practices such as the phenomenon of the absent narrator, claiming that it encourages a sense of innocent unobtrusiveness in the viewer: 'By identifying with the narrator, and with the perspective of the camera that so often appears to be the narrator's eye, the viewer is constructed as omniscient and capable of penetrating the most inaccessible reaches of the natural world' (p.232). As the metaphor of penetration might indicate, the illusion of unrestricted access into a mysterious or forbidden space produces a relation of subject to object that is structurally similar to pornography, in which the eye/I derives pleasure from a gaze that its object cannot challenge or return. In order to alleviate the naturalisation of this perspective, Armbruster advocates open admission that the documentary is a partial and particular construction of nature, with substantial technical demands. Interestingly, flagship BBC documentaries such *Planet Earth* (2006), produced since her critique, juxtapose traditional spectacle with a 'diary' element, although this is more a tribute to the technical prowess and adventuring spirit of the film crew than a reflexive commentary. A few documentaries, such as the gorgeous, enthralling *Microcosmos* (1996), eschew commentary almost entirely, revealing instead what the directors Claude Nuridsany and Marie Pérennou call 'le quotidien des insectes' (the everyday life of insects): not just predation but waking up and hanging around.

The phrase 'nature documentary' itself highlights a central concern about misrepresentation. As Brett Mills argues in *Animals on Television* (2017), 'nature' is commonly understood as ahistorical, inevitable, and immune to change (as in 'human nature'), whereas ecocriticism and related fields attempt 'to problematise and dismantle the naturalisation of the concept of nature' (p.89) (cf. ch.4). If the term 'documentary' encourages an assumption of veracity and accuracy, then a 'nature documentary' would be uniquely empowered to make claims about reality that could be highly 'naturalised' and hard to challenge. One of these, for Mills, is the idea that the 'natural world' is nothing but a resource for humans, an assumption of instrumental value bolstered by nature documentaries in which:

> ... animals are resources for human entertainment and education, and the technical wizardry used to capture animals' behaviour is often celebrated as evidence of human ingenuity. That the ways in which animals are captured within human forms of representation has analogies with how animals are captured within human forms of real-world domination evidences an overarching discourse which legitimises the categorisation of animals as resources.
>
> (p.96)

Mills's argument is surely too simplistic. The book you are reading is an educational 'resource' that has a retail value, but its *educational value* to a specific reader is unrelated to the cover price. Unobtrusively filming an animal for our excitement or edification is not very much like shooting it to make a fur coat. The vital work of assessing the environmental value of nature documentaries is little advanced by Mills's weak analogy.

Derek Bousé denies that these are 'documentaries' at all, as the title of his book, *Wildlife Films* (2000), indicates. They are so profoundly shaped by the commercial demands of spectacle and narrative coherence that they are not only, as Armbruster argues, unrealistically exciting, but also far too narrativised (much like *Tarka the Otter*). Bousé's detailed history ranges from Disney's *True Life Adventures* (1948–1960) through the BBC's acclaimed 'blue chip' series that started with *Life on Earth* (1979) to the explosion of formats in the mid-1990s with the advent of *Animal Planet* on cable TV. He shows how wildlife films have responded to commercial imperatives, technological developments and broader cultural changes. For example, the BBC's Natural History Unit (NHU), founded in Bristol in 1957 and still operational today as 'BBC Earth', not only 'assembled more talented people under one roof than any other wildlife film company' (2000: 76), but was increasingly called upon to exemplify the BBC's public service mandate and to justify the TV licence fee paid by Britons. Over time, Bousé argues, wildlife films have come to resemble other such films, rather than reality itself:

> The use of formal artifice such as varying camera angles, continuity editing, montage editing, slow-motion, 'impossible' close-ups, voice-over narration, dramatic or ethnic music, and the like should by no means be off-limits to wildlife filmmakers, but by the same token we should not avoid critical reflection on the overall image of nature and wildlife that emerges, cumulatively, from the long-term and systematic use of such devices.
>
> (p.8)

He concludes, with John Berger and Armbruster, that 'wildlife films may do less to acquaint us with nature than to alienate us from it' (p.8).

Bousé goes on to detail how, for example, unrelated clips are edited to create a wholly fictional narrative, albeit one presumably 'true to life'. Synchronised sound cannot be recorded alongside telephoto shots, and so the edited sequence also must be knitted together with dramatic music or sounds (crunching bones or rustling twigs) made in the studio. Bousé's most persuasive example of misrepresentation, though, is his critique of what he calls 'symbolic Darwinism', which illustrates population-level evolutionary abstractions such as 'sexual selection' and 'inclusive fitness' by means of 'dramatic vignettes depicting the actions of individuals' (p.33). Biologists disagree about what, exactly, 'natural selection' selects, be it genes, organisms, populations or – the least likely – species as such (Sterelny and Griffiths 2012). Whatever the preferred answer, Bousé is right to say that:

> Although an individual's physical survival may be at stake in [a depicted conflict], the survival of the species or genotype is not. Such battles simply do not illustrate the evolutionary 'struggle to survive'.
>
> (p.34)

Symbolic Darwinism provides the rationale for slow-motion hunting scenes that supposedly represent, as exemplary part of the larger whole, 'survival of the fittest', even though this circular statement is devoid of biological significance.

David Attenborough's genial presence, and more recently voiceover, on BBC wildlife films has been their seal of cultural value and assurance of scientific accuracy for over 40 years. He is the foremost of the select group discussed in Graham Huggan's *Nature's Saviours: Celebrity conservationists in the television age* (2013), as indicated by the chapter title 'A is for Attenborough'. Huggan adopts the cultural studies concept of the 'celebrity system' for his scrupulously balanced explanation of the role of presenters' 'cultural capital' in environmental politics. Even as he pays tribute to Attenborough's televisual and environmentalist accomplishments, Huggan draws attention to the ironies inherent in the presenter's role as a 'science media professional' (2013: 25). For example, Attenborough is invested with the authority of a scientist, even though he stopped doing science long ago and has himself, in interviews, underlined the dissensus and uncertainty inherent in scientific research. Huggan sums up the 'Attenborough persona' as 'simultaneously avuncular and aloof, alternately self-assured and self-effacing, combining the scientific authority of the expert with the passionate curiosity of the amateur' (p.24). Reflecting on criticisms that the BBC's sumptuous documentaries are simplistic and apolitical, Huggan responds:

> Attenborough's natural history films are more complex than this, sharing as they do the discrepant goals of romantic and realist documentary, and reflecting to some extent on the conflicting ideologies that drive them: capitalism and anti-capitalism, colonialism and anti-

colonialism, scientific-materialist and romantic-idealist conceptions and historical trajectories of the natural world.

(p.51)

Such tensions are especially evident in *Our Planet,* a series made for Netflix in collaboration with the World Wildlife Fund (WWF), narrated by Attenborough and produced by NHU alumni. A quantitative analysis by Julia Jones and colleagues shows that it mentions threats to the natural world far more often than *Planet Earth II* (2016), and also includes more 'positive tales of species recoveries and conservation interventions' (p.421). While *Our Planet* remains, in Huggan's words, as 'thoroughly aestheticized' (p.23) as previous documentaries, its emotional terrain is more demanding, transitioning from familiar wonder and amusement (at the birds' extraordinary mating dances in episodes one and three, for instance) to solemn elegy and fragile hope. If the linked WWF website falls short of calling for the end of capitalism, it does encourage political engagement as well as individual action and support for the charity.

Wildlife films' emotional contour is the focus of a new mode of eco-critical attention pioneered by Alexa Weik von Mossner: 'affective eco-criticism', which draws on neuropsychology to demonstrate that our *shared biology* ... enables us to cognitively read the emotional expressions of other animals' bodies' and share 'their affective states on the subconscious level through emotional contagion, affective mimicry and other processes of embodied simulation' (2018: 164). At best, wildlife films encourage 'trans-species empathy' (p.170) in ways that may encourage critical anthropomorphism. Meanwhile, the potential emotional entanglement of *filmmakers* and their animal subjects is the topic of Bart Welling's startlingly original essay, which looks at two unusual documentaries: *Being Caribou* (2004), a low-budget documentary in which a couple follow the Porcupine caribou herd across the Yukon and Alaska, and *Winged Migration* (2001), which used trained migratory birds and a plethora of human technologies to film avian migrations. Rejecting crude anthropomorphism, Welling shows how empathic, yet critical, relationships can form across species boundaries, thereby providing 'viewers with heavily mediated but potentially transformative modes of access to the emotional lives of our non-human kin' (2014: 82) Like Mossner, Welling calls for theoretical-empirical **'biocultural'** research that treats anthropomorphism as 'a dynamic process based on affective, historical, ecological, economic, and other kinds of *relationships* between animals, film-makers, and viewers' (p.91).

If the appeals of wildlife films are unsuccessful, innumerable species are at risk. Many biologists believe that we are in the early stages of the greatest mass extinction episode since the annihilation of the dinosaurs at the end of the Cretaceous Period 65 million years ago (Kolbert 2015), though *recorded* anthropogenic extinctions are so far concentrated in a few taxa, notably birds, amphibians and mammals. Prehistoric human settlers were primarily responsible for extinction episodes in Madagascar, Hawaii, Aotearoa New Zealand and elsewhere, and, more controversially, the distant ancestors of modern Indigenous people in Australia and the Americas are thought to have contributed to 'megafauna' extinctions in the late Pleistocene and early Holocene epochs (70–20Ka ago) in which at least 177 species of large animal died out (ch.7). In the era of European colonialism and industrial modernity, though, many more extinctions, especially of island species, were recorded far more quickly: at least 900 in five centuries (Ritchie and Roser 2021). A mass extinction requires that 75% of extant species are wiped out in a period that seems brief to geologists: less than two million years. Anthony Barnosky and colleagues ask how long it would take, on present trends, to reach this threshold in the case of well-studied taxa like birds, mammals and amphibians, and find that 'the recent loss of species is dramatic and serious but does not yet qualify as a mass extinction in the palaeontological sense' (2011: 56). Many more species are on the brink of extinction, however, and so the rate of loss could accelerate still further:

> ... [L]osing species now in the [International Union for Conservation of Nature's] 'critically endangered' category would propel the world to a state of mass extinction that has previously been seen only five times in about 540 million years. Additional losses of species in the 'endangered' and 'vulnerable' categories could accomplish the sixth mass extinction in just a few centuries.

Ursula Heise's groundbreaking *Imagining Extinction: The Cultural Meaning of Endangered Species* (2016) provides both a model and roadmap for eco-critics to address this daunting topic. Heise acknowledges both the scale of the crisis and the methodological challenges in estimating it, whilst advocating for cultural forms that go beyond the familiar elegies for lost species and cautionary tales about future decline. Rather than lamenting our failure to care more for non-human species, she takes it as given that many people *do* care, and asks: 'How, when, and why do we invest culturally, emotionally, and economically in the fate of threatened species?' (2016: 4). She makes the bold assertion that 'biodiversity, endangered species, and extinction are primarily cultural issues, questions of what we value and what stories we tell, and only secondarily issues of science' (p.5), and then backs it up with wide-ranging analyses of species databases, biodiversity laws, paintings and photographs, as well as novels such as Julia Leigh's *The Hunter* (2000) and Amitav Ghosh's *The Hungry Tide* (2004). Whereas scientific conservationists advocate the forlorn project of valuing *every* species 'purely for its own sake', Heise concludes that species:

> ... come to matter when they become associated with stories that particular cultures tell about their own origins, history, modernization, and futures, as well as about their relation to a broader 'humanity,' to different humans, and to the species that form part of the understanding of human identity in particular cultural contexts.
>
> (p.237)

Concern for endangered species is not lacking, but nor can it be conjured merely by placing a species on scientifically-determined list.

Heise is asking kindred questions to Gregg Mitman's afterword to the 2009 edition of *Reel Nature*:

> ... are the stories we tell familiar tales of violence and sex, love and family, Edenic Nature and ecological apocalypse that garner audience ratings and reinforce well-worn stereotypes? Or are they stories that challenge us to see the environment in new and surprising ways, inspiring action and hope on a planet, beautiful in its diversity of life, but also troubled by unprecedented environmental change and injustice?
>
> (p.220)

These are the same questions this book asks of environmental representations more broadly. In the case of nature films, though, scholars such as

Mossner, Ivakhiv and Welling have arrived at a consensus that 'The actual effects of film can hardly be measured without talking to those most affected by them' (Ivakhiv 2013: 223): audiences, in other words. Theoretical critique and close analysis, they argue, must be complemented with sophisticated empirical study that follows 'viewers' relations with cinematic images, ideas, and rhythms over time' (p.223). Ecocritics should want to know what works, but they also need to frame what it *means* for a book or film to 'work' in complex, rounded, not simplistic or reductive ways. The 'Conclusion' returns to this question.

7

INDIGENEITY

ACKNOWLEDGEMENTS

'I am writing this chapter on the traditional and unceded territory of the Syilx Okanagan people. I acknowledge that I am an uninvited guest in this land, and I accept the responsibility to be a good neighbour and a good ancestor.' This is a written version of the land acknowledgement that is frequently heard in settler colonial societies, at academic gatherings especially. It could be dismissed as liberal virtue signalling, or 'moral exhibitionism' (Wood 2021). If uttered in good faith, though, it accomplishes several things: first, it expresses the speaker's sense of their status in a colonised region whose prior Indigenous inhabitants were dispossessed. 'Unceded' means that settler-Indigenous relations were never codified in a treaty; rather, the Indigenous inhabitants were coerced into relinquishing their land without any recompense. The acknowledgement sometimes includes a longer statement of positionality that lists the speaker's demographic attributes: a White, straight, cis, presently able-bodied male, in my case. Second, it could be read as a 'constative' speech act (i.e. the statement about my location might be true or false) followed by a 'performative' speech act, which 'is not setting out to *describe* a situation, an event or an action: it *is* an event or an action' (Loxley 2007: 8). If we imagine

DOI: 10.4324/9781003174011-7

adding the word 'hereby' before the verb 'acknowledge', we can see that the speaker is making a promise. You can take it that, in addition to *quoting* this acknowledgement, it is true and I mean it.

There is a thorny question – the first of several – about whether my positionality means I shouldn't presume to introduce, let alone question, 'Indigeneity,' or if my acknowledgement only equips you, the reader, to decide how much to trust my authority. Clearly, I don't accept the first option. I know that many advantages have come with being a White male raised in an upper-middle class home, and I have learned that some of my ancestors fought in colonial wars while others settled in what is now British Columbia in 1905 and 1948. Still, demography is not destiny, and culpability is not heritable; colonial and other forms of privilege should be acknowledged, not to shut down discussion but to enable it on more honest terms. I am also no expert on Indigenous literature and culture, specifically, and so you should consider whether my summary and critique ought to be discounted as an instance of White colonial entitlement. As I say in the Introduction, this book departs from the activist norm in the environmental humanities in setting out to be **multi-partial**.

The question of authority, of speaking about or for Indigenous people, draws attention to a crucial difference between this trope and the others in this book: whereas animals cannot question our constructs of animality, Indigenous people have *actively shaped* the idea of Indigeneity, albeit under conditions of colonial violence and racial discrimination. When it comes to wilderness, say, ecocritical readings tend to 'zigzag,' as Timothy Clark suggests, between 'a culturalist and a realist reading':

> What any writer calls 'nature' can always be read as a cultural/political construction.
> But
> culture always depends on and is encompassed by actual nature, which requires recognition.
> But
> that 'nature' can always be read as a cultural/political construction.
> But
> ... etc.
>
> (Clark 2011: 94)

Indigeneity, though, is what Ian Hacking calls an 'interactive kind' of classification thanks to 'the almost-too-boring-to-state fact that people are aware of what is said about them, thought about them, done to them' (1999: 31). It therefore takes the form of a loop in which, in recent decades especially, Indigenous people themselves have rejected colonial stereotypes and demanded the right to self-definition.

THE 'ECOLOGICAL INDIAN' AND ECOLOGICAL INDIGENEITY

The White anthropologist Shepard Krech III sets out to support that effort in *The Ecological Indian: Myth and History* (1999). Krech tells the history of what he sees as a stereotype of European origin, which begins with Renaissance and Romantic celebrations of the 'noble savage' and issues in the late twentieth century in a 'dominant image of the Indian in nature who understands the systemic consequences of his actions, feels deep sympathy with all living forms, and takes steps to conserve so that earth's harmonies are never imbalanced and resources never in doubt' (p.21). The 'Ecological Indian' is not only historically inaccurate, according to Krech, but 'ultimately dehumanizing' in that it 'den[ies] both variation within human groups and commonalities between them' (p.26). He cites evidence of culturally-sanctioned overkill and over-harvesting of buffalo (aka bison), beaver and deer, for instance, that contradicts the stereotype. Reviewing the debate about the role played by the probable ancestors of modern Indigenes, known as Paleoindians, in the extinction of 35 mammalian genera (predominantly large species like mammoths and ground sloths) in the Americas, Krech concludes that climate change was most likely the dominant factor, but that Paleoindians may well have 'pushed certain species already heading toward their doom over the edge to extinction' (p.41). Outside the Americas, there is ample evidence that hunting, agriculture, use of fire and companion species introductions contributed to prehistoric mega-faunal and avian extinctions in Madagascar, Aotearoa New Zealand[1], and many Pacific Islands, and plausible arguments in the case of Australia. A 'comprehensive species-level, fine-grained global macroecological analysis' of Quaternary extinctions and continental extirpations of large mammals confirms 'humans as the key driver of extinction' and finds 'little association between climate change severity and the proportion of extinct large mammals' (Sandom et al. 2014: 3, 7). A separate statistical study of the relationship of body mass to the probability of terrestrial mammal extinction shows that 'body mass was rarely significantly associated with the probability of extinction before the late Pleistocene' (Smith et al. 2018: 1), whereas bigger animals were far more likely to become extinct on every continent *including Africa* after hominin species (latterly including *Homo sapiens*) evolved 2.6 million years ago. The Pleistocene and Holocene epochs have seen 'severe body size downgrading—a truncation of more than two orders of magnitude' (p.3), a trend that the researchers expect to accelerate in the Anthropocene epoch (ch.8). 'The distinctive selectivity signature,' the team concludes, 'implicates hominin activity as a primary driver of taxonomic losses and ecosystem homogenization' (p.1). Daniel Heath Justice (Cherokee) phrases a similarly depressing insight more colloquially:

> The only thing that really seems to be unique about humans as a species is our capacity for wilful, self-deluding destruction. We're *really good* at killing, maiming, and spoiling things, and doing it with pleasure. And we always have been – Indigenous traditions are well stocked with warnings against human destructiveness and lessons for more respectful co-existence with our other-than-human relatives.
>
> (2018: 38–9)

It is a striking suggestion: that those cautionary tales, widespread in Indigenous cultures, are oral records of Paleoindians' experience of extinctions and other failures, rather than proof positive of environmental virtue. The Ten Commandments, after all, are hardly evidence of Judaeo-Christians' superior moral character.

Vine Deloria Jr. (Standing Rock Sioux) (1933–2005), though, rejects the role of Paleoindians – what he dubs 'Mythical Pleistocene Hit Men' – in North American megafaunal extinctions in *Red Earth, White Lies: Native Americans and the Myth of Scientific Fact* (1997). He energetically contests the available paleontological evidence, in part because 'Conservative newspaper columnists, right-wing fanatics, sportsmen's groups, and scholars in general tend to see the "overkill" hypothesis as symptomatic of a lack of moral fiber and ethical concern for the Earth among Indians' (p.90). Intentionally privileging Indigenous oral traditions as opposed to scientific evidence, Deloria argues that volcanoes and floods were responsible for Pleistocene extinctions, and he suggests that, if we accept a Delaware Indian story concerning skeletal remains in Kentucky, 'there were mammoths or mastodons still living in the eastern United States at the time the Pilgrims landed' (p.114) in 1620. To Deloria, 'Krech's status as an outsider, a non-Indian, makes it inappropriate in the first place to address questions relating to the presumed ancestors of Native Americans' (Harkin and Lewis 2007: xxiii).

Other Indigenous authors find Krech's thesis both persuasive and liberating. Kimberley TallBear (Sisseton Wahpeton Oyate) contends that 'native people should diligently monitor for [race-based] power inequities, but we should not reject as worthless the knowledge to be had from scholarship undertaken by non-Indians' (p.3), and she commends Krech for 'challenging a stereotype that, while it may be healing to an extent, helps perpetuate divisive identity politics underway in Indian Country, and de-legitimizes the efforts of tribes to govern ourselves if we are not perceived as traditional according to a narrow, generic, and romanticized view of what is traditional' (2000: 2). She also points out that, far from seeking to condemn Indigenous people for failing to conform to a modern standard, *The Ecological Indian* understands tribal practices in the context of beliefs actually held at the time. Krech's conclusion supports TallBear's reading:

> Native people clearly possessed vast knowledge of their environment. They understood relationships among living things in the environment, and to this extent their knowledge was 'ecological.' But knowledge is cultural, and each group in its own way made the environment and its relationships cultural. Their ecologies were premised on theories of animal behavior and animal population dynamics unfamiliar to Western science, beginning, for some, with the belief in reincarnation. And their ecological systems embraced components like underground prairies [where bison lived in winter], which were absent from the ecological systems of Western scientists. Their actions, while perfectly reasonable in light of their beliefs and larger goals, were not necessarily rational according to the premises of Western ecological conservation.
>
> (p.212)

Krech is right to observe that the Ecological Indian is the descendant of the much older image of the 'Noble Savage', a benign, Romantic counter to the historically-dominant colonial stereotype of 'cannibalistic, bloodthirsty, inhuman' (p.16) Ignoble Savages. However, he underestimates Indigenous agency in 'interactively' constructing and contesting what I prefer to call 'Ecological Indigeneity'. Taking a long historical view, Jace Weaver (Cherokee) argues that what he calls the 'Red Atlantic' was 'a multilane, two-way bridge across which traveled ideas and things that changed both Europeans and American indigenes' (2014: 30) in the centuries between Viking settlement and the advent of air travel in the 1920s. A colonial traveller such as **Louis-Armand de Lom d'Arce, Baron de Lahontan** (c.1666–c.1716) influenced the Romantic conception of the noble savage with his popular published dialogues, which were based on actual encounters with the Huron Chief **Kondiaronk** (c.1649–1701). Lahontan 'coined the word "anarchy" to describe the Huron's political system' (Wilson 1999: 120), a confederacy of independent nations that may have inspired elements of the US constitution (pp.121–2). A century later, a Mohawk chief of Cherokee and Scottish ancestry, **Teyoninhokarawen (aka John Norton)** (1770–1831), travelled to Britain to advocate – unsuccessfully, as it turned out – for the same Six Nations confederacy, or *Haudenosaunee*, to gain legal title to the land conferred on them by the British Crown to thank them for military support in the American War of Independence. At this time, 'in the North American contact zone between whites and Indians', as Tim Fulford says, 'cross-cultural partnerships and mixed race children were not uncommon' (2006: 141). Teyoninhokarawen knew he had to take advantage of British Romantic assumptions about Indians, in his writings as much as his diplomacy, whilst selectively contradicting damaging myths like the assumption that his people were hunters not farmers. Fulford concludes that:

> British Romantic texts shaped ... Indian lives and writing, giving them terms with which to challenge colonial policies and prejudices, even if those terms were neither indigenous to them nor free of limiting assumptions. In responding to these texts some Indians themselves became Romantic writers, finding both leverage and difficulty in appropriating/being appropriated by this white discourse.
>
> (p.148)

During Teyoninhokarawen's life and afterwards, the Grand River Six Nations reserve was diminished by 95% by the sale of land, squatting by colonists and Crown-supported settlement.

In 1492, when Europeans glimpsed the Caribbean Islands for the first time, 'the western hemisphere was larger, richer, and more populous than Europe' (Wilson 1999: 57). Indeed, as Charles C. Mann explains (2011, 2nd edn), research in the last few decades suggests 'Indians were here far longer than previously thought ... and in much greater numbers. And they were so successful at imposing their will on the landscape that in 1492 Columbus set foot in a hemisphere thoroughly marked by mankind' (p.4). Almost immediately Eurasian diseases, to which Indigenous people had no immunity, began to spread through Indigenous populations, whereupon:

> ... the balance between the two sides tipped in Europe's favour. ... The draining of wealth, ideas and products from the New World to the old fuelled an enormous extension of European global power and contributed to a rapid and continuing rise in population, prosperity and cultural vitality. Native America, on the other hand, experienced an almost unimaginably catastrophic collapse as a result of conquest and disease.
>
> (p.57)

Europeans brought many organisms besides microbial pathogens. As Alfred Crosby argues in *Ecological Imperialism* (2004, 2nd edn), European colonists travelled the world with a 'portmanteau biota' (p.270) that included domestic, feral and wild animals and plants as well as epidemic and epizootic pathogens. On the Plains of North America, a European biota ultimately supplanted the native one in a well-documented campaign of combined genocide and ecocide in the late nineteenth century: Whites brought ploughs, livestock, tough short-stemmed grasses, arable crops and, unintentionally, European weeds, smallpox and measles, and they annihilated Plains Indians, tall grasses and bison. Wherever the climate was less temperate or the native flora and fauna more resilient, as in most parts of Africa, biological colonisation was less complete and slower. In temperate and subtropical regions of North America, Australia and Aotearoa New Zealand (Crosby's case study), the transformation of landscapes into what Crosby calls 'Neo-Europes' (p.2) was rapid, widespread and astonishingly destructive. The ecological impact of colonisation may have been planetary: Earth system scientists, Simon Lewis and Mark Maslin, argue that sixteenth- and seventeenth-century colonisation, centred on densely populated Mesoamerica, killed around 50 million people 'via exposure to diseases carried by Europeans, plus war, enslavement and famine', and the ensuing regrowth of forests and grasslands caused a 'dip in atmospheric CO_2 [that is] the most prominent feature ... in pre-industrial atmospheric CO_2 records over the past 2,000 years' (2015: 175). They therefore argue that the 1610 CO_2 minimum should be adopted as the beginning of the Anthropocene epoch (ch.8).

Even at the nadir of their populations and power in North America in the late nineteenth century, though, Indigenous people continued to insist on their right to stewardship of their traditional territories, which they articulated in terms we recognise as ecological. The ecofeminist **Annette Kolodny** (1941–2019) claims that 'Native people themselves had originally fashioned and deployed their own construction of the Ecological Indian for their own ends' (2007: 3), as for example in *The Life and Traditions of the Red Man* (1893) by the Penobscot Elder and political leader **Joseph Nicolar** (1827–1894). Nicolar deliberately constructs his version of the prophecies of the Algonkian culture hero Klose-kur-beh so as to emphasise 'a vision of the wholeness, interdependence, and indwelling sanctity of the "Red man's world"' (p.12). Kolodny is careful to dissociate this politicised self-presentation from any claim that the Penobscots were 'real-life *ecological saints*' (p.16), not least because colonisation had left them, by the end of the nineteenth century, with 'no good choices' (p.17). Nevertheless, Nicolar did provide his people with 'a set of traditions and an ethical system worth the struggle of preservation' (p.17). Moving on to twenty-first-century Native politics, Darren J. Ranco (Penobscot) critiques Krech in forthright terms for his failure to 'recognize ... identity claims [such as the Ecological Indian] and the context and resistance to them as an object for cultural analysis', as, for example, when modern-day 'Penobscot bureaucrats use the ecological Indian stereotype as a strategic intervention' (p.42) to legitimate their positions. Krech, in Ranco's account, represents Indigenous people today as reproducing a stereotype they had no part in creating, which ignores both Penobscot agency and the reality that, for them, 'ecological legitimacy and recognition are matters of life and death' (p.43). The Penobscot Indian Nation reservation in Maine is downstream from a paper mill, now closed down, which poisoned the fish in the Penobscot River with dioxins. In Ranco's account, colonial states impose a 'logic of recognition' (p.45) that forces

Indigenous communities to deploy such stereotypes, 'however weak and mythical' (p.46), in struggles for environmental justice.

Ecological Indigeneity is therefore a dynamic, 'looping' trope that is propagated and contested under specific historical and geographical conditions. Structures of colonial governance make a difference: Australia was declared *terra nullius* (empty land) by **Captain James Cook** (1728–1779), hence open to colonisation without negotiation, whereas in Canada, as Shawn Wilson (Opaskwayak Cree) reminds us, the Crown 'negotiated questionable treaties with the Indigenous peoples ... thus forming a *treaty commonwealth*' (2008: 46). Spanish colonies in the Americas were controlled primarily by *hidalgos* (gentlemen) who spurned labour and trade, whereas the British settler population was 'seeking escape from religious persecution, commercial opportunities or a plot of land which they could work to provide for their own family' (Wilson 1999: 194). During the colonial period, 'Britain was undergoing a population explosion ... producing enough people to grow the population dramatically at home while exporting millions to the colonies and beyond. Spain had never been able to do this' (Morland 2019: loc.967). Hence the emergence of *mestizo* (mixed race) cultures across Latin America, and the existence of an Indigenous-majority state in Bolivia. Any particular form of Indigeneity was, and is, produced by a 'colonial apparatus that is assembled to order the relationships between particular peoples, lands, the "natural world," and "civilization"' (Tuck and Yang 2012: 21). Patrick Wolfe explains how settler colonial objectives in the USA required that Black and Indigenous people be racialised in *opposite* ways, one expansive and the other subtractive:

> Black people's enslavement produced an inclusive taxonomy that automatically enslaved the offspring of a slave and any other parent. In the wake of slavery, this taxonomy became fully racialized in the 'one-drop rule,' whereby any amount of African ancestry, no matter how remote, and regardless of phenotypical appearance, makes a person Black. ... As opposed to enslaved people, whose reproduction augmented their owners' wealth, Indigenous people obstructed settlers' access to land, so their increase was counterproductive. In this way, the restrictive racial classification of Indians straightforwardly furthered the logic of elimination.
>
> (2006: 387–8)

The Indigenous cultures threatened by European colonialism were enormously diverse, and yet are frequently said to share common features. James Wilson says of Native American origin stories:

> When you set them alongside the biblical Genesis, the common features suddenly appear in sharp relief: they seem to glow with the newness and immediacy of creation, offering vivid explanations for the behaviour of an animal, the shape of a rock or a mountain, which you can still encounter in the here and now. Many tribes and nations call themselves, in their own languages, 'the first people,' 'the original people' or the 'real people,' and their stories locate them firmly in a place of special power and significance.
>
> (1999: 8)

In her popular *Braiding Sweetgrass: Indigenous Wisdom, Scientific Knowledge, and the Teachings of Plants* (2013), Robin Wall Kimmerer (Potawatomi) retells the Skywoman origin story common to First Nations in the Great Lakes region, and contrasts it with Eve's disobedience and ejection from Eden in the Biblical Genesis:

> One story [Skywoman] leads to the generous embrace of the living world, the other [Eve] to banishment. One woman is our ancestral gardener, a cocreator of the good green world that would be the home of her descendants. The other was an exile, just passing through an alien world on a rough road to her real home in heaven.
>
> (p.7)

Citing a Laguna Pueblo origin story, Daniel Heath Justice writes that 'while the details differ across geographies and cultures, stories like this are common in every Indigenous story tradition I know: we learned to be human in large part from the land and our other-than-human relatives' (p.76). Shawn Wilson agrees that 'We could not *be* without *being in relationship* with everything that surrounds us and is within us. ... Identity for Indigenous peoples is grounded in their relationships with the land, with their ancestors who have returned to the land and with future generations who will come into being on the land' (p.76, 80). He argues that this worldview, which anthropologists call 'animistic', is the basis of an Indigenous research methodology founded in 'relational accountability' (p.99), as distinct from Western objectivity.

'All my relations' is a common expression amongst Indigenous peoples of North America. It conveys a widening circle of relationship: from family to other humans to, as Thomas King (Cherokee) explains, 'the animals, to the birds, to the fish, to the plants, to all the animate and inanimate forms that can be seen or imagined' (1990: ix). For King, the phrase is 'an encouragement' to live our lives 'in a harmonious and moral manner (a common admonishment is to say of someone that they act as if they have no relations)'.

It seems obvious that relational accountability is an environmental ethic, and yet what counts as a harmonious existence depends on much more than people's general worldview, as Ernest S. Burch shows in a fascinating ethnohistorical comparison of the Alaskan Iñupiat and the Caribou Inuit in the early post-contact period. He notes that 'in the Arctic and subarctic, major fluctuations in the size of fish and game populations could and did throw even the most well-adjusted human populations out of harmony with their environments' (2007: 124). Nevertheless, the Iñupiat did 'fit the stereotype of Native people living in ecological harmony' (p.132), whereas the Caribou Inuit had come to reject seal meat and blubber (p.140) and to focus almost exclusively on hunting muskoxen. They also had a taboo against the use of gill nets, which 'meant that they had no effective means of exploiting the substantial population of fish that inhabited the large lakes in the region' (p.142). These culturally contingent differences, which are hard fully to reconstruct let alone explain by historical scholarship, had a dramatic effect on the Caribou Inuit: having wiped out the muskoxen in their region, they were acutely vulnerable to a crash in the caribou population, which caused famine when it occurred in 1919. Meanwhile, the Iñupiat's early adoption of breech-loading rifles enabled them to overkill caribou and mountain sheep herds in the 1870s and 1880s. Euro-Americans had taken most of the whales and walruses, and so 'Repeated overkills of [land] mammals soon resulted in overharvest, and eventually in widespread starvation and loss of human life' (p.136). The key points here are, first, that the details of people's cultures can make an enormous difference to their sustainability in particular ecosystems, and second, that technological change can radically disrupt whatever existing harmony there is. Notions like 'respect' and 'relationship' can shift in meaning over time: in the case of

Kwakwaka'wakw salmon fishing (Harkin 2007), these ideas formerly implied that hunters were *obliged* to kill any and all creatures that 'offered themselves', whereas later they were reinterpreted (perhaps after bitter experience) to require *restraint*, though both interpretations were embedded in ceremonies of symbolic reciprocity with the prey species.

The truth is that 'sustainability' is a moving target for any society, since it represents an assessment of aggregated human impact on a particular ecosystem, which is itself in flux. The human side of sustainability is sometimes simplified using the acronym PLOT, or Population x Lifestyle x (social) Organization x Technology, though 'lifestyle' is scarcely adequate to capture the richness and complexity of Indigenous cosmologies and practices. While popular environmentalism still talks about 'ecological balance' and Indigenous peoples' 'harmony' with nature, scientific ecologists mostly reject that rhetoric today (ch.3). In that context, Ecological Indigeneity, historical or contemporary, ought to be an open question rather than an assumption.

NORTH AMERICAN INDIGENOUS LITERATURES

'At the end of the fifteenth century,' writes James Wilson, 'there were probably more than six hundred autonomous societies in what is now the United States and Canada, each following its own way of life' (p.21). In some respects, Indigenous people were more diverse than the Christian Indo-European language-speakers who colonised the continent. Today, there are thousands of Indigenous societies in the Americas, Africa, Asia, Australasia and the Pacific Islands that define themselves and are defined by colonial nation-states, and there are flourishing Indigenous literary cultures, primarily Anglophone but also using Indigenous languages, in North America, Australia and Aotearoa New Zealand. I focus here on the accomplished and influential Indigenous literature of modern-day Canada and the USA because the limits of my expertise and experience would be too glaring if I went further afield. This literature emerges on a single, albeit hugely varied, land mass, and from an interwoven history of French, Spanish and British colonisation. One of the causes of the Revolutionary War (1775–1783) was resentment in the 13 American colonies at the Royal Proclamation of 1763, by which the British Crown tried to control westward migration and illegal settlement in Indigenous territories (Dickason and Newbigging

2019: 127). Whilst the defeat of the British by the American separatists was a catastrophe for their Indigenous allies, such as the Haudenosaunee (Six Nations Confederacy) and the Cherokee, the Proclamation did establish a 'procedure ... for acquiring Indian land [that] has remained an important legal precedent in both the United States and Canada' (Wilson 1999: 128). During the eighteenth and nineteenth centuries, there were numerous 'Indian Wars' and genocidal campaigns in the USA (notably in Florida, California and the Great Plains) and, according to Dickason and Newbigging, only one in the territory of Canada in which a tribe fought on its own land in its own defence: the Mi'kmaw War (1749–1755) (pp.115–7). Despite this difference in the level and extent of violence, the dispossession and attempted obliteration of Indigenous peoples took parallel courses in both nations after the 1783 Treaty of Paris brought the United States of America and British North America (later Canada) into existence.

The settler colonial imagination tends to be fascinated by moments of 'discovery', such as the first sight of land from **Christopher Columbus**'s (1451–1506) ship *Pinta* on October 12, 1492, or the stunning defeat of the Inka **Atawallpa** (c.1502–1533), fresh from victory in his own civil war, by the Spanish *conquistador***Francisco Pizarro** (1478–1541) on November 16, 1532 (Mann 2011: 85–93). Indigenous writers, though, downplay 'pristine encounters' (Dickason and Newbigging 2019: 43) in favour of nuanced stories of 'collisions, relationships, and contacts' (p.42) unfolding over much longer periods. Indeed, the Inka civil war was precipitated by a smallpox epidemic that killed the Inka emperor seven years *before* his son met Pizarro. In the Arctic, 'first meetings with Inuit occurred, off and on, over a period of more than 900 years' (p.42), from the first Viking settlements to the early twentieth century, and Indigenous peoples across North America are still fighting colonisation today.

For this reason, perhaps, historical novels such as James Welch's (Piikani) *Fool's Crow* (1986) and Louise Erdrich's (Chippewa) *Tracks* (1994) are uncommon. An Indigenous novelist of present-day Australia, Kim Scott (Noongar), has written a remarkable 'post-contact' novel, *That Deadman Dance* (2010), that narrates the mutual fascination and emergent relationships, as well as the escalating colonial violence, of the frontier in Western Australia in 1826–1844. The main narrative begins with the protagonist Bobby Wabalanginy returning home in 1833 on a ship, which he has come to love:

His language grew and his thinking shifted the longer he was at sea. Gunnels and galley. Thwarts and midships. Tiller and keel; shrouds, mast, sail.

(p.26)

Bobby's Aboriginal name, which means 'all of us playing together', suggests the possibilities of these early relationships, especially the friendship of Dr Cross, a settler colonist, and the Noongar Wunyeran. Cultural differences are highlighted by shifting **focalisation**, as when the crafty settler Geordie Chaine sights land from the ship carrying Bobby: 'Empty, he thought. Trackless. Waiting for him. A few columns of smoke were visible inland' (p.15). Chaine's perspective ironically combines the colonial doctrine of *terra nullius* and the contradictory reality of Indigenous presence. Watching an Aboriginal guide move through the strange, prickly Australian landscape, Chaine notes that:

Sometimes Wooral addressed the bush as if he were walking through a crowd of diverse personalities, his tone variously playful, scolding, reverential, affectionate. It was most confusing. Did he see something else?

(p.43)

Laura White argues that such animism anticipates New Materialism (ch.2), in that 'Noongar language and **ontology** engage an animate world without strict boundaries between human and nonhuman matter, encouraging awareness of human participation in a communicative world rather than figuring language as a feature that distances humans from a mute, inert world' (2018: 91). The even-handed focalisation, though, allows readers to situate themselves freely within the characters' various cosmologies.

While Chaine is ultimately a catalyst for the deteriorating relationship between Noongar and the colonists, he is never vilified. Instead, Scott depicts a series of missed opportunities for understanding and peaceful coexistence by disrupting the linear order of the narrative: long after the main story ends in 1844, Bobby is still telling stories of first contact, before he was born:

Old Bobby Wabalanginy, telling this true story of before he was born but of what gave birth to him, wanted his listeners to appreciate how

> it was for his Uncle Wunyeran to experience, for the first time, ... the boat sitting upon the sea's skin; oars walking across it; the bristling rope ladder; the slap of waves on timber ...
>
> (p.76)

Dr Cross and Wunyeran converse, in part by singing to one another, and the latter is intrigued by the way that learning English (his choice, not yet a colonial imposition) changes him: 'The questions you ask, learning a new way of speech. How it drives your thinking' (p.119). When the friends die of tuberculosis a few years apart, they are buried in one grave according to their own funereal customs.

The Noongar have long treasured whales that beached themselves on their shores, and so they are impressed by the colonists' ability to hunt them at sea. Bobby composes a song, in Noongar and English, that celebrates the 'solidarity' (p.280) of the hunt: 'His song had them in a boat suddenly made small and frail, dodging tail and fins and a great head as waves and whale threw them about and showered them in clotted, hot blood and they heard a brother whale's low-down dying groan' (p.280). Yet Bobby finds he is unable to kill or skin the whales, and eventually the marvellous efficiency and excess of the hunt disrupts Noongar lifeways and attracts unfriendly Aboriginal peoples from far afield.

By 1844, the whales have been extirpated and the colony of King George Town is reinventing itself as a site of unquestioned White supremacy. Walking up to the shared grave of Wunyeran and Dr Cross, Bobby reflects that:

> The difference in their skin colour had seemed just one among many other things – but maybe it was the most important, after all. No one said Noongar no more; it was all *blackfellas* and *whitefellas*. The grave was surrounded by holes for rubbish. A man with a shovel was poking right into their shared grave.
>
> (pp.311–2)

Bobby's observation is a reminder that the uncompromising *racial* construction of Indigeneity (as opposed to striking, yet negotiable, ethnic difference made up of 'many ... things') is a specific phase of settler colonialism that was dominant in the late nineteenth and twentieth centuries. In the context of the novel, racialisation marks the demise of a moment of fragile, often tense, reciprocity. Dr Cross's coffin is dug up and re-buried in the town graveyard, with a headstone celebrating his role as 'pioneer'.

The novel ends with Bobby's failed effort at diplomacy, and yet Scott has insisted that he wanted to create 'an ending, and a novel, that neither conforms to the traditional script of defeat and victimization nor simply inverts that trajectory by supplying an upbeat closure' (White 2018: 95). The effect is achieved, in part, by the frequent appearance of Old Bobby throughout the novel, who charms and challenges 'the tourists' long after the Noongar have been consigned to reservations:

> I am the only Noongar alive today who is mentioned in Dr Cross's papers, published in your own mother country. *Your* mother country, he said to the tourists, not mine because my country is here, and belonged to my father, and his father, and his father before him, too. ... Me and my people ... We learned your words and songs and stories, and never knew you didn't want to hear ours.
>
> (p.95)

That Deadman Dance is fictional, and yet Scott has given several characters the names of his Noongar ancestors. His novel, written in English, invites us to 'hear' their imagined stories, and to consider how restitution of Aboriginal land could allow lost opportunities for peaceful co-existence to be negotiated in the present.

Like *That Deadman Dance,* **Herman Melville**'s (1819–1891) epic *Moby Dick* (1851) represents Indigenous people, accurately, as prominent in nineteenth-century whaling, though as the industry mechanised in the twentieth century, their skills became dispensable. Industrial whaling has been under a moratorium agreed by the International Whaling Commission since 1985, when most large species were on the brink of extinction. The IWC also regulates 'Aboriginal Subsistence' (AS) whaling, though not in Canada, which left in 1981. It is likely that fewer whales were killed by 'industrialised' Japan, Iceland and Norway in the last decade, under various exemptions and objections, than the annual 'aboriginal' take in most years, though the Inuit do not provide exact numbers of belugas and narwhals killed in the Canadian Arctic. The IWC considers that 'aboriginal subsistence whaling is not the same as commercial whaling' (IWC 2022), and yet Arne Kalland points out that, just as in Indigenous cultures, whales are venerated in Japan, where 'the whale is seen as a manifestation of Ebisu, the patron deity of fishing' (2009: 155). Whilst Indigenous whalers in the Arctic and Bering Seas have continued whaling unhindered by the moratorium, the Makah nation in Washington state was permitted to kill just one gray whale in 1999, the first since the species was extirpated in the 1920s, and has been embroiled in legal action to recover their treaty right to hunt whales ever since.

Linda Hogan (Chickasaw) has written four novels that engage directly with environmental issues affecting Indigenous people in the USA. Lisa Udel describes her as an exponent of 'Indigenism', which presupposes that 'indigenous people worldwide share a common experience of colonization and subsumption into a capitalist and hegemonic nation state, a shared investment in the attainment of sovereign nationhood, and a fundamentally nondisruptive, integrative relationship with the natural habitat' (2007). Her novels exemplify 'the ideological novel, or *roman à these*', a didactic genre that seeks to convey a particular message about a topical event: *Power* (1999) fictionalises the prosecution in 1987 of a Seminole man for the killing of a critically endangered Florida panther, and *People of the Whale* (2008) embeds a version of the Makah saga within a fictional narrative of the rediscovery of Indigenous spirituality by a traumatised Vietnam War veteran, Thomas Witka Just.

The fictional A'atsika consider 'the whale' to be their ancestor:

> All their stories clung like barnacles to the great whale, the whale they loved enough to watch pass by. They were people of the whale. They worshiped the whales. Whalebones had once been the homes of their ancestors who covered the giant ribs with skins and slept inside the shelters. The whales were their lives, their comfort. The swordfish, their friends, sometimes wounded a whale and it would come to shore to die, or arrive already dead. It was an offering to the hungry people by their mother sea and friend, the swordfish.
>
> (p.42)

A'atsika cosmology, in which whales offer themselves to the People if they are worthy, is invested with narrative authority throughout the novel. Indeed, predictions always come true (p.90) and an old woman stops a forest fire by lying down in front of it and singing (p.140).

When the shifty tribal leader Dwight persuades Thomas to help kill a young gray whale without fasting and singing, the traditional preparations, it brings a curse on the village that alters the weather:

> They think about the whale and what they've done, who they have become in time, each person examining their own world. They do not feel the spirits that once lived in the fogs and clouds around them. The alive world is unfelt. They feel abandoned.
>
> Nor do they know, as the stench of rotting seaweed stings their noses, about the flooding on small islands on the other side of the ocean, as if the earth has tilted somehow, been thrown off course.
>
> Who would have thought this drought might continue past any remembered by the people before written history? It may last longer than the one that followed the signing of the treaty by the wrong people, those who were not the true leaders.
>
> (p.128)

The killing of the whale becomes a parable of global environmental violence and injustice, and climate change is framed in turn, by analogy, as a curse. Thomas's estranged wife Ruth, who opposed the whale hunt, sacrifices her fishing boat to bring a Rain Priest to the village, and the drought ends.

People of the Whale is therefore an environmental jeremiad that represents biogeophysical changes as supernaturally linked to moral failings: specifically colonial oppression of Indigenous peoples. What Kate Rigby calls the 'punishment paradigm' (2015: loc.1384) also prevailed in European cultures until it was largely displaced by secularism in the eighteenth and nineteenth centuries (ch.5). The punishment paradigm is distinct from New Materialism which, though it allies itself with Indigenous cosmologies, does not assert that non-human agents literally respond to humans' prayers, songs and moral character. Ecocritical readings of Hogan's novel, though, ignore or downplay its supernatural elements: Jonathan Steinwand's postcolonial analysis says only that 'For Hogan, the human animal lives and suffers in relationship to other animals and any violation of this relationship disrupts and damages the system and especially those who cut themselves off' (2011: 189). However, this vague notion of interconnectedness is quite different from both historical Indigenous cosmologies and the moral-spiritual economy endowed with narrative authority in *People of the Whale*. Furthermore, claims by both Steinwand and Lydia R. Cooper (2011) that Hogan counteracts the Ecological Indian stereotype because A'atsika men, led by Dwight, are the ones who kill the whale are unconvincing given the extent to which the authenticity of these tribal members is undermined by the authorial narrator. Not only has Dwight arranged to sell the whale meat to the Japanese (which the real-life Makah did not do), but his invocation of Indigenous traditions is directly contradicted:

> 'When one is killed, its spirit is born again into another whale. This is our belief. It is our way.' He was bringing in the old beliefs, trying to sound like a traditionalist. In truth, Dwight wanted desperately to believe the old ways, to be a part of them, but he had become a soldier and a businessman and he had not retained the old way of being in the world.
>
> (p.69)

The suggestion that a *real* Indigenous person, who retains 'the old way of being in the world', could never behave in an anti-environmental way seems to reinforce the most reductive version of the Ecological Indian which, as TallBear suggests above, 'helps perpetuate divisive identity politics ... in Indian Country'.

Leslie Marmon Silko's (Laguna Pueblo) *Ceremony* (1977) likewise includes a drought and a traumatised war veteran – of the Allies' war against the Japanese (1941–1945) in this case. It is also a story of recuperation by rediscovery of traditional knowledge, albeit with some crucial differences from Hogan's novel. Tayo, the mixed-race protagonist, believes that he caused the drought on his reservation in New Mexico by cursing the incessant rain falling on his wounded brother in the Philippines: 'So he had prayed the rain away, and for the sixth year it was dry; the grass turned yellow and it did not grow' (2020: 13). His reflection is juxtaposed with one of the novel's many 'tribal story-poems containing traditional legends about threats to the natural world and to Laguna people' (Stein 2002: 195) interspersed with prose narrative: in this case, how an argument between Corn Woman and her sister Iktoa'ak'o'ya-Reed Woman caused the drought. Feeling demoralised and bewildered, Tayo asks Betonie, a 'half-breed' medicine man, 'what good Indian ceremonies can do against [White people's] sickness which comes from their wars, their bombs, their lies?' (p.122) In response, Betonie tells a story in which *'white skin people / like the belly of a fish'* (p.125) were conjured into being by an Indigenous witch, and loosed upon the world to destroy it. As Rachel Stein explains, 'In this poem, white-skin peoples' detachment from nature causes all their violent actions' (p.201). Tayo comes to see the world in terms of an apocalyptic confrontation between the 'witchery' of the 'destroyers' (p.228), of whatever race, and adherents of Indigenous stories of reciprocity and respect for all our relations.

While *Ceremony* shares a morally dualistic vision with *People of the Whale*, its resolution comes about, not through *recovery* of traditional ceremonies and beliefs, but with the elaboration of updated ones that combine Indigenous and Euro-American elements. As Betonie says, 'in many ways, the ceremonies have always been changing' (p.116). It is true that 'witchery' structures the plot and several medicine men appear as characters, yet occurrences that secular readers would consider 'supernatural' are infrequent. Even the drought comes to seem neither a curse nor mere craziness: '[Tayo] had only seen and heard the world as it always was: no boundaries, only transitions through all distances and time' (p.229). The war and the drought *are* connected, if not necessarily causally.

Indigenous literature's recurrent features, then, include supernatural agency; unsparing depiction of colonial discrimination and violence; alienation from both White-dominated society and Indigenous community (often experienced by mixed-race characters); and recuperation through reconnection with 'all our relations'. Justice helpfully distils these aspects into four questions, which encompass 'some of the more widely held ideas about relationship, kinship, respect, and responsibility that Indigenous peoples articulate, separately and together': 'How do we learn to be human? ... behave as good relatives? ... become good ancestors? ... learn to live together?' (p.28) The second and third questions, in particular, are central to the project of ecocriticism. He goes on to acknowledge that:

> For secular, post-Enlightenment readers of the industrialized West, the very ideas of spirit beings and little people, individualized and speaking animals, stones, and plants with powers to shape the reality around them and motivations of their own, human actions changing

weather and affecting various elemental forces, and other worlds of being and kinship with other-than-human peoples, are the stuff of childish make-believe or even pathology, not generally understood as the mature, experiential realities they are in most traditional Indigenous systems.

(p.141)

Indigenous authors frame such realities in quite different ways, however. *Love Medicine* (1994, 2nd edn) by Louise Erdrich (Ojibwe), for example, employs multiple narrators, some of whom are explicitly sceptical of spiritual realities. Young Lipsha Morrissey says he heals people by laying on his hands and talks about the Christian God and the 'Indian Gods ... like tricky Nanabozho or the water monster, Missepeshu' (1994: 236) as if they are neighbours. His Grandma Kashpaw, who 'will not admit she has a scrap of Indian blood in her' (p.240), nevertheless predicts the death of another boy thanks to a vision 'in the polished-up tin of her bread toaster' (p.240). Lipsha decides to use 'love medicine' – the hearts of a pair of Canada geese that 'mate for life' (p.242) – to switch his errant grandfather's affection back from glamorous Lulu Lamartine to his Grandma, but ends up feeding them hearts from a frozen supermarket turkey instead. When Grandpa Kashpaw dies by choking on the heart and later appears as a ghost to his wife, Lipsha is forced to explain his substitution and reassure Grandma Kashpaw that 'true feeling, not no magic' brought him back (p.257). Throughout his narration, Lipsha vacillates between treating magic as common sense and telling himself (and us) 'the old superstitions was just that – strange beliefs' (p.245). In this way, Erdrich's novel is compelling in its spirituality without being 'authoritarian', the term Udel uses (though apparently not as a criticism) of explicitly activist writing such as Hogan's.

Few Indigenous novels are more deeply infused with Indigenous spirituality than Eden Robinson's *Monkey Beach* (2000), which takes place in the author's Haisla territory around Kitimat in the Pacific Northwestern coastal rainforest. The protagonist Lisamarie Hill, an endearingly foul-mouthed 'tomboy,' narrates being repeatedly visited by a terrifying 'little man' (p.20) with red hair from early childhood on. Sometimes he is dressed 'like a leprechaun' in green plaid; other times in a 'strange cedar tunic with little amulets' (p.132). Often, his visits portend disaster, including a tsunami; the death of her beloved, rascally, Elvis-loving Uncle Mick; and the demise of her grandmother Ma-ma-oo in a house fire. Lisamarie spends most of the novel searching for her missing brother Jimmy, and she is haunted by both past and future, making her narration dense, occasionally bewildering, with memory and foreshadowing. Her people, too, are haunted, as Jodey Castricano explains, 'by the legacy of European contact':

> For the Haisla, the 'unspeakable' consists of the real and material effects of the forced relocation of Aboriginal people by the government of Canada pursuant to the *Indian Act*; the loss of traditional land and water rights; the pollution of the environment ...; and ... the psychological and emotional damage to Aboriginal children in residential schools ...
>
> (2006: 802)

Ma-ma-oo provides the Haisla explanation for Lisamarie's visions: out on a walk gathering traditional medicines, she describes a tree spirit with red hair, which she describes as 'a guide, but not a reliable one' (p.153). Lisamarie's parents, though, make the obvious secular assumption – that she is suffering from a mental pathology – and send her to a 'shrink' (p.272). The session is a remarkable piece of storytelling: even as 'Ms. Jenkins' is suggesting that 'these ghosts you dream about aren't really ghosts, but are your attempt to deal with death' (p.273), Lisamarie can see a 'thing beside her, whispering in her ear' that has 'no flesh, just tight, thin skin over bones' (p.272). When the thing notices her, it floats over and starts telling her what to say to Ms. Jenkins so she will think Lisamarie is attention-seeking, rather than perceiving an Indigenous 'experiential reality'.

Lisamarie discovers the truth about Jimmy's disappearance by giving her own blood to monstrous beings at Monkey Beach (perhaps the 'b'gwus' (sasquatches) who are occasionally sighted there) and is saved from drowning by the spirits of her family. It is therefore unsurprising, as Castricano admits, that critics have discussed the novel in terms of the Gothic genre, which likewise 'deals with ghosts, spirits, altered states of consciousness, precognition, dreams, visions, and trance states' (p.806). Yet that designation invokes, she says, a Euro-American opposition between Gothic fantasy, which permits supernatural agency, and secular literary realism, within which it is consigned to mental pathology (or childhood, as Justice observes), and as we have already seen, Robinson has anticipated and defused that reading in the scene with Ms. Jenkins. *Monkey Beach* seems both to invite and to deter reading in terms of settler colonial conceptual categories.

It is frequently argued (by Justice, in this instance) that supernatural elements 'challenge oppressive lived realities through the intentional employment of the fantastic to imagine otherwise' (p.143). Perhaps, though such an effect depends on the interaction between a particular author's choice of narrative techniques and readers' existing orientation towards Indigenous cosmologies. Secularism is a matter of degree, not a yes or no, and all readers, Indigenous or not, come to literary texts with a wide variety of cultural assumptions in tow. I used to be a militant atheist, though I've mellowed with age, and although I confess much of Justice's list of 'experiential realities' strikes me as 'make-believe', I find the agency and intelligence of living beings perfectly plausible, and an ethic of kinship eminently desirable. Indigenous people are also diverse: many belong to Christian denominations, whilst others are presumably more secular and sceptical (though still 'real Indians'). The central question, which is too seldom asked, is how readers' existing beliefs shape their understanding of 'the fantastic,' and are altered by it in turn. I could ascribe my impatient dismissiveness towards *People of the Whale* and affection for *Monkey Beach* to differences of literary quality and narrative technique, or I could turn my critical gaze inward and ask why I refuse to suspend my disbelief in one case but not the other. Hogan strikes me as uncompromisingly literalistic, whereas Robinson neutralises my scepticism by allowing space for it – yet this distinction necessarily draws attention to an obduracy in me. Lurking behind this interpretive quandary is the much wider one of respecting and integrating Indigenous knowledge in pluralistic, secular settler colonial societies.

It may be an effect of his sardonic humour, but I suspect Thomas King (Cherokee) has a sceptical disposition. *The Back of the Turtle* (2014) begins where many other Indigenous fictions conclude: with a deracinated Indigenous character, later identified as Gabriel Quinn, seeking to reconnect with tradition by drumming and singing a 'memorial song' (2014: 5) on a beach. In fact, it is a suicide attempt, which is disrupted when he has to pull several other people out of the ocean. Not surprisingly considering the strangeness of the situation, he reaches for a mythic interpretation:

... he knew these people. They were the sea people. The first people. The ones who had come from the ocean when the world was new. The long black hair. The fierce eyes. They had heard his song, and they had come to be with him at his dying.

Or perhaps he had summoned them. Perhaps it was time for a new beginning. Perhaps it was time for the twins to walk the earth again and restore the balance that had been lost.

(p.9)

The 'twins' are the left- and right-handed children of 'The Woman who Fell from the Sky' (discussed above as 'Skywoman') in the Haudenosaunee creation story, which is 'the novel's leitmotif' (Fraile-Marcos 2020: 481). The mysterious people disappear, though, and Gabriel's suicide is postponed.

The novel has five focalisers: Gabriel, an Indigenous scientist on the run from his corporate job; Mara, an Indigenous artist returning to Samaritan Bay in the Pacific Northwest; Sonny, a 'salvager' with an implied disability; Dorian Ashe, the CEO of Domidion, an agri-industrial conglomerate based in Toronto; and Nicholas Crisp, a 'red-bearded man of archaic expressions who revels in equal measure in the lushness of biblical stories, the English classics, and Indigenous orature, [and] commemorates the environmental catastrophe he calls "The Ruin" with his recital of the Sky Woman story at the hot springs' (Fraile-Marcos 2020: 482). Crisp represents settler-Indigenous synthesis, albeit in an enjoyably caricatured form.

In the course of the novel, we learn that Gabriel is partly responsible for the poisoning of the entire Indian reserve at Samaritan Bay, including his mother, sister and nephew, by a Domidion herbicide called, ironically, 'GreenSweep'. Unlike Thomas Witka Just and Tayo, whose complicity in America's wars is hardly culpable, Gabriel loves science, and even reconsiders the water people soon afterwards:

One human being didn't sing other human beings up out of the water. Their appearance in the high tide was unexpected, but there was a scientific answer for every anomaly.

Stories were stories. They were not the laws of the universe.

(p.185)

Yet working for Domidion has so compromised his ethics that he introduces himself to Mara with an allusion to the scientist who led the development of the nuclear bomb:

> Mara cupped her coffee in her hands and leaned forward. 'So,' she said, 'what is it exactly that you do.'
> Gabriel put the muffin on the plate and licked his fingers. 'Worlds,' he said. 'I destroy worlds.'

> (p.168)

Dorian Ashe is a bold choice as well as a comic masterstroke. His bemused cynicism helps defray the 'sanctimony and sincerity' (Seymour 2018: 2) popularly attributed to environmentalists, and not infrequently found in environmental writing, even as he emerges as a satirical study in corporate environmental image-management. (He does have excellent taste in suits, however.) The Samaritan Bay disaster is only the first of Domidion's eco-crimes: the remaining stock of GreenSweep was loaded onto a barge, the *Anguis*, which is missing at sea, and then a tailings pond on the Alberta oil patch accidentally drains into the Athabaska River. As he prepares for an interview on CBC, Dorian runs through his talking points:

> Athabaska River? Tragedy.
> Oil extraction? National priority.
> Safety protocols? The best in the industry.
> Environmental damage? Minimal.
> Legal liability? Unfortunate accident.
> It was all a waste of time. North American Norm didn't give a damn about the environment. Cancel a favourite television show. Slap another tax on cigarettes. Stop serving beer at baseball and hockey games. That was serious.

> (p.422)

As Ana María Fraile-Marcos shows, Dorian is a master of 'post-truth' strategies that 'mangle the truth, corrupt knowledge, twist ethics, and control the [sic] public opinion' (p.477). He thinks, wrongly as it turns out, that how he looks and sounds, rather than what he says, will matter in the interview.

Dorian is still not a villain, though. He is troubled by mysterious ailments throughout the novel, which he thinks can be resolved by finding a more compliant doctor. He is so estranged from his own body that he can't even lust after his attractive, yet remote, personal assistant Winter: 'Capable assistants were rare, Dorian reminded himself, while lovers and wives were easy enough to find. Always best to maintain the line between the two' (p.442). His strategy for protecting Domidion's reputation is successful, and he suffers no comeuppance, though we suspect his health problem will not concede to image management, and the reappearance of the *Anguis* hints at disasters yet to come.

The narrative resolution involves Gabriel and Mara's return to the Indian reserve, and the revelation that the mysterious sea people are actually the Taiwanese crew of the *Anguis*, who had to abandon ship off shore. Welcoming them into the reserve re-establishes the hospitality and reciprocity embodied in the story of Skywoman, although, as Susie O'Brien points out, the story (like Mara and Gabriel) has been transplanted from its Haudenosaunee source in the East to the West Coast, where it blends with 'other stories and creative practices, including movie and literary references, traditional songs, and Mara's paintings of the former residents of the Smoke River reserve' (2020: 49). The truth about the sea people could be seen as demythologising – the 'anomaly' has a prosaic, if improbable, explanation – or as ironically *re*-mythologising, in that the rescued foreigners help to heal the community.

The book's title alludes to the turtle's back where Skywoman first lands, and also to 'Turtle Island', the name given by some Indigenous peoples to the continent settlers call North America. Kimmerer employs the same metaphor when she reflects on her mixed settler and Indigenous ancestry: 'And here we all are, on Turtle Island, trying to make a home' (p.8). Whereas Kimmerer seeks to 'inculcate "proper" environmentalist feelings' like 'reverence, love, and wonder' with her lengthy series of botanical parables, King's novel exemplifies what Nicole Seymour approvingly calls 'bad environmentalism' characterised by 'affects and sensibilities such as irreverence, ambivalence, camp, frivolity, indecorum, awkwardness, sardonicism, perversity, playfulness, and glee' (p.4). Its humour is anything but apolitical, though, in that Mara cajoles Gabriel to tell 'the [story] you don't want to tell' (p.502) about pride, shame and complicity with colonial violence. Thus, as O'Brien concludes, 'storytelling helps to create the conditions for living on in the years to come, which start with responsibly inhabiting the devastation of the present' (p.50).

This discussion is limited to prose fiction, a medium in which Indigenous writers are particularly distinguished, and yet it must be acknowledged that Indigenous literatures 'include a wide array of other texts, such as cane baskets, wampum belts, birchbark scrolls, gourd masks, sand paintings, rock art, carved and painted cedar poles, stones and whale bones, culturally modified trees, and so on' (Justice 2018: 22). Norton, whose poetry anthologies define the canon, finally published *When the Light of the World Was Subdued, Our Songs Came Through: A Norton Anthology of Native Nations Poetry* in 2020, which encompasses every part of the USA, though not Canada or Mexico. Indigenous eco-cinema is particularly strong in present-day Canada, including screen adaptations of Indigenous novels such as *Monkey Beach* and documentaries including *Qapirangajuq* (dir. Zacharias Kunuk, 2009), an Inuktitut-language treatment of climate change, and Warren Cariou's (Métis) study of the Alberta tar/oil sands, *Land of Oil and Water* (2009). *Angry Inuk* (dir. Alethea Arnquq-Baril, 2016) powerfully illustrates how the European Union's 2009 ban on seal products undermines Inuit self-reliance, and challenges animal rights' organisations' emotive and misleading adverts that 'align white women [e.g. Brigitte Bardot and Pamela Anderson] and white harp seal pups through a narrative of purity and innocence against the unknowable barbarism of seal hunting' (Burelle 2020: 155). (NB: killing white seal pups has been banned in Canada since 1987.) The documentary highlights how traditional ethics and community relations are interwoven with modern technologies, as in the Twitter #sealfie campaign that advocated for Inuit seal-hunting. Moving into digital media, Iñupiaq stories and knowledge are exquisitely rendered by *Never Alone (Kisima Ingitchuna)* (E-Line 2016), while other examples of contemporary Indigenous media are discussed by Salma Monani, Renata Ryan Burchfield (Cherokee), Danika Medak-Saltzman (Chippewa) and William Lempert (Monani et al. 2021).

Indigenous science fiction and cinema with environmental implications, especially with futuristic dystopian and post-apocalyptic settings, are growing in popularity. Novels include *Moon of the Crusted Snow* (2018) by Waubgeshig Rice (Anishinaabe), Cherie Dimaline's (Métis) lauded young adult novel *The Marrow Thieves* (2017), and Louise Erdrich's ambitious, flawed *Future Home of the Living God* (2017), a would-be example of 'cli-fi' (cf. ch.5 and 10). Often, these futuristic fictions revisit historical injustices in allegorical form, especially the cultural genocide inflicted on First Nations by Canadian residential schools in the late nineteenth and twentieth centuries, which prompted the federally-funded Truth and Reconciliation Commission's (TRC) enquiry and report (2007–2015). (Similar schools existed in the USA, Australia and Aotearoa New Zealand.) *Night Raiders* (dir. Danis Goulet (Cree-Métis) 2021), a feature film, depicts an Indigenous mother trying to save her daughter from an authoritarian state called 'Emerson' that controls all of North America, which requires parents to surrender their children for indoctrination. Goulet previously directed *Wakening* (2013), an eco-horror short in which an Indigenous woman warrior confronts a cannibalistic monster in an abandoned theatre. The woman is identified as Weesageechak, a Cree trickster figure, and the elk-like creature is its long-time nemesis Weetigo. Its Anishinaabe cousin Wendigo appears frequently in both Indigenous and settler colonial narratives, though in the latter it is, according to Salma Monani, 'laden with colonially problematic appropriations' that 'make Indigenous peoples both hypervisible', due to the folkloric source of the figure, and 'invisible, in that there is little effort to further engage Native issues' (2016: 9). In Goulet's film, the Weetigo has been corralled in the theatre, which it calls its 'palace', by the colonial 'Occupiers', but then instead of battling the creature, Weesageechak persuades it that their ancient enmity has been superseded by the present dystopia. The Weetigo heads off to eat some more Occupiers, a fate they presumably deserve.

Indigenous dystopias are 'less about the spectre of a new future and more like the experience of déjà vu' (Seymour 2018: 9) because, as Kyle Powys Whyte underlines, 'the hardships many non-Indigenous people dread most of the climate crisis are ones that Indigenous peoples have endured already due to different forms of colonialism: ecosystem collapse, species loss, economic crash, drastic relocation, and cultural disintegration' (Whyte 2018: 226). Concepts of finality, like the 'end of the world', or epochal change, such as 'the Anthropocene' (ch.10), will be understood and represented differently 'by Indigenous persons who see their societies as already having endured one *or many more* apocalypses—perhaps some of these apocalypses happened before European colonialism' (p.236). It remains to be seen how successfully Indigenous artists can intervene in, and redefine, the obdurate trope of apocalypse (ch.5).

DECOLONISATION, INDIGENISATION AND ECOCRITICS

As we have seen, historical questions about Ecological Indigeneity are complex and context-specific. In contemporary environmental justice contexts, as Ranco suggests above, Ecological Indigeneity can have strategic value provided it does not become an expectation that compromises First Nations' sovereignty. Settler-dominated arts and media celebrate the opposition of wealthier coastal tribes, such as the Tsleil-Waututh, to the expansion of the Trans-Mountain pipeline (TMX) in British Columbia, but largely ignore the 120 tribes that support or do not oppose it (Tasker 2020). Ranco points out that divisive resource projects must be seen in the context of 'intense poverty and hundreds of years of colonization that precipitated these activities' (p.34), while *Angry Inuk* confronts the demeaning insistence that Indigenous sealing or whaling should only be for 'subsistence'.

The importance of land is underscored by the influential article, 'Decolonization is not a Metaphor' by Eve Tuck (Unangax̂) and K. Wayne Yang, which sets out to challenge comforting invocations of decolonisation as primarily, if not wholly, mental and symbolic. The fashionable notion of 'decolonizing the mind, or the cultivation of critical consciousness' (p.19) is critiqued as one of several 'moves to innocence ... that attempt to relieve the settler of feelings of guilt or responsibility without giving up land or power or privilege, without having to change much at all' (p.10). This telling riposte is the prelude to Tuck and Yang's literal demand: 'decolonization in the settler colonial context must involve the repatriation of land simultaneous to the recognition of how land and relations to land have always already been differently understood and enacted; that is, all of the land, and not just symbolically' (p.7). Tuck and Yang refuse to address the practicality of ensuring that 'all land is repatriated and all settlers become landless' (p.27) because, they argue, 'decolonization is not accountable to settlers, or settler futurity' (p.35), and they admit no ethical or political qualms themselves. Still, the moral of Tuck and Yang's ironic parable of literality is that questions of land and sovereignty *precede* the ones of primary interest to ecocritics: of culture, narrative, nomenclature and sustainability.

Sovereignty implies the right to decide who is and is not Indigenous. Early colonial relations took ethnic self-definition for granted, and then later, colonial bureaucracies imposed racialised identities that minimised

Indigenous presence, as well as carceral regimes like residential schools that destroyed familial and communal inheritance. Thus, in the modern era, many Indigenous people are having to rediscover and reconnect with their cultures: the *ur*-plot of Indigenous literatures. At the same time, genetic testing encourages White people to discover their 'Indian princess grandmother,' a phenomenon Tuck and Yang dismiss as 'settler nativism' (pp.10–3). Tribal citizenship would seem to be firm grounds for saying who *is* Indigenous, and so the *Norton Anthology of Native Nations Poetry* restricts the included poets to enrolled members of federally-recognised tribes in order to keep 'Pretendians' out. Yet Joy Harjo's editorial admits that 'The question "Who is Native?" has become more and more complex as culture lines and bloodlines have thinned and mixed' (Harjo, Howe and Foerster 2020: 4). There are tribes fighting for federal recognition in both Canada and the USA, such as the Sinixt of British Columbia, some of whose claims are rejected by existing First Nations (e.g. the 'Eastern Métis' of Quebec). STS scholar Kim TallBear summarises 'indigenous peoples' "ancestry" [as] not simply genetic ancestry evidenced in "populations" but biological, cultural, and political groupings constituted in dynamic, long-standing relationships with each other and with living landscapes that define their people-specific identities and, more broadly, their indigeneity' (2015: 131). The questionable claims to Indigeneity of Joseph Boyden, one of Canada's most distinguished novelists, led me to exclude *Through Black Spruce* (2008) from this discussion, though his particular case and the broader issue are far from settled.

Disputes about identity overlap, in universities especially, with questions of knowledge, voice and authority. Given the uniqueness of Indigenous societies, scholars from specific nations should not be asked to 'speak for' or represent Indigenous perspectives in general, though that is frequently expected of them. Then again, Indigenous authors, too, cross those lines: King's novel relocates the Skywoman story from the Great Lakes to the Pacific Northwest, and Linda Hogan, a citizen of the Chickasaw nation, fictionalises real-life Seminole and Makah environmental conflicts, which could be considered a form of cultural appropriation. It would be disastrous for imaginative literature if authors could only write about themselves, though, and so thoughtful cross-cultural efforts should be approached sympathetically, including work by non-Indigenous authors such as Annie Proulx, whose novel *Barkskins* includes an ancestral line of Mi'kmaw characters (ch.4). There is no consensus about how to distinguish creative inhabitation of others' lifeworlds from egregious misrepresentation or cultural appropriation, and the polarising outrage machine of social media will never yield one. I believe that patient, honest, respectful discussion in scholarly criticism and the classroom just might.

Indigenous social scientists such as Shawn Wilson articulate research paradigms founded on the '3 Rs': respect, reciprocity and relationality. In working with Indigenous communities, 'respect' means that 'it is not culturally appropriate to criticize or judge other people or their work' (2008: 134), a deferential approach at odds, as he says, with the 'adversarial dialogue' (p.57) expected of scholars and students. Challenge and debate are more acceptable when texts, rather than Elders and other community members, are at stake: Justice encourages us to 'hold each other to account as we hold each other up – they needn't be mutually exclusive practices' (p.xxi). His notion of 'accountable kindness' aligns with non-Indigenous scholar Kathleen Fitzpatrick's advocacy of 'generous thinking', as distinct from 'suspicious' (2019: 29) or 'pugilistic forms of critique' (p.129) which are 'inescapably masculinist' (p.107) and 'over-determined by the internalized competitive structures of contemporary life' (p.129). Indeed, it would be more productive if criticism were directed at what authors *do* attempt in their writing, well or badly, and not just what they supposedly 'omit' or 'elide'.

Indigenous methodologies are more difficult to reconcile with those of the natural sciences, which stress dispassionate observation and orga-nised scepticism (aka 'objectivity'), and yet writers with bi-cultural training stress their compatibility: Kimmerer, an Indigenous environ-mental biologist, remarks that 'Doing science with awe and humility is a powerful act of reciprocity with the more-than-human world' (p.252). Her ideal of mutualism, though, depends on distinct and separate domains that recall the long-standing Western distinction of fact and value: 'I dream of a world guided by a lens of stories rooted in the revela-tions of science and framed with an Indigenous worldview – stories in which matter and spirit are both given voice' (p.346). In some contexts, this complementarity is impossible: TallBear's review of the implications of 'genomic articulations of Indigeneity' (which some tribes have adopted themselves) describes how the scientific narrative of 'one global human history and set of migrations' (p.134) conflicts with Indigenous concep-tions of Indigeneity: 'Indigenous notions of *peoplehood* as emerging *in relation with* particular lands and waters and their nonhuman actors differ from the concept of a genetic *population,* defined as moving *upon* or *through* landscapes' (p.137). A related conflict that TallBear does not discuss is that Indigenous origin stories are typically creationist rather than evolutionary.

In other contexts, though, the supposed dichotomy of 'science' and 'Indigenous Knowledges' (IK) 'falsely indicate[s] entirely separable spaces within which to produce accounts of reality', as Annette Watson, an academic geographer, and Orville H. Huntington, a scientifically-trained Koyukon hunter, show in a startling co-authored article that narrates 'a single moose hunting event as [a] human–nonhuman (post-humanist) assemblage: the acceptance of a moose's body and its spirit by the hunter' (2008: 259). Not only is the article presented in the form of an autobiographical story, 'permeated by theoretical arguments derived from the academy' (p.259), but the narrative viewpoint switches abruptly between the first-person perspectives of Annette and Orville. In the context of both the hunt and the story, 'A moose is not just an object of knowledge, but an active agent in the world, politically equal with humans' (p.272), which offers itself to the Koyukon hunter to be killed. Orville's acceptance of the gift (in secular terms, locating and shooting the bull) is 'informed by Koyukon traditions – but also by his education and employment in Western wildlife biology' (p.276). For Annette and Orville, IK is not a distinct 'epistemic space' from science, either historically or personally (pp.275–6). We should add that, as STS scholars have illustrated, the sciences themselves are far from monolithic or epistemically unified, though they do benefit from topping an implicit hierarchy that has the humanities and fine arts at the bottom. Despite the emollient intentions of phrases like 'ways of knowing', which celebrate epistemic equality without advancing it, Indigenisation is presently advancing most quickly in the least prestigious disciplines. It is inevitable that the epistemic hierarchy of the university will struggle to comprehend Ecological Indigeneity because, while Indigenous nations increasingly demand the right to define 'Indigeneity', what counts as 'ecological' is likely to default to a scientific benchmark. The challenge of Indigenisation is therefore comparable (not identical) to that of integrating environmental humanities' perspectives in multidisciplinary contexts where scientific truth claims are expected to predominate. Again, sustained open debate, cognisant of power hierarchies, is the way forward.

And so we return to my territorial acknowledgement. For me, being a good neighbour implies a responsibility to learn about the land, history and culture of the Syilx Okanagan people so as to rectify my colonial *mis*-education. As Justice says, alluding to the TRC, 'It's simple: no truth, no reconciliation' (p.159). I am frankly undecided, though, whether living on unceded territory ought to imply intellectual deference on my part, and I don't know if it is expected. A further neighbourly action is to make the privileges and resources of the university available to support the purposes of First Nations, displacing the dominant historical model of extracting Indigenous knowledges in service of the advancement of learning (and careers and institutional reputations). Recognising that we are uninvited guests, non-Indigenous scholars have to decide, in Paulette Regan's words, 'whether we will remain colonizer-perpetrators or strive to become more ethical allies in solidarity with Indigenous people' (2010: 234). The latter must involve commitment to 'actual material redress – return of land, meaningful correction of wrongs against Indigenous communities – or sophisticated moral reckoning' if the land acknowledgement is not to be insultingly superficial or evasive (Wood 2021). Fortunately, in my limited experience, Indigenous people are gracious and accepting of respectful actions undertaken 'with a good heart'. Tuck and Yang disclaim responsibility for 'settler futurity', when the difficult truth is that it is inextricable, practically, politically and climatically, from Indigenous futurity. In the coming decades, students of ecocriticism will continue to be instructed by Indigenous writers what it means to be a 'good ancestor' to our descendants as well as our predecessors. We would do well to listen.

NOTE

1 'Aotearoa' is the Indigenous Māori name for the North Island, now commonly used for the nation-state as a whole.

8

THE EARTH

IMAGES

We begin with *An Inconvenient Truth* (dir. Davis Guggenheim, 2006), an influential documentary in which former US Vice-President Al Gore introduces the science of climate change and advocates for political and personal action. John Parham's detailed examination calls it 'one of the most iconic green media texts, one of the few to have had audience reception research, [which] has been applauded for its green production credentials' (Parham 2015: 189). Whilst Gore does a lot of lecturing with Powerpoint slides, the movie also includes narrative anecdotes that highlight Gore's personal knowledge and connection with the issue, such as a moving sequence about his sister's death from lung cancer, which prompted his Tennessee farming family to stop growing tobacco. The story functions, like all the narrative sequences, as a parable, which illuminates the gap between *knowing* that scientists identify smoking as a cause of cancer and, later, bitter personal experience. He reflects that 'It's just human nature to take time to connect the dots ... but I know there can also be a day of reckoning when you wish you had connected the dots more quickly'. As *An Inconvenient Truth* draws to a close, Gore criticises Republican administrations in the USA for opposing climate

DOI: 10.4324/9781003174011-8

action, recalls inspirational examples of liberal political and scientific progress, and then invites 'us', the audience, to 'rise above ourselves'. The affective appeal of his exhortation hinges on a series of images of the Earth. The first is a 'pale blue dot', a photo taken by the Voyager 1 space probe from four billion miles away in which Earth is just a single pixel. 'That's us,' says Gore, and 'It's our only home. And that is what is at stake.' Next, Gore returns to two photos he showed at the beginning of the movie: 'Earthrise', taken by Apollo 8 astronauts in December 1968 from lunar orbit, and NASA photo 22727, an image of the whole earth taken from Apollo 17 in 1972. Gore's voiceover urges that climate change is a 'moral issue' to which 'we' must respond.

For Gore, the image of Earth from space has an unequivocal meaning. It functions as a rhetorical silver bullet intended to bypass interpretation and argument. Gore says of 'Earthrise': 'That one picture exploded in the consciousness of humankind.' Indeed, John Hannigan cites evidence that 'the single most effective environmental message of the century was totally inadvertent: the 1969 [sic] view from the moon of a fragile, finite "Spaceship Earth"' (2014: 105). While the Earth images' wide circulation is unquestionable, though, their origin and meaning remain contentious. Gore implies that the Earth photos capture an astonished human perspective, when in fact none of the astronauts saw the planet as pictured: the cameras were held 'at the hip of the astronaut' in the cramped spacecraft, and the images were later cropped and reorientated so as 'to reduce the strangeness of the imaging' (Russill 2016: 237, 40). Furthermore, as Denis Cosgrove argues in *Apollo's Eye* (2001), the images draw on 'longstanding ... themes of global unity and perfection, imperial authority to "the ends of the earth," heroic individual telos, and a redeemed humanity' (p.236). In addition to vaunting American technology, the Apollo missions were explicitly intended to elevate the USA over the Soviet Union in their Cold War struggle over symbolism, hence Cosgrove's sceptical reading of 'Earthrise': 'The small disk hanging delicately in velvet space becomes visual confirmation of American democracy's redemptive world-historical mission, namely, to realize the universal brotherhood of a common humanity' (pp.259–60). Sure enough, Gore's motivational list of things 'we' have achieved before, which precedes his use of the Earth images, switches unconsciously between *American* accomplishments and ones that might be credited to 'humanity' more generally. Cosgrove suggests that as the Earth images spread, through advertising especially, they accumulated two related, but distinct, meanings: 'A "whole-earth" discourse stresses the globe's organic unity and matters of life, dwelling, and rootedness' (pp.262–3) whereas 'A "one-world" discourse ... concentrates on the global surface, on circulation, connectivity, and communication' (p.263). The Earth images serve, we might say, both planetary and globalising capitalist discourses.

For Gore, an environmental moderniser and liberal internationalist, these discourses are potentially compatible, though both eco-Marxists and sceptical conservatives would disagree. Writing before *An Inconvenient Truth,* Cosgrove argues that a 'liberal mission of universal redemption' projects 'ideas and beliefs forged in one locale across global space' and so 'is inescapably ethnocentric and imperial, able to admit "other" voices only if they speak and are spoken by the language of the (self-denying) center' (pp.265–6). The documentary's visual repertoire is dominated by what Andrew Ross calls 'images of ecology': 'on the one hand, belching smokestacks, seabirds mired in petrochemical sludge, fish floating belly-up, traffic jams in Los Angeles and Mexico City, and clearcut forests; on the other hand, the redeeming repertoire of pastoral imagery, pristine, green, and unspoiled by human habitation, crowned by the ultimate global spectacle, the fragile, vulnerable ball of spaceship earth' (1994: 171). The superficial allure of striking photos should not distract us, Ross warns, from the 'ecology of images' (p.172), or the socio-ecological processes by which they are acquired, circulated, and received, such as the 770 thousand litres of kerosene in each Saturn V rocket. But then, climate science, as delivered by the IPCC (ch.6), is not *merely* local knowledge projected imperially across 'global space', as Mike Hulme explains:

> Scientific knowledge is made in places. But by making this knowledge commensurable – by describing climatic phenomena using the language of mathematics – science also makes things scalable.
>
> (2021: loc.1486–7)

Thereafter, climate science knowledge 'moves unevenly around the world through material networks, embodied agents, news and social media, and encultured discourses and artefacts' encountering 'frictions which slow or modify' it (loc.3609–10). Moreover, climate governance must construct and sustain global agreement through the United

Nations' annual 'Conference of the Parties' (COP) meetings to avert a climate catastrophe. This chapter takes seriously both the globalising claims, without which we'd just be experiencing a lot of bafflingly weird weather, and their disreputable histories and contemporary exclusions.

Most of Ross's 'images of ecology' began circulating in the 1960s and 70s. In 1975, the environmental NGO Greenpeace pioneered the strategy of putting their Zodiac dinghies in between Soviet whaling vessels and the animals they were hunting, and filming it. Kevin Michael DeLuca calls the outcome an 'image event' (1999: 1), and he claims that the 'sophisticated media artists' (p.5) in Greenpeace used it to accomplish 'the banning of commercial whaling, harvesting of baby harp seals, and ocean dumping of nuclear wastes; the establishment of a moratorium in Antarctica on mineral and oil exploration and their extraction' (p.3) and many other objectives, though it is arguable that nowadays environmentalist image events are too hackneyed to have impact (see Parham 2015: 108–9). Ursula Heise's history of the Earth images in *Sense of Place and Sense of Planet* (2008) points out that in the 1970s they were as likely to invoke apocalyptic anxieties (ch.6) as utopian plans for rational global governance. Of the latter, the high point is probably *Our Common Future* (aka 'the Brundtland Report') in 1987, a UN-sponsored report on environment and development that claims 'this [whole Earth] vision had a greater impact on thought than did the Copernican Revolution' (cited Heise 2008: 23). Even at that time, though, American environmentalism was prioritising localisms, such as bioregionalism (ch.2), on the assumption that environmental ethics could only emerge in the context of knowledge of, and attachment to, particular locales: what Heise calls an 'ethic of proximity' (p.33). In the 1990s and after, increasing attention to gender, racial and other axes of difference gave rise to critiques (such as Cosgrove's) of universalism. Heise, though, questions the value, and even the coherence, of a 'sense of place', calling it 'a kind of hobby' that cannot account for the ways in which 'political, economic, technological, social, cultural, and ecological networks [beyond the locale] shape daily routines' (p.55). She advocates instead a 'sense of planet' that is 'eco-cosmopolitan', or 'an attempt to envision individuals and groups as part of planetary "imagined communities" of both human and nonhuman kinds' (p.61).

We might get a sense of planet from digital representations such as Google Earth, a 'metamorphosis of the Blue Planet image into a searchable and zoomable database in the shape of a virtual globe' that can 'display the whole planet as well as the minute details of particular places in such a way that the user can zoom from one to the other and focus on different types of information' (p.67). Google Earth is obviously more sophisticated and interactive than a still image, and it also allows users to experience Earth at multiple scales in no particular order. It contrasts in this respect with *An Inconvenient Truth*, which zooms from the 'pale blue dot' to the Apollo Earth images, and concludes back at the Caney Fork River in Tennessee, which anchors Gore's environmental nostalgia through its family associations. In parallel, Gore frames climate action first as a matter of 'political will' (meaning, implicitly, support for the Democratic party), and then zooms in to the moral, individual scale. However, the modest (one might say infinitesimal) actions recommended during the credits ('When you can, walk or ride a bicycle') are absurdly inadequate compared to the epic scale of the challenge Gore describes. Timothy Clark calls this type of disjunction a 'derangement of scale', and he finds it implicit in the 'pale blue dot' image itself. According to Clark, Earthly existence in a medium-sized primate body profoundly, if usually unconsciously, defines the way we talk about 'the world' (a term that itself equivocates between Earth and a cosmic context). Thus *'Terrestriality*, defined as that "normal" prereflective sense of scale inherent to embodied human life on the Earth's surface, forms a kind of transcendental, one that both underlies and exceeds any view that it is merely our social context that determines our understanding of ourselves' (2015: 33). We can only view the pale blue dot *from* our terrestrial viewpoint (sitting in front of a TV, say), and yet Gore invites us to see, not only ourselves (invisible) on it, but also 'everything that has ever happened in all of human history'. To take this statement seriously is to experience a kind of vertigo in which, as Clark remarks:

> ... the Earth is read solely as an index of the human ('That's us'), but one now collapsed towards an impossible experience of overload, in which we are forced to imagine everything about human life at once and at the one site — the myriad incommensurable horizons shrinking down upon each other to a point, like water down a plughole.
>
> (p.32)

Whereas Heise sees artistic and media representations as capable of integrating different scales into multiple, overlapping eco-cosmopolitan cultures around the world, Clark describes 'a loss of proportion *tout court*, vertiginously and as yet without a conceived alternative' (p.23). We might also describe the disjunction, less dramatically, as ironic, as Nicole Seymour suggests in her funny and insightful book, *Bad Environmentalism: Irony and Irreverence in the Ecological Age* (2018). She notes that 'environmentalists (and feminists) have long been the butt of cultural jokes in the West—skewered, sometimes rightfully so, for their sanctimony and sincerity' (p.2), and proposes that even when Gore does use humour in his presentation, he conveys superiority rather than reflexivity: he 'points out the hypocrises [sic] of antienvironmental politicians and climate change deniers, while never admitting that his own position or that of environmentalists might be fraught' (p.54). In my experience, students watching *An Inconvenient Truth* are swayed by Gore's accurate, accessible presentation of climate science, but seldom fail to note the irony that he spends much of the movie in an airplane or the back of a limo. Gore justly draws attention to the influence of fossil fuel lobbyists on politicians, and gets a laugh from his sympathetic audience for this Upton Sinclair quotation: 'It is difficult to get a man to understand something when his salary depends upon his not understanding it.' But climate scientists and Greenpeace staffers get salaries too, don't they? And isn't it ironic that left-leaning environmentalists and scholars such as Bruno Latour used to encourage scepticism towards scientific claims, whereas now, in opposition to the populist right, they deny that they meant to undermine scientific authority (e.g. Latour 2004b) and urge the public to 'trust the science' with regard to global heating and the COVID-19 pandemic? We return to this point in the Conclusion.

Seymour discusses a handful of 'vivid examples' of what she calls '"bad environmentalism": environmental thought that employs dissident, often-denigrated affects and sensibilities' (p.6), whilst claiming there are plenty more. Heise identifies only a few instances of eco-cosmopolitanism, while Parham's survey of 'the interrelationship and balance of power between a dominant global media culture and its "eco-cosmopolitan alternatives"' (loc.241) struggles, in the case of television especially, to identify many others. It is true that 'all too often, all too easily, environmentalist critics loathe media and popular culture' (loc.133), in part because they seem so constrained by the dominant anti-environmentalist ideology of capitalism. Popular culture may be dispiriting to ecocritics like Parham who consider ecological modernisation (ch.2) inadequate to address climate change, but it is, as he says, 'one of the central ways we shape our relationship to other animals, our place on Earth, and the social structures that arise from these understandings' (p.1).

The primary visual medium for climate-related content is news and factual programming, which has been extensively studied by scholars of Environmental Communications (EC), a branch of social studies. Where ecocriticism focuses (too much, says Parham) on literary fiction and poetry using close reading of individual texts, EC research uses population-scale empirical methodologies such as opinion polls and discourse analysis. Taking climate change communication as an example, Juliet Pinto, Robert E. Gutsche, Jr and Paola Prado explain why it is a challenge for both journalists and the EC scholars who study their work:

> Journalists must navigate not only the complex science around accel-erating climate change, but also the politics, cultural shifts, technolo-gical innovations and commercial pressures that can influence publics' reception of such information. ... So, too, must be scrutinized the machinations of power and hegemony, and the structural inequal-ities underlying how these issues are constructed, disseminated, and received.
>
> (2019: 1)

The Guardian, a British newspaper, is committed to using unequivocal language about the climate crisis, and also to avoiding obvious images, such as 'a polar bear on melting ice', in favour of ones that show 'the direct impact of environmental issues on people's daily lives as well as trying to indicate the scale of the impact' (Shields 2019). Addressing the same issue, EC researchers studied sample groups' responses to photos of floods, solar panels, climate protests, celebrities and others, which they were asked to rank ('Q-sort') and then discuss with researchers. Comparison of results from the USA, UK and Australia found that 'imagery can play a role in either increasing the sense of importance of the issue of climate change (saliency), or in promoting feelings of being able to do something about climate change (efficacy) – but few, if any, images seem to do both' (O'Neill et al. 2013: 420). The trade-off between saliency and efficacy is probably a general conundrum for climate communication – the more we know, the more hopeless we feel, on the whole – though empirical methods, which could test the question, have only recently been adopted by ecocritics. EC has had much more impact outside academia than ecocriticism thanks to its scientific-seeming methodologies and population-level analyses.

EC researchers and ecocritics alike have been drawn to *The Day After Tomorrow*, which is still the only Hollywood movie actually *about* climate change as an atmospheric phenomenon (albeit wildly exaggerated) (ch.5). Many scholars and artists, though, are equally interested in the 'knowledge-action gap', the social phenomenon in which growing scientific knowledge about the causes and impacts of climate change is not accompanied by concerted political (and, usually, personal) action to avert it. Unlike global heating itself, the gap is human-scaled, thus more amenable to conventional narrative cinema. In *First Reformed* (dir. Paul Schrader, 2018), for example, Mary (Amanda Seyfried) invites Reverend Ernst Toller (Ethan Hawke) to counsel her environmentalist husband Michael (Philip Ettinger), who wants her to terminate her pregnancy because he cannot bear to bring a child onto such a degraded Earth. Their discussion of faith, hope and despair goes on for seven minutes, an eternity in a mainstream movie. Towards the end, Michael asks Toller: 'Can God forgive us? For what we've done to this world?' The next day, Mary shows Toller an explosive suicide vest Michael made in their garage. The day after that, Michael kills himself with a shotgun. Driven by guilt and horror, Toller eventually comes to agree that puncturing complacency and confronting fossil fuel interests might justify violence. The movie's stunning conclusion holds in tension Toller's disillusioned fury and the possibility, deluded as it may be, of redemption.

Schrader's unconventionally sparse 'transcendental style,' which minimises camera movement and lacks a musical soundtrack, puts Toller's spiritual, psychological and political dilemma at its centre, leaving the viewer to decide what degree of doubt, despair or violence is appropriate to the scale of the crisis. At the opposite extreme, *Don't Look Up* (dir. Adam McKay, 2021) is a clamorous, big-budget satire that translates the knowledge-action gap into a comic allegory: astronomers discover that a comet is going to destroy the Earth in six months and 14 days, but they are unable to convince politicians or the media to concentrate long enough to avert disaster. While the movie effectively captures scientists' frustration that their reasoned arguments have failed to motivate commensurate social change, the immediate and spectacular threat from the comet seems a terrible analogue for climate change. Audience research is needed to know whether the satire hit home.

Climate movies have not yet identified an appropriate visual language with which to communicate vast, slow, uneven changes in the Earth system. *The Day After Tomorrow* depicts a 'global superstorm' being modelled on American supercomputers and then unfolding in apocalyptic fashion across the whole planet (but mainly New York City) in just a few days. The allegorical framing of *Don't Look Up* translates the vast complexity of climate models into relatively simple calculations of the comet's trajectory carried out on a whiteboard. In *First Reformed,* Michael explains to Toller the 'unliveability' of the world his child will experience with awful fervour, while a laptop is visible over his right shoulder running through what Heather Houser describes in *Infowhelm* (2020) as 'an animated visualization of a global map changing color from white and pale blues and yellows to orange and vermillion as the years 1960 to 2030 tick away' (p.3). Houser argues that, in addition to informing the audience, 'The visualizations … convey how climate data participates [sic] in religious debates, generate contradictory emotions, and possibly even drive someone to environmental martyrdom' (p.4). She goes on to explain how climate visualisations in general:

> … process data through affectivity and not only through computational algorithms. They employ color, sophistication, sound, interactivity, temporal difficulty, and genre conventions in ways that render data experiential because they produce emotional responses.
>
> (p.32)

In this way, they share in the seeming objectivity of data whilst also suffusing them, usually surreptitiously, with meaning. It is striking that, in *First Reformed,* the visualisation supplements a sustained dialogue, presumably because climate data are considered indigestible by cinematic narrative in their own right.

DATA

The contemporary idea of climate, and especially global climatic change, is bound up in scientific data and projections thanks to the work of the IPCC (ch.5). However, as Mike Hulme reminds us, every society constructs 'shared collective knowledge – cultural knowledge – of how and why the weather of a particular place behaves the way it does' (2021: 4–5). Looking for patterns in the weather, and trying to predict the future, is a necessity for every human society, yet this practical notion of climate as 'a descriptive index of aggregated weather' is just one of its many cultural functions. Thus, Canadian adverts promoting products 'Tested for Life in Canada' reflect a 'northern' national identity inspired by a challenging continental climate. Climate can extend well beyond 'a narrow description of expected weather': 'for Australian Aboriginal Aboriginals and Torres Strait Islanders', according to Hulme, 'climate is connoted as "country," an Aboriginal English word that embraces the weather, seasons, places, people, and their wider relationships, which, together, constitute a homeland' (p.6). He concludes that people's 'encounter with landscapes, their social and animal relationships, their livelihood practices, their imaginations, memories and stories, their gods and spirits … all these matter for the task of making sense of the weather' (p.5). This is why the scientific conception (or *re*-conception) of climate encounters innumerable points of 'friction', interference or amplification as it acquires local significance in diverse social contexts.

The universal practice of naming and predicting the weather was first systematised during the European colonial period. British authorities were particularly interested in the diverse climates of their colonies and maritime trading posts, which could increasingly be recorded and compared to one another. Just as **Carl Linnaeus** (1707–1778) developed a universal binomial system for classifying all living creatures, so **Francis Beaufort** (1774–1857) introduced a 13-point scale that enabled Royal Navy officers to record wind force systematically. Climates had always been distinctively grounded in particular places and their human and other-than-human inhabitants. European colonists, though, tried to 'improve' colonial natures by moving useful species between empirically defined climatic zones. Alan Bewell (ch.3) writes of European colonial natural history: 'Embodying a fundamental transformation in Europeans' relationship to nature, its revolutionary character lay in the project of *producing natures that could travel*' (p.26). Indeed, this was the explicit project of 'acclimatization societies,' which intentionally introduced European species to colonies (such as starlings to North America, which now number 150–200 million). Thus, Hulme argues, 'climate became a globally interconnected idea *conceptually* at the same time as empires and colonies were themselves becoming connected *materially* through the infrastructures of transglobal trade, mobility, and communication' (p.33). To put it another way, planetary environmental consciousness was made possible by imperial globalisation.

Even though Europe's empires successfully reconceptualised climate as a universal statistical index (Hulme 2021: 8–9), by the time they unravelled after World War Two there was still no such thing as 'global climate'. Instead, global climate had to be *produced* as an object of knowledge, laboriously over many decades, before the IPCC could provide a consensus judgement on global climate *change*, past and future. Paul N. Edwards calls this extraordinary project '"a vast machine": a sociotechnical system that collects data, models physical processes, tests theories, and ultimately generates a widely shared understanding of climate and climate change' (2010: 9). Edwards's history of the 'infrastructural globalism' (p.25) required by the system highlights the fiendish difficulty of extracting a homogenous dataset from heterogeneous historical weather information, recorded in numerous forms and languages, collected by ships using various methods (p.318); weather stations using different instruments and recording protocols dotted around the globe (pp.312–4); and, later, satellites (pp.413–8). (Edwards discusses only the historical 'instrumental' record, whereas climate scientists also draw on longer term 'proxy' records from ice cores, lake sediments, tree rings and so on.) In addition, these data sources are not spread out evenly over the planet (lots in Europe, very few in Africa or Antarctica), and so models and algorithms must be used 'to blend and smooth out diverse, heterogeneous data' (p.321) and fill in gaps in the record. 'Empirical' knowledge of global climate is impossible without modelling because 'Raw "data" are noisy, shapeless, and uninterpretable' (p.418). And this arduous process only provides an historical image of global climate: Edwards goes on to describe the still greater challenge of modelling future climates, and to explain how a reliable consensus can develop out of the unavoidable 'shimmering' of different climate models:

If you understand why climate data shimmer, now and always, and why climate predictions too will always shimmer, you may come to accept *proliferation within convergence*. Today, an Enlightenment ideal of knowledge as perfect certainty still holds us back from this acceptance. Oddly enough, so too does a widespread relativism – promoted not least by some of my colleagues in Science and Technology Studies (STS) – that elevates virtually any skeptical view to the same status as the expert consensus.

(p.436)

One of those 'colleagues,' Stephen Yearley, explains how claims about climate change are 'socially constructed' (I discuss 'cultural construction' in ch.1), but protests: 'This is not to say that they are fictions, mere conventions or conclusions arrived at in tendentious ways. In this area there can only be constructions' (2009: 393). The problem is that, as Latour explains in *The Politics of Nature* (2004), the Enlightenment ideal of scientific knowledge requires that politics must not be allowed to 'contaminate' it: 'There exists [in this ideal] no possible continuity between the world of human beings and access to truths "not made by human hands"' (2004a: 10). In the 'Two-House Collective' that insists on the distinction between the social and natural worlds, 'On the one hand, we have the chattering of fictions; on the other, the silence of reality' (p.14). However, reviewing apparently simple empirical questions in climate science shows that this separation is untenable. Global heating is happening primarily because greenhouse gases, principally carbon dioxide, are being emitted more quickly that they can be absorbed by natural 'sinks' such as oceans and forests. 'Anthropogenic' emissions of CO_2 make up roughly 4% of the global carbon cycle (G.P. Wayne 2022). But what counts as 'anthropogenic'? Wildfires in western North America and Australia, for example, are ignited naturally by lightning, but also by arson or accident. They are growing in scale and ferocity because previous Indigenous practices, which Stephen Pyne sums up as 'burn early, burn light, burn often' (2019: 52), were suppressed in the colonial era. Today, patterns of forest density (aka 'fuel load') are heavily dependent on economics and policy, especially the extent and latitude of Indigenous stewardship, and yet only prescribed burns, not 'natural' ones, are added to these settler nation-states' (already large) tally of anthropogenic emissions.

The homogeneity of anthropogenic emissions is also contested by Anil Agarwal and Sunita Narain, who describe 'scientific' calculations of various countries' emissions (in 1990) as 'A Case of Environmental Colonialism'. They ask:

Can we really equate the carbon dioxide contributions of gas guzzling automobiles in Europe and North America or, for that matter, anywhere in the Third World with the methane emissions of draught cattle and rice fields of subsistence farmers in West Bengal or Thailand?

(1991: 82, it.orig.)

At the same time, they challenge the globalisation of climate knowledge, emphasising that Third World nations 'cannot depend on Western institutions to present a true picture of the global situation and safeguard their interests' (p.87). Their distinction between 'survival' and 'luxury' emissions is intuitively plausible, if questionable, not least because there is no cross-cultural definition of adequate wealth. Still, these considerations show that climate justice does not arrive *after* the empirical reality has been described, when costs and benefits are worked out, but is an aspect of the empirical problem in the first place. As Hulme observes, 'Institutions like the IPCC require the rhetorical boundary between science and politics to be constantly reiterated. Yet in practice the location of this boundary is constantly being withdrawn' (p.45). STS scholarship on climate change is critical of what Yearley defines as 'scientification' (aka 'scientisation'): *'The conviction that science speaks objectively and disinterestedly means that one need have no qualms about excluding other people from decision-making since they would, in any event, have arrived at the same conclusions as oneself'* (1996: 113, it.orig.). To counter scientification, STS scholarship humanises and historicises climate science: Edwards, for instance, shows why and how the IPCC 'explicitly recognizes the provisional nature of climate knowledge by bringing *controversy within consensus,* and by articulating the climate's past and its future as ranges and likelihoods, not bright lines' (p.438). The social reality of science is more humble, more nuanced, but not less impressive, than the Enlightenment ideal.

The role of data in environmental representations is examined at the intersection of ecocriticism and Digital Humanities (DH), a space designated 'EcoDH' by Jeffrey Jerome Cohen and Stephanie LeMenager (2020) that aligns, in their telling, with the philosophy of New Materialism (ch.2). EcoDH highlights the enormous environmental impact of digital media (Maxwell and Miller 2012), despite the intangibility suggested by terms like 'world wide web' and 'cloud computing'. This 'ecology of media' (Carruth 2020: 369) recalls Ross's critique of the 'ecology of images', though given our profound dependence on digital media for research and writing, it is hard to see what we can do about it. Sean Cubitt admits that 'our discussions of data, truth and climate change simultaneously rely on and contribute to global warming, but do so in the margins of a system devoted to an overwhelmingly mechanical internal dialogue, where humans have a diminishing statistical and perhaps semantic role' (2021: 56). Our efforts to measure our impact on global climate have, he suggests, displaced humanity to the periphery of a vast machine:

> ... the planet-scale instruments we now employ – relays of satellites, automatic buoys in mid-ocean, remote anemometers equipped with cellular communications, all reporting to international computer networks – produce more data than whole cadres of technicians can observe, in granular detail sifted through by devices trained by machine learning to seek patterns that, in their increasing autonomy from direct human design, no longer exclusively conform to the requirements of the science they were built for.
>
> (p.57)

The infrastructural globalism that Edwards describes, in which scientists wrestle with instruments and data sets, is invoked by Cubitt to decentre human intention altogether. Yet his breathless invocation of a 'single mass image of the world' (p.65) in which we are dissolved, as 'data subjects' tracked in a GPS mapping app for instance, is the type of exaggeration decried as 'worship of the algorithm' by Ian Bogost (2015). Google Maps, for Bogost, is:

> ... not just mapping software running via computer—it also involves geographical information systems, geolocation satellites and transponders, human-driven automobiles, roof-mounted panoramic optical recording systems, international recording and privacy law, physical- and data-network routing systems, and web/mobile presentational apparatuses. That's not algorithmic culture—it's just, well, culture.

Existing DH scholars like Bogost can help EcoDH balance analysis of the awesome power of data with critical attention to the all-too-human, and corporate, infrastructure of 'algorithmic culture.'

The scale of 'big data', and the wealth and influence of the 'big four' tech companies (Alphabet, Amazon, Apple and Meta), are truly intimidating.

So, in a different domain, is the multi-dimensional environmental crisis, which encompasses the whole planet and extends into the distant, unthinkable future. It is this 'infowhelm' of bewildering scale that, Heather Houser suggests, environmental art helps to mediate. Alenda Chang's *Playing Nature: Ecology in Video Games* (2019) points out that 'Environmental thinking has always been an exercise in scalar understanding. How much is too much, and when is enough enough?' (p.70) She argues plausibly that video games 'are tailor-made to develop scalar environmental consciousness, for instance by bridging local and global, micro and macro domains' (p.71). Ecocritics like Chang analyse examples as different as *Spore* (Maxis, 2008), *Flower* (Thatgamecompany, 2009), *Journey* (Thatgamecompany, 2012), *Eco* (Strange Loop, 2018), and *Beyond Blue* (E-line, 2020) in terms of their 'potential to create meaningful interaction within artificially intelligent environments, to model ecological dynamics based on interdependence and limitation, and to allow players to explore manifold ecological futures—not all of them dystopian' (p.16; cf. Parham 2015: 205–29). Increased scholarly attention may also, Chang hopes, nudge games companies towards more sophisticated ecological engagements.

We seem a long way from Wordsworth and Thoreau's experience of sublime bewilderment, of embodied 'contact!' (ch.4), although Chang's book begins with a discussion of *Walden, a game* (2017), a video game linked to the book and the location that is, she claims, 'not as heretical as it sounds' (p.1). Questions of scale permeate all academic disciplines, and can therefore become interdisciplinary conversation points, or 'boundary objects' (Lundgren 2020). Chang, for example, criticises the way that 'scientists usually design ecological studies on scales appropriate to human experience and perception, rather than to the species or subjects in question' (p.75). *Ecocriticism on the Edge* (2015), Timothy Clark's seminal argument for scale-consciousness, underlines that:

> With climate change ... we have a map whose scale includes the whole Earth but, when it comes to relating the threat to daily questions of politics, ethics or specific interpretations of history, culture, literature or other areas, the map is almost mockingly useless. Even the climatology works on a less than helpful scale. For, paradoxically, it is simpler to predict futures for the planet as a whole, a closed system, than to make forecasts for specific areas.
>
> (2015: 71)

Regional projections have to be 'downscaled' from global models, with consequent loss of predictive accuracy (Koutsoyiannis et al. 2008; cf. Garrard et al. 2019: 231–3). If models and visualisations have specific limitations in terms of representing climate change, though, we might expect human (or 'meso') scaled narratives to be wholly useless.

NARRATIVES

According to geologists, I am writing this book during the Holocene epoch, which began 11,700 years ago with the end of the last ice age. In all likelihood, you are reading it in the Anthropocene, a prospective epoch moving towards acceptance by geologists that could replace the Holocene (Group 2019). They will have to decide when it *will have begun*: candidate beginnings include the advent of agriculture (Ruddiman 2017), the seventeenth century ecological transformations caused by European colonialism (Lewis and Maslin 2015) (ch.7), and the late-eighteenth century Industrial Revolution (Crutzen 2002), though the stratigraphers prefer 1950CE because plutonium isotopes from atmospheric nuclear testing will be detectable for aeons in the geologic record. The name itself is controversial: it seems anthropocentric, and it appears to blame all humans ('anthropos') for ecological impacts that Marxist, postcolonial and other critics attribute to specific groups or systems (Crist 2013). As Marco Caracciolo acknowledges, 'Talk of "humanity" becoming a geological agent thus risks sidelining the moral responsibilities that come with our capitalist and neoliberal economic system, whose roots lie in Western colonialist practices and in various forms of exploitation of human and nonhuman subjects' (2021: 9–10). Proposed alternative epochs include the Capitalocene (Moore 2017), Plantationocene (Davis et al. 2019), Pyrocene (Pyne 2021) and Chthulucene (Haraway 2016). The most moving suggestion is biologist E.O. Wilson's 'Eremozoic', or 'age of loneliness', inaugurated by biodiversity loss (Wilson 2006). Perhaps, though, 'Anthropos' is not quite 'humanity'. Hannes Bergthaller suggests that 'To recognise the human as a geological force is to see ourselves as on the same level with the cyanobacteria and methanosarcina', which also dramatically altered the planet's atmosphere. Thus, 'We encounter ourselves as an alien force' (2021: 213). Cubitt 'codes' *Anthropos*, no longer as confidently human, but as a cyborg that is 'increasingly reliant not only on prosthetic senses but also on prosthetic memory and prosthetic understanding' (p.58). Or, to look at it another way, the Anthropocene can be seen as 'quintessentially ironic insofar as it constitutes unintended and unexpected consequences of human actions' (Seymour 2018: 8). The epoch is not even a novel proposal: Laura Dassow Walls shows that humans were already identified as a geological force in the nineteenth century, when the term 'Anthropozoic' was coined, and concludes that 'The problem historians face ... is not how to account for the emergence of Anthropocenic discourse, but to understand how it emerged, repeatedly, only to be repeatedly marginalised and subsequently forgotten' (Walls 2021: 26). Whether as *déja vu* or shocking (if backdated) novelty, the Anthropocene is, in several senses, here to stay, if only as, in Clark's terms, a 'catchphrase, used as both intellectual shortcut and expanded question mark to refer to the novel situation we are in' (p.3).

Any account of the Anthropocene must refer to 'The Scale of Human Activity' (Rafferty 2018): not only climate change, but also land use, population (humans and livestock), ocean acidification, and increased extinction rates of wild animals. Taking it seriously challenges us, as Dipesh Chakrabarty writes in 'The Climate of History: Four Theses,' to revise our 'disciplinary prejudices' (2009: 215); in his case, by reconsidering theories of globalisation in the Anthropocene context. His first thesis is that 'Anthropogenic Explanations of Climate Change Spell the Collapse of the Age-old Humanist Distinction between Natural History and Human History' (p.201). Human history has been conceived, since the eighteenth century at least, as saturated with intention, whereas nature is 'a silent and passive backdrop to ... historical narratives' (p.204). Chakrabarty acknowledges humans have always been 'biological agents', modifying ecosystems with fire-sticks, spears and later agriculture, but he points out that 'we can become geological agents only historically and collectively' (p.206). However, if we accept Rigby's argument (ch.5) that the idea of 'natural disaster' only emerged in the eighteenth century, and also Walls's account of the 'first Anthropocene' in the nineteenth century, we would dispute that the distinction is 'age-old' and admit that the threat of 'collapse' was there almost from the outset. Chakrabarty is right, though, to warn that 'The mansion of modern freedoms stands on an ever-expanding base of fossil-fuel use' (p.208), which implicates progressive scholars as much as oil barons, and he is bold in his willingness to blend historical critique of capitalism with the 'deep history' that has brought us to the brink of 'a shared catastrophe that we have all fallen into' (p.219). The essay ends on a note of intellectual humility in the face of 'a figure of the universal [i.e. the Anthropocene] that escapes our capacity to experience the world' (p.222).

Literary narratives are all about experiences, both those evoked through fictional characters and, indirectly, those of readers. 'Climate Apocalypse' was discussed in chapter 5, so in the remainder of this section we focus on 'cli-fi' that avoids this familiar trope. As recently as 2016, Amitav Ghosh worried about 'the peculiar forms of resistance that climate change presents to what is now regarded as serious fiction' and warned that 'if certain literary forms are unable to negotiate these torrents, then they will have failed—and their failures will have to be counted as an aspect of the broader imaginative and cultural failure that lies at the heart of the climate crisis' (p.8). Since then, dozens of authors have risen to the challenge. For some, the intention is to 'translate,' as Caracciolo puts it, 'science into the human-scale, embodied language of everyday perception' (p.12): they write to effect social change. Others worry about becoming an unofficial creative branch of the IPCC, and choose to make art that, Hulme contends, 'is about "thickening" people's understanding of climate change rather than disciplining it' (p.155).

Caracciolo's *Narrating the Mesh: Form and Story in the Anthropocene* (2021) is intrigued by, and sceptical of, New Materialist claims that 'nonhuman matter can take on narrativity' (pp.17–8) (ch.2), so he develops an 'eco-narratological' framework that thinks 'with and about narrative form, in its intersection with scientific models and patterns of affectivity' (p.19). A chapter co-authored with Andrei Ionescu and Ruben Fransoo displays an 'algorithmic' method of reading the patterns of metaphor in three climate fictions, including Atwood's *Oryx and Crake* (ch.5 and 6) and Ian McEwan's *Solar* (2010). They argue that 'creative metaphor [is] the primary stylistic form through which narrative may realize multiscalarity, one of the main features of complex systems and of the human-nonhuman **mesh**' (p.140). An ecocritical assessment of *Solar* by Richard Kerridge that employs close reading sees the personal vices of 'anti-hero protagonist' (2019: 161) Michael Beard, including gluttony, avarice, pride and lust, as emblems of broader human failings that prevent us from addressing climate change. By contrast with Kerridge, Caracciolo and colleagues 'map' all the metaphors in the novel, such as this passage comparing Beard's body (coded

LH) to a landscape (W): 'He went home to his flat and lay brooding in the scum-rimmed bath, gazing through steam clouds at the archipelago of his disrupted selfhood—mountainous paunch, penis tip, unruly toes—scattered in a line across a soapy grey sea' (McEwan 2010: 164). Reviewing the pattern, they conclude that 'The protagonist becomes an unlikely, and to a large extent unsuspecting, embodiment of climate change—where the word "embodiment" refers to Beard's actual body, not to a merely conceptual or symbolic connection with the environment' (p.156). Their findings, using a quantitative method borrowed from DH, complement Kerridge's discussion of *Solar* as a comic allegory.

We have seen that allegory is employed in Lydia Millet's *The Children's Bible* (ch.6), *Solar* and *Don't Look Up* to anatomise and lambast our failure to prevent climate change. Another way for writers to manage the forbidding complexity of the topic is to identify a telling symbol. The beautiful, enigmatic monarch butterfly symbolises climatic disruption in Barbara Kingsolver's *Flight Behaviour* (2012), the most celebrated example of climate fiction in a realist mode. Dellarobia Turnbow, a mother of two, comes across a flock of migratory monarchs as she traipses up a mountain in high-heeled boots intending to have an affair with a telephone lineman. Out of vanity, she has left her glasses at home, and so the clouds of orange butterflies clustered on conifers strike her as a baffling yet exhilarating apparition:

> Trees turned to fire, a burning bush. Moses came to mind, and Ezekiel, words from Scripture that occupied a certain space in her brain but no longer carried honest weight, if they ever had. *Burning coals of fire went up and down among the living creatures.*
>
> (p.14)

Dellarobia feels trapped by her gentle 'slow motion' husband, Cub (p.7) and her poor, conservative, Christian hometown. By contrast, the 'orange boughs' look to her 'like the inside of joy, if a person could see that' (pp.15–6), so she resolves to ditch the lineman and pursue the meaning of the vision.

Returning to the site with Hester and Bear, her parents-in-law, she realises what they are:

> The drooping branches seemed bent to the breaking point under their weight. Of *butterflies*. The verity of that took her breath. A million times

nothing weighed nothing. Her mind confronted a mathematics she'd always thought to be the domain of teachers and pure invention.

"Great day in the morning," Hester said, looking stricken.

"There you go," Bear said, "Whatever the hell that is, it can't be a damn bit of good for logging."

"I'd say it would gum up their equipment," Norwood agreed. "Or we might run into one of those government deals. Something endangered."

"No sir," said Bear, "I believe there's more of them than we've got people.'

(p.53)

Media coverage of the butterflies brings Ovid Byron, a charismatic, handsome Black lepidopterist who resembles Barack Obama, to Feathertown to study their anomalous behaviour. As Dellarobia becomes involved in his research, her 'hopes for the survival of the butterflies through the Tennessee winter and for her own future personal happiness and possible career seem to become closely intertwined' (Clark 2015: 171). So much so that, as Byron describes the marvel of the monarchs' migration, she is choked with emotion, and asks herself: 'How was that even normal, to cry over insects?' (p.146) Dellarobia's self-consciousness here reflects what Kari Norgaard calls a 'norm of emotion' that facilitates 'socially organized denial', in which people 'collectively distance themselves from information' about the effects of global heating that is too upsetting to acknowledge (2011: 259).

Ovid Byron, too, cares deeply about the mortal threat to the butterflies, asking Dellarobia: "'If someone you loved was dying, what would you do?'" (p.319) Shortly afterwards, though, he says that 'Science doesn't tell us what we should do. It only tells us what *is*' (p.320). Like many scientists and non-scientists, Byron confuses the vital institutional safeguards of impartiality (collaboration, blind peer review, public funding) with the *rhetoric* of dispassionate impartiality, which is by no means essential to it. Hence he is caught, like many environmental scientists, in an excruciating double-bind: deeply committed to the survival and flourishing of the monarch butterflies, whilst imagining himself bound by scientific protocols *not to feel* for them. By placing this quandary at the centre of Dellarobia and Byron's relationship, *Flight Behaviour* elevates it into a metanarrative that shows why such novels *need* to exist: to get past social and scientific norms of emotion that rule out feelings of panic, love and grief.

Dellarobia challenges him to engage with 'climate deniers' like her neighbours, whom she represents compassionately as members of a different cultural 'team', not ignoramuses:

> "Team camo, we get the right to bear arms and John Deere and the canning jars and tough love and taking care of our own. The other side wears I don't know what, something expensive. They get recycling and population control and lattes and as many second chances as anybody wants. Students emailing to say they deserve their A's."
>
> (p.321)

Dellarobia's conciliatory effort seems forlorn in light of the cultural polarisation in America, which has only worsened since 2012. Still, it aligns with Dan Kahan's research, which suggests Americans' cultural identity, not their knowledge of science, is the best predictor of their professed opinions on hot-button questions: 'whether people "believe in" climate change, like whether they "believe in" evolution, expresses who they are' (2015: 11). Dellarobia's mediation between Byron and her Appalachian neighbours is motivated by concern for her children's future, in that, as Adeline Johns-Putra argues, she 'combines her experience of poverty-stricken parenthood with her new ecological understanding of the threatened global environment into a very particular view of posterity' (2019: 160). The novel itself refrains from mentioning the underlying threat to the butterflies until page 147, and then as an object of suspicion: 'Climate change, she knew to be wary of that'. *Flight Behaviour* is finely balanced between enthusiasm for scientific methods and understanding of conservative scepticism; between perceptive sardonic humour and wrenching grief for an unravelling world.

The butterflies appear in the novel collectively as 'orange boughs', 'golden darts', (p.52) 'a whole butterfly forest' (p.94) and so on. One butterfly is individualised though, just as Dellarobia confronts the fear of the butterflies' extinction:

> Dellarobia suddenly found she could scarcely bear this day at all. She stepped out in the rain to pick up one of the pitiful survivors and bring it under their roof. She held it close to her face. A female. And ladylike, with its slender velvet abdomen, its black eyes huge and dolorous. The proboscis curled and uncurled like a spring.
>
> (p.319)

This exquisite moment counterbalances both the mass depictions and the accumulation of symbolic resonances attached to the monarchs by numerous characters, including Christian locals, biology grad students, Mexican migrants, British hippies and others.

The novel's ending, in which Dellarobia decides to get divorced and go to college and the region is flooded by torrential rain, has divided ecocritical opinion. The remaining monarchs stream away to the south:

> The numbers astonished her. Maybe a million. The shards of a wrecked generation had rested alive like a heartbeat in trees, snow-covered, charged with resistance. Now the sun blinked open on a long impossible time, and here was the exodus. They would gather on other fields and risk other odds, probably no better or worse than hers.
>
> (p.433)

For Clark, the symbolic association of the monarchs with the protagonist's fate inevitably reduces them to 'a kind of visual background music for Dellarobia's story' (p.177). He goes on to ask: 'why is the trajectory of one, individual fictional life still felt by the reader to be so much more powerful ... than that of the natural history of the insects whose strange behaviour would still remain a harbinger of ecosystem collapse and extinction?' (pp.177–8) Johns-Putra, though, disagrees that this is a 'happy ending of human triumph' (p.162), and claims that the pointed focus on the butterflies 'shocks the reader out of an emotional connection with Dellarobia' (p.163), giving the novel an 'ecocentric' ending after all.

Superficially, Charlotte McConaghy's *Migrations* (2020) resembles *Flight Behaviour*: it centres on a female protagonist, the narrator Franny Stone, and employs a migratory species, the Artic tern, as a central symbol. Where Kingsolver's central narrative is linear and progressive, though, McConaghy switches abruptly between the narrated present, spent on a fishing boat following the terns from Greenland to South America, and several interwoven past plots in which she falls in love with Niall, an ornithologist, and undergoes a traumatic event for which she is imprisoned as a murderer in Ireland. The predominant mood is different too: where *Flight Behaviour* is compassionately realistic about the lives of rural working people, *Migrations* is a vivid fantasy with Gothic overtones, including haunting, suicide, sexual violence, repressed trauma, and a seemingly inherited death wish. Though no dates are revealed, and there are no futuristic elements (the fishing boat still uses DVDs), Franny is stranded in the Eremozoic from the first line: 'The animals are dying. Soon we will be alone here' (McConaghy 2020: 3). Some of the extinctions seem far-fetched, including deer and crows as well as wolves. Still, this and other implausibilities are swept aside by the romantic (and Romantic) plot that drives forward, in search of the last Arctic terns on Earth, and backward to unearth, and perhaps redeem, the narrator's crime. *Migrations* is a relentlessly **declensionist** narrative, though not apocalyptic, and it returns often to the theme of powerlessness, as when Niall is lecturing in Galway:

> He said it's hard, sometimes, to finish. The bile rises in his throat and he could break the lectern beneath his hands, overcome with a profound sense of loathing of what we are, all of us, and the poison of our species. He called himself a hypocrite for always talking, never doing, and he said he hates himself as much as anyone ... I wish I could ease it for him somehow, smooth it away with a touch of my fingers or the whisper of my lips, but it's bigger than I am, it's an anger to swallow the world.
>
> (p.166)

Niall's sense of guilt and implication is understandable – the cry of 'hypocrisy' is considered a knockdown criticism even of environmentalists who drive to protests – but as Timothy Morton movingly explains, 'Humans have entered an era of *hypocrisy*' (2013: 148). Since neither capitalism nor climate change have any 'outside,' both complicity and vulnerability are universal, though not evenly distributed. Morton is impatient with cynicism:

> Doing nothing evidently won't do at all. Drive a Prius? Why not (I do)? But it won't solve the problem in the long run. Sit around criticizing Prius drivers? Won't help at all. Form a people's army and seize control of the state? Will the new society have the time and resources to tackle global warming? Solar panels? They take a lot of energy to make. Nuclear power? Fukushima and Chernobyl, anyone? Stop burning all fossil fuels now? Are we ready for such a colossal transition? Every position is 'wrong': every position, including and

especially the know-it-all cynicism that thinks that it knows better than anything else.

(p.136)

Morton advocates for hypocrisy and admission of weakness because 'The hypocrite understands that she is caught in her own failure' (p.148). Franny's discovery of her own weakness comes as she gets to know the fishermen and woman on the boat that takes her south, whom she despises as killers at first. The terrible truth about her 'murders' is revealed just before the pursuit of the terns reaches an optimistic conclusion, freeing Franny from her 'endless drowning shame' (p.252) to keep living and striving. Whereas Dellarobia's personal fulfilment seems to leave the butterflies behind, Franny is revived by the birds' perdurance and the claim it makes on her.

There could be few greater contrasts to the metaphoric density of *Flight Behaviour* and lyrical beauty of *Migrations* than Kim Stanley Robinson's punishingly literalistic *The Ministry for the Future* (2020), a doorstopper novel that explores what it might take to slow down global heating as it accelerates in the coming decades. There are only two substantial characters: Mary Murphy, director of the eponymous ministry, a fictional United Nations agency based in Zurich, Switzerland, and Frank May, an American NGO worker who survives the catastrophic Indian heatwave described in the opening chapter. Hanging from this filament of plot are several other kinds of chapters: anonymous narratives, usually in the first person plural, evoke global stories of suffering, resistance and adaptation, such as chapter 65 in which Africans enslaved in a Namibian mine are freed by drones sent by the 'African Union Peace and Security Council' (p.324). Other first-person stories, not anonymous but barely characterised, describe extraordinary projects to avert disaster, including pumping vast amounts of seawater to the base of Antarctic glaciers to slow their slide into the ocean. There are occasional chapters, in the form of riddles, that introduce other-than-human beings like the Sun (ch.2) and the capitalist market (ch.46), also (uncannily) in the first person, and many more voiced by an authorial persona that discuss philosophy, politics, psychology and, especially, economics: chapter 40 explains 'Jevons Paradox', which 'proposes that increases in efficiency in the use of a resource lead to an overall increase in the use of that resource, not a decrease' (p.165). The authorial narrator states, therefore, that 'it is naïve to expect that technological improvements alone will slow the impacts of growth and reduce the burden on the biosphere' (p.166). Thus, while Robinson displays the geeky fascinations of a science fiction author and ecological moderniser (ch.2), he subsumes science and technology within a larger narrative of radical social and economic change: a roadmap for global climate justice, in fact.

The Indian heatwave, which kills 20 million people in two weeks, inspires a ruthless and highly effective eco-terrorist movement, the Children of Kali. By the 2030s, we are told, 'fear and anger, denial and guilt, shame and regret' (p.227) are universal, and yet people 'still drove cars, ate meat, flew in jets, did all the things that caused the heatwave and would cause the next one' (p.228). And so the Children of Kali shoot down 60 passenger jets all around the world with drones. The narrator acknowledges, but does not describe, the 'people, innocent people, flying for all kinds of reasons: all dead' (p.228). Next, diesel-powered container ships are sunk, 'often where they could form the foundations for new coral reefs', and mad cow disease is 'cultured and introduced by drone dart into millions of cattle all over the world' (p.229). The Children also claim responsibility for assassinations of fossil fuel executives and other 'carbon burners' (p.368). Later on, Frank May reflects that 'people', presumably including himself, see the Children as 'resistance warriors, fighting for the Earth itself' (p.368):

If a few people got killed for flying, no one felt much sympathy. Fools conspicuously burning carbon, killed from out of the sky somehow? So what. Death from the sky had been the American way ever since Clinton and Bush and Obama, which was to say ever since it became technologically feasible. People were angry, people were scared. People were not fastidious.

(p.369)

Robinson tries to neutralise our moral qualms in advance by describing the heatwave in gruelling detail, and by ensuring the flawlessly targeted murders happen mostly off-stage, which suggests that he endorses the Children's campaign: Murphy's ministry even has a deniable back-channel of communication with the organisation. He is, though, naïve about the precision and effectiveness of political violence, to say nothing of its ethics, and he imagines that catastrophe will catalyse solidarity, as when India renounces conservative Hindu nationalism (politically dominant at present) overnight, becoming a model of socialist ecology (ch.31). The unfolding narrative of climate justice is, in that way, curiously *apolitical*: 'people', from Africa to the American Midwest, get with the program, and we never hear from narrators who disagree with it. As a novel, some readers will consider it refreshingly clear-eyed, plausible, even optimistic; others will find it lifeless and interminable. At its best, though, *The Ministry for the Future* asks, not 'What if?' but 'If not this solution, then what?'

Clade (2015) by James Bradley illuminates the Anthropocene by disrupting narrative temporality. Its ten chapters appear in linear order separated by unstated gaps in time (or 'ellipses'), and whilst the action seems to begin in the present or near future, the precise timescale cannot easily be deduced, though it seems to span the twenty-first century. 'Clade' is a biological term for a group of organisms with a common ancestor, most obviously Adam (as in the Biblical Genesis), the paleobotanist in the first chapter, yet the chapters' shifting focalisers are Adam's kith as well as kin, all the way to the last chapter in which Izzie, Adam's friend Lijuan's daughter, hears of his death. In common with other examples of cli-fi, *Clade* depicts disastrous climate-related impacts including a pandemic of Acute Viral Respiratory Syndrome (AVRS) that, like COVID-19, starts in China (p.195); a new Accelerated Colony Collapse Disorder that wipes out bees (p.166); and a dramatic flood in the East of England that Adam, his daughter Summer and grandson Noah survive together (pp.123–37). One chapter delicately juxtaposes the fate of bees with the precarious existence of Amir, a Bangladeshi doctor and climate refugee who takes up beekeeping.

Still, *Clade* is not apocalyptic. There is no macho survivalism, few futuristic gadgets, and although the carnage of the pandemic occurs 'off-stage', as in many apocalyptic texts, some individual AVRS deaths are marked and mourned. The devastating death of a child, Declan, drives a wedge between his parents, Tom and Maddie, and though climate change is not to blame, Bradley depicts everyday griefs as woven into the larger pattern of loss:

The last time Tom came up here he stood on the deck and watched the birds. He looked old, his face haggard.

'They're dying, you know,' he said, glancing at her as he spoke.

He waited for her to answer and when she did not he said, 'Not just here but all over the world.'

'They look fine to me,' she said, irritated.

'They might look fine but they've stopped breeding, or if they're still breeding their eggs aren't hatching, or the heat is killing the chicks. The ones you can see here are adults because they're all that's left, and when they're gone that will be the end of them. They're a ghost species.'

'Get out,' she said, 'I don't want you here.'

(pp.74–5)

We may know that climate impacts will encompass, not supersede, the ordinary suffering of human existence, but it is startling to be shown it with such compassion and finesse. There is, moreover, beauty even in catastrophe, as Adam recognises one morning in flood-torn England:

He wakes early, the light from the windows filling the room. Outside the moon is still visible, and in the dawn the water's expanse spreads like ruffled silk beneath the colourless sky. Not for the first time he is struck by the beauty of the planet's transformation, the indifferent majesty of the change that is taking place.

(p.134)

Bradley's economical prose attaches the reader emotionally to the various focalisers, and the elliptical narrative structure leaves mysteries unresolved and gaps for us to colour in, though some readers may find the connections stretch too thin to sustain their interest.

This novel has an Adam and a Noah, and a breath-taking surprise near the end, but, like Millet's *A Children's Bible* (ch.6), no revelation. The characters witness appalling losses of humans and Earth Others, and still Adam refuses the apocalyptic frame:

'... There are so many of us, and resources are stretched so thin the system can't survive unless there's some kind of radical change. The problem is we're so busy stumbling from one disaster to the next we can't get any distance, can't see what's happening for what it is.'

'You mean the end?'

'A point of transition.'

(p.131)

Clade is scary enough to work as a jeremiad, yet still the predominant affect is anticipatory grief for what Lijuan lists as 'the things we've lost' (p.207). Far from conveying, in Heather Hicks's words, the 'sort of exasperated throwing up of hands' associated with 'totalizing annihilation' (p.15), Bradley stays with the trouble through catastrophe (ch.5) because, as Izzy concludes at the end of the novel, 'It is always a beginning' (p.297).

Global heating has also been tackled in several graphic novels, including Philippe Squarzoni's documentary-style *Climate Changed: A Personal Journey Through the Science* (2014). Richard McGuire's *Here* (2014), though, expands the specific possibilities of the medium to remarkable effect by depicting a single location throughout: a corner of the author's childhood living room in Perth Amboy, New Jersey. In most graphic novels, as Laura Moncion explains, 'each panel is a moment but is also strung together into a narrative, much like words in a sentence: time is laid out spatially as a progression from one image to the next' (2016: 200). *Here,* by contrast, is anchored by a spread showing the corner of the room in 2014, and thereafter the spreads, all of them labelled with dates from 3,000,500,000BCE to 22,175CE, are in non-linear order, some including inset panels from other years. The space alone unites them; the site has, Moncion suggests, 'its own presence and personality, its own material existence through time' (p.204). Caracciolo describes *Here* as a rhizomic narrative (see Preface) that 'employs a highly decentralized form of narrative organization: because temporal sequentiality and causal coherence exist only at the local level (between specific panels or inserts), the text fosters a plurality of connections and a sense of playful open-endedness' (2012: 73). Global heating is introduced in a spread of the 1949 room in which someone calls someone else a 'drip,' whilst 16 other small inset panels from different years include insults from other eras.[1] A large inset panel on the left shows flood waters pouring through the window in 2111. A later spread from 2213 shows future brown-skinned humans standing on a boardwalk over a swamp viewing a holographic image of the room. While *Here* is centred on humans, it nonetheless blends, as Jon Hegglund points out, 'narrative expectations about individual human character with a more detached sense of humanity's species existence within the deep historical time registers implied by the Anthropocene' (2019: 186–7). It is a superb example of an Anthropocene fiction in which we appear, to recall Bergthaller's phrase, as a transient, alien, if undeniably fascinating, force.

It would be a mistake to ponder each book and movie only in isolation, and find them all lacking. If instead we consider them in aggregate, we might be encouraged to find that, while most are depressing in their own right, together these climate fictions constitute a striking riposte to Ghosh's assertion of an 'imaginative and cultural failure that lies at the heart of the climate crisis'. There are enormous obstacles to mitigating and adapting to climate change, which cultural artefacts can do nothing, directly, to overcome: matters of power generation, agricultural production, carbon taxation, global governance and many more. John Parham is right to reject the idea of an artistic or rhetorical silver bullet in favour of *Kairos*, the ancient Greek notion of the 'opportune moment', or 'the principle that environmentalism demands different rhetorical strategies for different situations' (p.44). If nothing else, these fictions 'thicken,' as Hulme puts it, our understanding of climate change, and suggest what it might mean to dwell less anthropocentrically in the Anthropocene.

NOTE

1 *Here* has no page numbers.

9

CONCLUSION

ECOCRITICISM IN THE FUTURE

In the years since the first edition of this book, ecocriticism has spread around the world, delving into diverse cultures of nature and developing a plethora of distinctive theoretical positions. Timothy Morton has acquired celebrity status, and many other scholars have engaged people outside their universities, as well as their own students, in conversations about culture and sustainability. Ecocriticism is a key element of the environmental humanities (ch.1) and a contributor to the 'public humanities'; it is also learning from Animal Studies (ch.6), Indigenous scholarship (ch.7) and the Digital Humanities (ch.8). These cross-fertilisations and coalitions respond to the sense of crisis in the humanities, which centre on 'how we justify the resources dedicated to our work, reading, teaching, and writing about literature in an age of neoliberal austerity and STEM ascendance' (Menely and Taylor 2017: 10). They are also opportunities though: public engagement can progress from conveying our findings to a grateful world into real co-production of knowledge, while a closer alliance with environmental history, for example, can yield new ideas and methodologies. Ecocriticism is hybridising with Science and Technology Studies, an inherently interdisciplinary field, as it learns to work in critical, but constructive, ways with the natural sciences.

DOI: 10.4324/9781003174011-9

The most promising new directions in ecocriticism are methodological, rather than thematic, historical or geographical. I have mentioned Caracciolo and colleagues' algorithmic analysis of *Solar*, part of an eco-narratological study that also draws on cognitive science. Innovators such as Erin James, Alexa Weik von Mossner, Jon Hegglund and W.P. Małecki, too, draw on contemporary psychology and experiment with empirical methods in eco-criticism. Sarah McFarland Taylor's *Ecopiety: Green Media and the Dilemma of Environmental Virtue* (2019) develops a critique of 'green consumerism' by way of delightfully original studies of popular culture, including, improbably, E.L. James's blockbuster erotic romance *Fifty Shades of Grey* (2011). McFarland draws widely on scholarship from psychology and media studies, and discusses 'Digital "prosumers" (simultaneously producers and consumers of media)' who 'engage in disruptions or in-breaks into a lulled consumer conscience' (p.25). *Fifty Shades* prosumers, for instance, write online fictions featuring 'an authentically green romantic hero in contrast to James's greenwashed [protagonist Christian] Grey' (p.60). The peak oil movement, the subject of Matthew Schneider-Mayerson's *Peak Oil* (2015), may itself have peaked, and yet the book remains a model for mixed methods research. Schneider-Mayerson draws on 'interviews with peak oil leaders and rank-and-file believers; discourse analysis of movement Web sites and online forums; visits to Transition Towns, where peakists attempted to build resilient, sustainable communities in preparation for peak oil and climate change; ... literary analysis of peak oil novels and nonfiction works' and the results of 'two large-scale online surveys' (p.12). *Peak Oil* is, in other words, as much a work of ethnography and Environmental Communication as literary ecocriticism. Where Schneider-Mayerson is engaged and particular, Serenella Iovino is passionately present throughout her New Materialist masterpiece (or *maestra*-piece) of **narrative scholarship**, *Ecocriticism and Italy* (2016). Texts with human authors are submerged within the 'trans-corporeal' (ch.1) mesh of 'storied matter' (p.9) mapped in the book. Iovino reads books and sites alike as 'forces, signs, wounds, and messages of creativity dispersed on Italy's body' (p.1). Such innovations are exciting, but also daunting. Just imagine responding to Menely and Taylor's assertion that 'in the Anthropocene, all scholars are called upon to become Earth system humanists, which involves thinking about how [naturalcultural] systems interrelate with, internalize, and destabilize one another' (p.4). In this ever-expanding **material-semiotic** universe, what is the value of ecocriticism (Clark 2019)? The historical 'mission of "English"' (i.e. literary studies), in Richard

Kerridge's account, is to imbue students with empathy whilst discouraging overt politicisation of literature:

> In the tradition of 'practical criticism' and close evaluative reading, literary study offers the experiential intensity of emotional identification with fictional characters or poetic personae, combined with an ethic of detachment from direct personal interest.
>
> (2012: 16)

Feminist, Marxist and environmental critics draw on the same methods, but they refuse to pretend to be detached or impartial. So do I, and yet I dislike 'thesis novels' (cf. ch.7) and I strive, in my teaching and my criticism, for **multi-partiality**. Teachers should not, in my view, be preachers.

This book models an abbreviated version of 'close reading,' a practice that reads quoted passages in relation to a wider historical, philosophical or, increasingly, scientific context, then makes some mixture of aesthetic and ethical judgments about the work as a whole. Reviewing challenges to this 'method,' Mark C. Long wonders how many ecocritics are prepared to transcend 'the disciplinary limits of professional training as well as the personal investments in humanist identities and ideological commitments' (2021: 79). He suggests instead that close reading shift from a solo performance of interpretive insight for a few scholarly peers towards 'a fundamentally collective project within the everyday collaboration of teachers and students' (p.80). Kerridge invites instructors to highlight the difference between the 'instrumentality of literary scholarship as practised by students and career researchers' (2012: 21) – reading quickly, extracting material for essays, and moving on – and 'slow reading', in which 'A text is for life, not just for the degree'. The contrast relates to a much wider quandary in relation to climate change: we are called to respond with both 'slow, deep changes [of culture and society] and fast, pragmatic ones – the open, non-pre-emptive encounter with otherness *and* a rapid, utilitarian response' (p.21).

As Helena Feder points out, closeness and distance are hard to calibrate in the aftermath (is it?) of the COVID-19 pandemic:

> The world is ... more-than-human and more than our measure of it. Scale itself expands and recedes almost infinitely, while 'close' has

become uncomfortably closer from toxins inherited *in utero* to cultivated misinformation sweeping the globe faster than any disease ...
Living in increasingly polarized countries, amid torrents of ... partisan
acrimony and misinformation, in the ever-widening trench between
the rich and the poor, we were already socially *distant*.

(2021: 8, 12)

In *The Ministry of the Future*, Robinson portrays a heatwave so horrific
and unequivocal that it brings political unity, and yet innumerable
people have died in the COVID-19 pandemic thanks to partisan 'epidemiology'. An acquaintance of mine died of the disease whilst continuing to deny its existence, just one of 20.7 million excess deaths
attributable to the disease worldwide as of April 14, 2022, according to
The Economist. Perhaps the 'derangements of scale' attributed to the
Anthropocene (ch.8) also afflict meso-scaled humans stuck at the mid-
point between molecular-scale viral reproduction and global pandemic
(geo)politics. If we consider the pandemic response as a speeded-up
allegory of global heating, it does not bode well.

Reading is in question as well as closeness. As N. Katherine Hayles
explains, students born into the Internet age are better at 'hyper attention' – 'switching focus rapidly among different tasks, preferring multiple information streams, seeking a high level of stimulation, and
having a low tolerance for boredom' – than the kind of deep attention
required by close reading, which involves 'concentrating on a single
object for long periods (say, a novel by Dickens), ignoring outside stimuli while so engaged, preferring a single information stream, and
having a high tolerance for long focus times' (2007: 107). Should
instructors and students strive to recover deep attention, which may
come to be valued as a kind of superpower, or accept that 'hyper attention is more adaptive than deep attention for many situations in contemporary developed societies' (p.194), in which case close reading is as
obsolete as blacksmithing? Just as new ecocritical methods combine
attention to singular texts with empirical, network, algorithmic and
'surface reading' methods, Hayles urges us to embrace the 'frustrating,
zesty, and intriguing ways in which the two cognitive modes interact'
(p.198).

Nicole Seymour points out that 'environmental crisis is, from certain
vantage points, laden with ironies and absurdities' (2018: 9). It is darkly

ironic that, in the years since the first edition of this book, ecocritical scholarship and environmental cultures have accelerated in tandem with global crisis. Reviewing the same period, though, David Boyd says he remains 'an optimistic environmentalist': 'From air pollution to safe drinking water, from greener cities to renewable energy, we've made remarkable but widely underacknowledged progress' (Boyd 2015: xi). It happened because people believed it was possible. Ecocritics can also make progress by opening ourselves to new methods and discourses, and by holding our theoretical commitments more humbly, or ironically, in the knowledge that wicked problems like global heating have neither simple causes, nor single solutions. Above all, this book shows we should celebrate with increased confidence and wonder the capacity of human imagination to evoke, or channel, the unextinguished beauty, complexity and diversity of the other-than-human world.

GLOSSARY OF SPECIALISED TERMS AND MEANINGS

Agency: the capacity to act. Western thought typically reserves agency for living beings that act autonomously, or sentient beings that act intentionally, whereas New Materialists argue that all matter possesses agency of some kind.

Assemblage: an aggregated group of things and/or persons. Whereas scientific rhetoric assumes the superior role of the impartial scientist (subject) with respect to the object of their research, 'assemblage', in STS scholarship, puts scientists, instruments, and the things they research on the same level.

Biocultural: describes phenomena in which biological and cultural factors interact. Cf. **material-semiotic, naturecultures**.

Biosemiotics: a branch of semiotics that explores the numerous forms of communication and signification employed in living systems. Biosemiotics considers molecular communication (e.g. DNA, pheromones) and other-than-human sign systems (e.g. whale song) on a continuum with symbolic sign systems (e.g. human languages).

DOI: 10.4324/9781003174011-10

Declensionism: historical or mythological narrative structure of decline from a preferable or ideal state.

Ecomimeticism: as described by Timothy Morton (p.58), the effort to represent nature transparently, or with minimal overt artifice.

Environmentality: a term derived from Michael Foucault's concept of 'governmentality'. Rather than taking 'the environment' for granted as an object of public concern and governance (somewhat like Passmore's 'problems in ecology'), analysis of environmentality shows how relations of power govern the production of ecological knowledge, discourse and policy (i,e. 'ecological problems').

Focaliser: in narratology, the character(s) whose point of view is conveyed by the narrative.

Instrumental Rationality: in philosophy, the adoption of appropriate means to one's ends. The Frankfurt School adapted the phrase to critique the reduction of all kinds of value to the economic under capitalism.

Mechanomorphism: representation of a living being as if it were a machine.

Material-semiotic: describes phenomena as simultaneously physically real and communicative. Cf. **biocultural, naturecultures.**

Mesh: in Morton's work, a term for naturalcultural interdependence in which 'Nothing exists all by itself, and so nothing is fully "itself"' (*The Ecological Thought*, p.15).

Millennialism: belief in the literal reign of Christ on Earth for 1000 years, but also more generally belief in imminent collective salvation or political transformation.

Multispecies ethnography: anti-anthropocentric method in anthropology that studies co-constitutive relationships between humans and Earth Others.

Multi-partiality: pedagogical approach that stresses fair representation of competing viewpoints without the pretence of impartiality.

Narrative Scholarship: scholarly writing that blends autobiographical and analytical elements.

Naturecultures: portmanteau term used by Bruno Latour and Donna Haraway to emphasise the inextricability and interpenetration of the supposedly distinct domains of nature and culture.

Neo-animism: relational cosmology, influenced both by Indigenous spirituality and aspects of Western science, populated by many kinds of other-than-human persons.

Ontology: in philosophy, the branch of metaphysics that studies the nature of being. In contemporary anthropology, 'ontologies' are enculturated beliefs about the kind of things that exist, e.g. Western positivist ontology depicts matter as real, mind as epiphenomenal and spirit as delusional.

SUGGESTED READING

ADDITIONAL INTRODUCTORY TEXTS

Timothy Clark. 2011. *The Cambridge Introduction to Literature and the Environment* (Cambridge University Press: Cambridge). A complementary introduction to this book that mostly covers different ground. Clark's 'quandaries' of environmental reading are well conceived and provocative.

John S. Dryzek. 2013. 3rd edn. *The Politics of the Earth: Environmental Discourses* (Oxford University Press: Oxford). Engages with the 'Positions' of chapter 1 from the perspective of political science.

Mike Hulme. 2022. *Climate Change* (Routledge: Abingdon). Excellent survey from the perspective of numerous disciplines, including literary studies.

Richard Kerridge. 2012. 'Ecocriticism and the Mission of "English"', in *Teaching Ecocriticism and Green Cultural Studies*, ed. Greg Garrard (Palgrave: London). Usefully situates ecocriticism within the history of English Literature.

Cheryl Lousley. 2020. 'Ecocriticism', in *Oxford Research Encyclopedia*. doi: https://doi.org/10.1093/acrefore/9780190201098.013.974 Superb nuanced examination of 'open conceptual problems ... within ecocriticism.'

John Parham. 2016. *Green Media and Popular Culture: An Introduction* (Palgrave: London). Spirited account of the need for ecocritical engagement with popular culture.

Sergio Sismondo. 2010, 2nd edn. *An Introduction to Science and Technology Studies* (Wiley-Blackwell: Chichester). Informed, accessible discussion of the history and key concepts of STS.

FURTHER READING

ASLE and ASLE-UKI's book awards reliably recommend outstanding critical texts.

Stacy Alaimo and Susan Hekman (eds). 2008. *Material Feminisms* (Indiana UP: Bloomington, IN.). Ground-breaking collection, including work from leading scholars at the intersection of feminism and science such as Grosz, Barad, Haraway, Mortimer-Sandilands and Alaimo herself.

Lawrence Buell. 2001. *Writing for an Endangered World: Literature, Culture, and Environment in the U.S. and Beyond* (Belknap Press: London). Together with Buell's earlier Thoreau book, constitutes a thorough basis for American literary ecocriticism.

Dipesh Chakrabarty. 2009. 'The Climate of History: Four Theses'. *Critical Inquiry* (35: 2), pp.197–222. Justly celebrated discussion of the collision of postcolonial and geological histories of the Earth.

Timothy Clark. 2015. *Ecocriticism on the Edge: The Anthropocene as a Threshold Concept* (Bloomsbury: London). Brilliantly original application of deconstructive thought to the idea of the Anthropocene.

Ursula Heise. 2008. *Sense of Place and Sense of Planet: The Environmental Imagination of the Global* (Oxford University Press: Oxford). Indispensable discussion of the globalisation of ecocriticism, which draws widely on sociology and political theory.

Ursula Heise. 2016. *Imagining Extinction: The Cultural Meanings of Endangered Species* (University of Chicago Press: Chicago). Foundational argument for the importance of culture in thinking about the biodiversity crisis.

Graham Huggan and Helen Tiffin. 2015. *Postcolonial Ecocriticism: Literature, Animals, Environment, 2nd edition* (Routledge: Abingdon). Balanced and informative discussion of ecocriticism and Animal Studies from a postcolonial perspective.

Serenella Iovino. 2016. *Ecocriticism and Italy* (Bloomsbury: London). Witty, propulsive and illuminating application of New Materialist theory to Italian culture.

Serenella Iovino and Serpil Oppermann. 2014. *Material Ecocriticism* (Indiana University Press: Bloomington, IN.). Seminal anthology that includes a who's who of New Materialist ecocritics, and a few sceptics.

Anthony Lioi. 2018. *Nerd Ecology: Defending the Earth with Unpopular Culture* (Bloomsbury: London). Sprightly, engaging ecocritical treatment of geeks and nerds' cultural favourites, including Tolkien and superhero comics.

Timothy Morton. 2010. *The Ecological Thought* (Harvard University Press: London). The most worthwhile of Morton's many books. More rewarding than his *Ecology Without Nature*; full of lively argument and interesting examples.

Rob Nixon. 2011. *Slow Violence and the Environmentalism of the Poor* (Harvard University Press: Cambridge, MA.). Nixon has worked as a journalist, and it shows. His transformative contribution to postcolonial ecocriticism is thoroughly readable and illuminating.

Paul Outka. 2008. *Race and Nature: From Transcendentalism to the Harlem Renaissance* (Palgrave: New York). Powerful, tightly-argued analysis of the racialisation of nature in American culture.

Kate Rigby. 2015. *Dancing with Disaster: Environmental Histories, Narratives, and Ethics for Perilous Times* (University of Virginia Press: Charlottesville, VA.). Compelling argument for an overhaul of the concept of 'natural disaster'.

Heidi Scott. 2014. *Chaos and Cosmos: Literary Roots of Modern Ecology in the British Nineteenth Century* (Pennsylvania State University Press: University Park, PA.). Cleverly reverses the usual flow of ecological concepts into ecocriticism by showing how ecology, too, absorbs culture into its scientific frameworks.

Kate Soper. 1998. *What is Nature?* (Blackwell: Oxford). Lucid, indispensable discussion of the various meanings and political implications of 'nature', and defence of 'critical realism'.

Robert N. Watson. 2006. *Back to Nature: The Green and the Real in the Late Renaissance* (University of Pennsylvania Press: Philadelphia). Stylish and thought-provoking historicisation of ecocritical concepts.

There are three journals of ecocriticism: *Interdisciplinary Studies in Literature and the Environment (ISLE)*; *Green Letters: Studies in Ecocriticism*; *Ecozon@*. The last of these is multilingual and online only.

BIBLIOGRAPHY

Abell, Stig. 2016. 'A family log book: Into the woods with Annie Proulx', *Times Literary Supplement*, Issue 5906. June 10, 2016. 23–24.

Abram, Christopher. 2019. *Evergreen Ash: Ecology and Catastrophe in Old Norse Myth and Literature* (University of Virginia Press: Charlottesville). Kindle book.

Adamson, Joni, Mei Mei Evans, and Rachel Stein. 2002. *The Environmental Justice Reader: Politics, Poetics, and Pedagogy* (University of Arizona Press: Tucson).

Agarwal, Anil, and Sunita Narain. 1991. 'Global warming in an unequal world: A case of environmental colonialism', in Navroz K. Dubash (ed.), *India in a Warming World* (Oxford University Press: New Delhi).

Alaimo, Stacy. 2010. *Bodily Natures: Science, Environment, and the Material Self* (Indiana University Press: Bloomington).

Alaimo, Stacy, and Susan Hekman. 2008. *Material Feminisms* (Indiana University Press: Bloomington).

Anderson, Colin L. 2019. 'Segregation, Popular Culture, and the Southern Pastoral: The Spatial and Racial Politics of American Sheet Music, 1870–1900', *The Journal of Southern History*, 85: 577–610.

Anthropocene Working Group. 2019. 'Results of binding vote'. *Subcommission on Quaternary Stratigraphy*. http://quaternary.stratigraphy.org/working-groups/anthropocene/ Accessed April 12, 2022.

Armbruster, Karla. 1998. 'Creating the world we must save: the paradox of television nature documentaries', in Richard Kerridge and Neil Sammells (eds), *Writing the Environment* (Zed Books: London).

Armstrong, Philip. 2008. *What Animals Mean in the Fiction of Modernity* (Routledge: London).

Atwood, Margaret. 1979. *Surfacing* (Virago: London).

Atwood, Margaret. 1991. *Wilderness Tips* (Virago: London).

Atwood, Margaret. 2003. *Oryx and Crake* (Virago: London).

Baarschers, William H. 1996. *Eco-Facts & Eco-Fiction: Understanding the Environmental Debate* (Routledge: London; New York).

Bagemihl, Bruce. 1999. *Biological Exuberance: Animal Homosexuality and Natural Diversity* (Macmillan: New York).

Baker, Steve. 1993. *Picturing the Beast: Animals, Identity, and Representation* (Manchester University Press: Manchester).

Banerjee, Damayanti and Michael Mayerfeld Bell. 2007. 'Ecogender: Locating Gender in Environmental Social Science', *Society & Natural Resources*, 20: 3–19.

Barad, Karen. 2007. *Meeting the Universe Halfway: Quantum Physics and the Entanglement of Matter and Meaning* (Duke University Press: Durham, N.C.).

Barnosky, Anthony D., Nicholas Matzke, Susumu Tomiya, Guinevere O.U. Wogan, Brian A. Swartz, Tiago B. Quental, Charles Marshall, Jenny L. McGuire, Emily

L. Lindsey, Kaitlin C. Maguire, Ben Mersey and Elizabeth A. Ferrer. 2011. 'Has the Earth's sixth mass extinction already arrived?', *Nature*, 471, 51–57. doi:10.1038/nature09678.

Bartosch, Roman. 2013. *EnvironMentality: Ecocriticism and the Event of Postcolonial Fiction* (Rodopi: Amsterdam).

Bate, Jonathan. 2000. *The Song of the Earth* (Picador: London).

Bate, Jonathan. 2013. *Romantic Ecology: Wordsworth and the Environmental Tradition* (Routledge: London).

Battersby, Christine. 2007. *The Sublime, Terror and Human Difference* (Routledge: London).

Beck, Ulrich. 1999. *World Risk Society* (Polity Press: Malden, MA.).

Beckerman, Wilfred. 1995. *Small is Stupid: Blowing the Whistle on the Greens* (Duckworth: London).

Bekoff, Marc. 2007. *The Emotional Lives of Animals* (New World: Novato, CA.). Kindle book.

Bennett, Jane. 2010. *Vibrant Matter: A Political Ecology of Things* (Duke University Press: Durham and London). Kindle book.

Berger, John. 2009. *Why Look at Animals?* (Penguin: London).

Bergthaller, Hannes. 2010. 'Housebreaking the human animal: Humanism and the problem of sustainability in Margaret Atwood's *Oryx and Crake* and *The Year of the Flood*', *English Studies*, 91: 728–743.

Bergthaller, Hannes. 2018. 'Malthusian Biopolitics, Ecological Immunity, and the Anthropocene//Biopolítica malthusiana, inmunidad ecológica y el antropoceno', *Ecozon@: European Journal of Literature, Culture and Environment*, 9: 37–52.

Bergthaller, Hannes. 2021. 'Humans' in John Parham (ed.), *The Cambridge Companion to Literature and the Anthropocene* (Cambridge University Press: Cambridge).

Bewell, Alan. 2017. *Natures in Translation: Romanticism and colonial natural history* (Johns Hopkins University Press: Baltimore, MD.).

Bindra, Prerna Singh. 2017. *The Vanishing: India's Wildlife Crisis* (Viking: New Delhi).

Bogost, Ian. 2015. 'The Cathedral of Computation', *The Atlantic*, January 15, 2015. https://www.theatlantic.com/technology/archive/2015/01/the-cathedral-of-computation/384300/ Accessed August 24, 2022.

Booker, Christopher. 2009. *The Real Global Warming Disaster: Is the Obsession with 'Climate Change' Turning Out to Be the Most Costly Scientific Blunder in History?* (Continuum: London). Kindle book.

Botkin, Daniel B. 1990. *Discordant Harmonies: a New Ecology for the Twenty-First Century* (Oxford University Press: Oxford).

Bousé, Derek. 2000. *Wildlife Films* (University of Pennsylvania Press: Philadelphia, PA.).

Bouson, J. Brooks. 2016. 'A "joke-filled romp" through end times: Radical environmentalism, deep ecology, and human extinction in Margaret Atwood's eco-apocalyptic MaddAddam trilogy', *The Journal of Commonwealth Literature*, 51: 341–357.

Boyd, David R. 2015. *The Optimistic Environmentalist: Progressing Towards a Greener Future* (ECW Press: Toronto, ON.).

Bradley, James. 2015. *Clade* (London: Titan).

Bradley, Nicholas and Ella Soper. 2013. *Greening the Maple: Canadian Ecocriticism in Context* (University of Calgary Press: Calgary, AB.).

Branch, Michael P. 2004. 'John Muir's My First Summer in the Sierra (1911)', *ISLE: Interdisciplinary Studies in Literature and Environment*, 11: 139–152.

Buell, Frederick. 2003. *From Apocalypse to Way of Life: Environmental Crisis in the American Century* (Routledge: London). Kindle book.

Buell, Lawrence. 1995. *The Environmental Imagination: Thoreau, Nature Writing, and the Formation of American Culture* (Belknap: Cambridge, MA.).

Buell, Lawrence. 2001. *Writing for an Endangered World: Literature, Culture, and Environment in the U.S. and Beyond* (Belknap: Cambridge, MA.).

Buell, Lawrence. 2005. *The Future of Environmental Criticism: Environmental Crisis and Literary Imagination* (Blackwell Publishing: Oxford).

Bullard, Robert D. 2019. *Dumping in Dixie: Race, Class, and Environmental Quality* (Routledge: Abingdon).

Burch, Ernest S. 2007. 'Rationality and Resource Use among Hunters: Some Eskimo Examples' in Michael Eugene Harkin and David Rich Lewis (eds), *Native Americans and the Environment: Perspectives on the Ecological Indian* (University of Nebraska Press: Lincoln, NE.).

Burelle, Julie. 2020. 'Inuit Visual and Sensate Sovereignty in Alethea Arnaquq-Baril's 'Angry Inuk'', *Canadian Journal of Film Studies*, 29: 145–162.

Burke, Edmund and Adam Phillips. 1990. *A Philosophical Enquiry into the Origin of Our Ideas of the Sublime and Beautiful* (Oxford University Press: Oxford).

Buss, David M. 2019. *Evolutionary Psychology: The New Science of the Mind* (Routledge: New York).

Butler, Judith. 1993. *Bodies that Matter: on the Discursive Limits of "Sex"* (Routledge: London).

Butler, Octavia and N.K. Jemisin. 2019. *Parable of the Sower* (Grand Central: New York).

Caminero-Santangelo, Byron. 2014. *Different Shades of Green: African Literature, Environmental Justice, and Political Ecology* (University of Virginia Press: Charlottesville, VA.).

Campbell, Neil. 2008. *The Rhizomatic West: Representing the American West in a Transnational, Global, Media Age* (University of Nebraska Press: Lincoln, NE.).

Canavan, Gerry. 2012. 'Hope, But Not for Us: Ecological Science Fiction and the End of the World in Margaret Atwood's Oryx and Crake and The Year of the Flood', *Literature, Interpretation, Theory*, 23: 138–159.

Caracciolo, Marco. 2019. 'Deus Ex Algorithmo: Narrative Form, Computation, and the Fate of the World in David Mitchell's Ghostwritten and Richard Powers's The Overstory', *Contemporary Literature*, 60: 47–71.

Caracciolo, Marco. 2021. *Narrating the Mesh: Form and Story in the Anthropocene* (University of Virginia Press: Charlottesville, VA.). Kindle book.

Carruth, Allison. 2020. 'Ecological Media Studies and the Matter of Digital Technologies', *PMLA*, 131: 364–372.

Carson, Rachel. 1999. *Silent Spring* (Penguin: London).

Castricano, Jodey. 2006. 'Learning to Talk with Ghosts: Canadian Gothic and the Poetics of Haunting in Eden Robinson's Monkey Beach', *University of Toronto Quarterly*, 75: 801–813.

Chabon, Michael. 2007. 'After the Apocalypse', *New York Review of Books*, February 15, 2007. https://www.nybooks.com/articles/2007/02/15/after-the-apocalypse/ Accessed July 12, 2022.

Chakrabarty, Dipesh. 2009. 'The climate of history: four theses', *Critical Inquiry*, 35: 197–222.

Chang, Alenda Y. 2019. *Playing Nature: Ecology in Video Games* (University of Minnesota Press: Minneapolis, MN.).

Charmantier, Isabelle. 2020. 'Linnaeus and Race', The Linnaean Society. https://www.linnean.org/learning/who-was-linnaeus/linnaeus-and-race. Accessed July 20, 2022.

Clark, John P. 1990. 'What is Social Ecology?' in John P. Clark (ed.), *Renewing the Earth: the Promise of Social Ecology* (Green Print: London).

Clark, Timothy. 2011. *The Cambridge Introduction to Literature and the Environment* (Cambridge University Press: Cambridge). Kindle book.

Clark, Timothy. 2015. *Ecocriticism on the Edge: The Anthropocene as a Threshold Concept* (Bloomsbury: London).

Clark, Timothy. 2019. *The Value of Ecocriticism* (Cambridge University Press: Cambridge).

Cocker, Mark. 2018. *Our Place: Can We Save Britain's Wildlife Before it Is Too Late?* (Jonathan Cape: London). Kindle book.

Cohen, Jeffrey Jerome. 2014. 'Foreword: Storied Matter' in Serenella Iovino and Serpil Oppermann (eds), *Material Ecocriticism* (Indiana University Press: Bloomington, IN.). Kindle book.

Cohen, Jeffrey Jerome, and Stephanie LeMenager. 2020. 'Introduction: Assembling the Ecological Digital Humanities', *PMLA*, 131: 340–346.

Cooper, Lydia R. 2011. '"Woman Chasing Her God": Ritual, Renewal, and Violence in Linda Hogan's Power', *ISLE: Interdisciplinary Studies in Literature and Environment*, 18: 143–159.

Cosgrove, Denis E. 2001. *Apollo's Eye: a Cartographic Genealogy of the Earth in the Western Imagination*. (Johns Hopkins University Press: Baltimore, MD.). Kindle book.

Crane, Kylie. 2012. *Myths of Wilderness in Contemporary Narratives: Environmental Postcolonialism in Australia and Canada* (Palgrave: New York).

Crist, Eileen. 2000. *Images of Animals: Anthropomorphism and the Animal Mind* (Temple University Press: Philadelphia, PA.). Kindle book.

Crist, Eileen. 2013. 'On the Poverty of Our Nomenclature', *Environmental Humanities*, 3: 129–147.

Cronon, William. 1996. 'The Trouble with Wilderness; Or, Getting Back to the Wrong Nature', *Environmental History*, 1: 7–28.

Crosby, Alfred W. 2004. *Ecological Imperialism: The Biological Expansion of Europe, 900–1900* (Cambridge University Press: Cambridge).

Crutzen, Paul J. 2002. 'Geology of mankind', *Nature*, 415: 23.

Cubitt, Sean. 2021. 'Data/Anecdote' in John Parham (ed.), *The Cambridge Companion to Literature and the Anthropocene* (Cambridge University Press: Cambridge).

Curry, Patrick. 2011. 2nd edn. *Ecological Ethics: An Introduction* (Polity: London).

Davies, Jeremy. 2018. 'Romantic ecocriticism: History and prospects', *Literature Compass*, 15: 1–15.

Davion, Victoria. 1994. 'Is ecofeminism feminist?' in Karen J. Warren and Barbara Wells-Howe (eds), *Ecological Feminism* (Routledge: London).

Davis, Janae, Alex A. Moulton, Levi Van Sant and Brian Williams. 2019. 'Anthropocene, Capitalocene, ... Plantationocene?: A Manifesto for Ecological Justice in an Age of Global Crises', *Geography Compass*, 13: e12438.

Deckard, Sharae. 2019. 'Water shocks: Neoliberal hydrofiction and the crisis of "cheap water"', *Atlantic Studies*, 16: 108–125.

Deleuze, Gilles, and Felix Guattari. 1987. *A Thousand Plateaus: Capitalism and Schizophrenia* (University of Minnesota Press: Minneapolis, MN.).

Deloria Jr, Vine. 1997. *Red Earth, White Lies: Native Americans and the Myth of Scientific Fact* (Fulcrum: Golden, CO.).

DeLoughrey, Elizabeth M. and George B. Handley. 2011. *Postcolonial Ecologies: Literatures of the Environment* (Oxford University Press: New York; Oxford).

DeLuca, Kevin Michael. 1999. *Image Politics: The New Rhetoric of Environmental Activism* (Guilford Press: New York).

Derrida, Jacques and Marie-Louise Mallet. 2008. *The Animal That Therefore I Am* (Fordham University Press: New York).

Diamond, Jared M. 1991. *The Rise and Fall of the Third Chimpanzee* (Vintage: London).

Dickason, Olive Patricia and William Newbigging. 2019. *Indigenous Peoples Within Canada: A Concise History* (Oxford University Press: Don Mills, ON.).

Doubiago, Sharon. 1989. 'Mama Coyote Talks to the Boys' in Judith Plant (ed.), *Healing the Wounds: the Promise of Ecofeminism* (Green Print: London).

Dungy, Camille T. 2009. *Black Nature: Four Centuries of African American Nature Poetry* (University of Georgia Press: Athens).

Eagleton, Terry. 1996. *Literary Theory: An Introduction* (Blackwell: Oxford).

Edney, Susannah and Tess Somervell (eds) 2022. *Georgic Literature and the Environment: Working Land, Reworking Genre* (Routledge: London).

Edwards, Paul N. 2010. *A Vast Machine: Computer Models, Climate Data, and the Politics of Global Warming* (MIT Press: Cambridge, MA.).

Egya, Sule Emmanuel. 2020. 'Out of Africa: Ecocriticism beyond the Boundary of Environmental Justice', *Ecozon@*, 11: 66–73.

Ehrlich, Paul R. 1971. *The Population Bomb* (Ballantine/Friends of the Earth: London).

Elder, John. 2019. "American Nature Writing" in *Oxford Research Encyclopedias: Literature* (Oxford University Press: Oxford) doi:10.1093/acrefore/9780190201098.013.552. Accessed March 12, 2022.

Emmett, Robert S. and David E. Nye. 2017. *The Environmental Humanities: A Critical Introduction* (MIT Press: Cambridge, MA.). Kindle book.

Erdrich, Louise. 1994. *Love Medicine* (Flamingo: London).

Ergin, Meliz. 2017. *The Ecopoetics of Entanglement in Contemporary Turkish and American Literatures* (Springer: Cham).

Farley, Paul and Michael Symmons Roberts. 2011. *Edgelands: Journeys into England's True Wilderness* (Vintage Digital: London). Kindle book.

Feder, Helena. 2021. *Close reading the Anthropocene* (Routledge: New York).

Finney, Carolyn. 2014. *Black Faces, White Spaces: Reimagining the Relationship of African Americans to the Great Outdoors* (The University of North Carolina Press: Chapel Hill, NC.). Kindle book.

Fitter, Chris. 1995. *Poetry, Space, Landscape: Toward a New Theory* (Cambridge University Press: Cambridge).

Fitzpatrick, Kathleen. 2019. *Generous Thinking: a Radical Approach to Saving the University* (Johns Hopkins University Press: Baltimore, MD.).

Flesch, William. 2007. *Comeuppance: Costly Signaling, Altruistic Punishment, and Other Biological Components of Fiction* (Harvard University Press: Cambridge, MA.).

Foreman, Christopher H. 1998. *The Promise and Peril of Environmental Justice* (Brookings Institution: Washington, D.C).

Foreman, Dave. 2011. *Man Swarm and the Killing of Wildlife* (Raven's Eye: Durango, CO.).

Fraile-Marcos, Ana María. 2020. 'Precarity and the stories we tell: Post-truth discourse and Indigenous epistemologies in Thomas King's "The Back of the Turtle"', *Journal of Postcolonial Writing*, 56: 473–487.

Fulford, Tim. 2006. 'Romantic Indians and their Inventors', *European Romantic Review*, 17: 139–150.

Gaard, G. 2010. 'New Directions for Ecofeminism: Toward a More Feminist Ecocriticism', *Interdisciplinary Studies in Literature and Environment*, 17: 643–665.

Gaard, Greta. 2017. *Critical Ecofeminism* (Lexington: Boulder, CO.). Kindle book.

Gallery, AnselAdams. n.d. 'The Story of Winter Sunrise, Sierra Nevada from Lone Pine'. https://www.anseladams.com/the-story-of-winter-sunrise-sierra-nevada-from-lone-pine/ Accessed March 23, 2022.

Gano, Geneva M. 2021. 'The Poetry of Ecological Witness: Robinson Jeffers and Camille T. Dungy', *Interdisciplinary Studies in Literature and Environment*, 28: 727–747.

Garrard, Greg. 2010. 'How Queer is Green?', *Configurations*, 18: 73–96.

Garrard, Greg. 2019. 'Never too soon, always too late: Reflections on climate temporality', *Wiley Interdisciplinary Reviews: Climate Change*, 10: e605.

Garrard, Greg. 2020. 'Brexit ecocriticism', *Green Letters*, 24: 110–124.

Garrard, Greg, Axel Goodbody, George B. Handley and Stephanie Posthumus. 2019. *Climate Change Scepticism: A Transnational Ecocritical Analysis* (Bloomsbury Academic: London).

Ghosh, Amitav. 2016. *The Great Derangement: Climate Change and the Unthinkable* (The University of Chicago Press: Chicago, IL.). Kindle book.

Gifford, Terry. 2017. 'The Environmental Humanities and the Pastoral Tradition' in Christopher Schliephake (ed.), *Ecocriticism, Ecology, and the Cultures of Antiquity* (Lexington: Boulder, CO.).

Gifford, Terry. 2019. *Pastoral* (Routledge: London). Kindle book.

Glotfelty, Cheryll and Harold Fromm. 1996. *The Ecocriticism Reader: Landmarks in Literary Ecology* (University of Georgia Press: Athens, GA.).

Gottschall, Jonathan and David Sloan Wilson. 2005. *The Literary Animal: Evolution and the Nature of Narrative* (Northwestern University Press: Evanston, IL.).

Grandin, Temple and Catherine Johnson. 2005. *Animals in Translation: Using the Mysteries of Autism to Decode Animal Behaviour* (Bloomsbury: London).

Gray, John. 2002. *Straw Dogs: Thoughts on Humans and Other Animals* (Granta: London).

Gregory, T. Ryan. 2009. 'The Argument from Design: A Guided Tour of William Paley's Natural Theology (1802)', *Evolution: Education and Outreach*, 2: 602–611.

Grewe-Volpp, Christa. 2013. 'Keep Moving: Place and Gender in a Post-Apocalyptic Environment.' in Greta Gaard, Simon C. Estok and Serpil Oppermann (eds), *International Perspectives in Feminist Ecocriticism* (Routledge: London).

Guha, Ramachandra and Joan Martínez Alier. 1998. *Varieties of Environmentalism: Essays North and South* (Oxford University Press: Delhi).

Hacking, Ian. 1999. *The Social Construction of What?* (Harvard University Press: Cambridge, MA.).

Haidt, Jonathan. 2006. *The Happiness Hypothesis: Finding Modern Truth in Ancient Wisdom* (Basic Books: New York).

Haidt, Jonathan. 2012. *The Righteous Mind: Why Good People Are Divided by Religion and Politics* (Vintage: New York).

Hall, Stuart. 2021. *The Hard Road to Renewal: Thatcherism and the Crisis of the Left* (Verso Books: London).

Handley, George. 2018. 'Anthropocentrism and the Postsecularity of the Environmental Humanities in Aronofsky's Noah', *Modern Fiction Studies*, 64: 617–638.

Handley, George B. 2014. 'Letter to a Student', *Interdisciplinary Studies in Literature and Environment*, 21: 22–32.

Hannigan, John A. 2014. *Environmental Sociology* (Routledge: London).

Haraway, Donna. 2007. *When Species Meet* (University of Minnesota Press: Minneapolis, MN.) Kindle book.

Haraway, Donna. 2016. *Staying With the Trouble: Making Kin in the Chthulucene* (Duke University Press: Durham). Kindle book.

Harjo, Joy, LeAnne Howe and Jennifer Elise Foerster. 2020. *When the Light of the World Was Subdued, Our Songs Came Through: A Norton Anthology of Native Nations Poetry* (W.W. Norton & Company: New York).

Harkin, Michael Eugene. 2007. 'Swallowing Wealth: Northwest Coast Beliefs and Ecological Practices.' in Michael Eugene Harkin and David Rich Lewis (eds), *Native Americans and the Environment: Perspectives on the Ecological Indian* (University of Nebraska Press: Lincoln, NE.).

Harkin, Michael Eugene and David Rich Lewis. 2007. *Native Americans and the Environment: Perspectives on the Ecological Indian* (University of Nebraska Press: Lincoln, NE.).

Harrison, Melissa 2018. *All Among the Barley* (Bloomsbury: London).

Hayes, Tanya and Elinor Ostrom. 2005. 'Conserving the world's forests: are protected areas the only way?', *Indiana Law Review*, 38: 595–617.

Hayles, N. Katherine. 2007. 'Hyper and Deep Attention: The Generational Divide in Cognitive Modes', *Profession*, 2007: 187–199.

Head, Dominic. 2020. 'The farming community revisited: complex nostalgia in Sarah Hall and Melissa Harrison', *Green Letters*, 24: 354–366.

Hegglund, Jon R. 2019. 'A Home for the Anthropocene: Planetary Time and Domestic Space in Richard McGuire's *Here*', *Literary Geographies*, 5(2): 185–199.

Heise, Ursula K. 2015. 'What's the Matter with Dystopia?', *Public Books*, February 2, 2015. https://www.publicbooks.org/whats-the-matter-with-dystopia/ Accessed August 13, 2022.

Heise, Ursula K. 2008. *Sense of Place and Sense of Planet: The Environmental Imagination of the Global* (Oxford University Press: Oxford).

Heise, Ursula K. 2016. *Imagining Extinction: the Cultural Meanings of Endangered Species* (The University of Chicago Press: Chicago).

Hesiod. 1914. *Homeric Hymns, Epic Cycle, Homerica*. Trans. H.G. Evelyn-White (William Heinemann: London). https://www.theoi.com/Text/HesiodWorksDays.html. Accessed Aug 19, 2022. eBook.

Hess, Scott. 2010. 'Imagining an Everyday Nature', *ISLE: Interdisciplinary Studies in Literature and Environment*, 17: 85–112.

Hicks, Heather J. 2016. *The Post-Apocalyptic Novel in the Twenty-First Century: Modernity Beyond Salvage* (Palgrave Macmillan: New York).

Hiltner, Ken. 2011. *What Else is Pastoral?: Renaissance Literature and the Environment* (Cornell University Press: Ithaca, NY.).

Hogan, Linda. 2008. *People of the Whale* (W.W. Norton: New York, NY.). Kindle book.

Holmes, Brooke. 2017. 'Before Nature?' in Christopher Schliephake (ed.), *Ecocriticism, Ecology, and the Cultures of Antiquity* (Lexington: Boulder, CO.).

Houser, Heather. 2020. *Infowhelm: Environmental Art and Literature in an Age of Data* (Columbia University Press: New York, NY.). Kindle book.

Huggan, Graham. 2013. *Nature's Saviours: Celebrity Conservationists in the Television Age* (Earthscan, Routledge: New York, NY.).

Huggan, Graham. 2016. 'From Arctic Dreams to Nightmares (and back again): Apocalyptic Thought and Planetary Consciousness in Three Contemporary American Environmentalist Texts', *Interdisciplinary Studies in Literature and Environment*, 23: 71–91.

Huggan, Graham and Helen Tiffin. 2015, 2nd edn. *Postcolonial Ecocriticism: Literature, Animals, Environment* (Routledge: London).

Hughes, Ted. 1995. *New Selected Poems 1957–1994* (Faber and Faber: London).

Hulme, M. 2009. *Why We Disagree About Climate Change: Understanding Controversy, Inaction and Opportunity* (Cambridge University Press: Cambridge).

Hulme, Mike. 2021. *Climate Change* (Routledge: London). Kindle book.

Hurley, Jessica and Dan Sinykin. 2018. 'Apocalypse: Introduction', *ASAP Journal*, 3: 451–466.

Iovino, Serenella. 2016. *Ecocriticism and Italy: Ecology, Resistance, and Liberation* (Bloomsbury Academic: London).

Iovino, Serenella and Serpil Oppermann. 2014. *Material Ecocriticism* (Indiana University Press: Bloomington). Kindle book.

Itäranta, Emmi. 2014. *Memory of Water* (HarperCollins: New York, NY.).

Ivakhiv, Adrian. 2008. 'Green film criticism and its futures', *Interdisciplinary Studies in Literature and Environment*, 15: 1–28.

Ivakhiv, Adrian J. 2013. *Ecologies of the Moving Image: Cinema, Affect, Nature* (Wilfrid Laurier University Press: Waterloo, ON.).

IWC. 2022. 'Aboriginal Subsistence Whaling', *International Whaling Commission*. https://iwc.int/management-and-conservation/whaling/aboriginal Accessed May 31, 2022.

James, Erin. 2022. *Narrative in the Anthropocene* (Ohio State University Press: Columbus, OH.).

James, Jennifer C. 2011. 'Ecomelancholia: Slavery, War, and Black Ecological Imaginings.' in Stephanie LeMenager, Teresa Shewry and Ken Hiltner (eds), *Environmental Criticism for the Twenty-First Century* (Routledge: London).

Jeffers, Robinson. 2002. *The Selected Poetry of Robinson Jeffers*, Tim Hunt (ed.) (Stanford University Press: London).

Johns-Putra, Adeline. 2019. *Climate Change and the Contemporary Novel* (Cambridge University Press: Cambridge).

Johnson, Eric Michael. 2014. 'How John Muir's Brand of Conservation Led to the Decline of Yosemite', *Scientific American*, August 13, 2014. https://blogs.scientificamerican.com/primate-diaries/how-john-muir-s-brand-of-conservation-led-to-the-decline-of-yosemite/ Accessed March 12, 2022.

Johnson, Shelton. 2009. *Gloryland: A Novel* (Counterpoint: Berkeley, CA.).

Jones, Sally-Ann Mair. 2013. 'Advertising wild Wales: turning the tables on 'greenwashing'', *Green Letters*, 17: 54–66.

Justice, Daniel Heath. 2018. *Why Indigenous Literatures Matter* (Wilfred Laurier University Press: Waterloo, ON.).

Kahan, Dan M. 2015. 'Climate-science communication and the measurement problem', *Political Psychology*, 36: 1–43.

Kalland, Arne. 2009. *Unveiling the Whale: Discourses on Whales and Whaling* (Berghahn Books: New York, NY.).

Kean, Hilda and Philip Howell (eds). 2018. *The Routledge Companion to Animal-Human History* (Routledge: Abingdon).

Kennedy, A.L. 1999. *On Bullfighting* (Yellow Jersey: London). Kindle book.

Kerridge, Richard. 2012. 'Ecocriticism and the Mission of "English"' in Greg Garrard (ed.), *Teaching Ecocriticism and Green Cultural Studies* (Palgrave Macmillan: Basingstoke, Hants.).

Kerridge, Richard. 2019. 'Ian McEwan's Solar (2010).' in Axel Goodbody and Adeline Johns-Putra (eds), *Cli-Fi: A Companion* (Peter Lang: Oxford).

Kimmerer, Robin Wall. 2013. *Braiding Sweetgrass: Indigenous Wisdom, Scientific Knowledge, and the Teachings of Plants* (Milkweed Editions: Minneapolis, MN.).

King, Thomas. 1990. *All My Relations: An Anthology of Contemporary Canadian Native Fiction* (University of Oklahoma Press: London).

King, Thomas. 2014. *The Back of the Turtle* (HarperCollins: Toronto, ON.).

Kingsnorth, Paul. 2015. *The Wake: A Novel* (Graywolf Press: n.p.). Kindle book.

Kingsnorth, Paul and Dougald Hine. 2009. 'Uncivilisation: The Dark Mountain Manifesto', *The Dark Mountain Project*. https://dark-mountain.net/about/manifesto/ Accessed July 19, 2022.

Kingsolver, Barbara. 2012. *Flight Behaviour* (Faber and Faber: London).

Kolbert, Elizabeth. 2015. *The Sixth Extinction: An Unnatural History* (Picador: New York). Kindle book.

Kolodny, Annette. 2007. 'Rethinking the "Ecological Indian": A Penobscot Precursor', *Interdisciplinary Studies in Literature and Environment*, 14: 1–23.

Koutsoyiannis, Demetris, A. Efstratiadis, N. Mamassis and A. Christofides. 2008. 'On the credibility of climate predictions', *Hydrological Sciences Journal*, 53: 671–684.

Krech, Shepard. 1999. *The Ecological Indian: myth and history* (Norton: New York, NY.).

Kricher, John C. 2009. *The Balance of Nature: Ecology's Enduring Myth* (Princeton University Press: Princeton, NJ.) Kindle book.

Ladino, Jennifer K. 2012. *Reclaiming Nostalgia: Longing for Nature in American Literature* (University of Virginia Press: Charlottesville, VA.) Kindle book.

Ladino, Jennifer K. 2019. *Memorials Matter: Emotion, Environment, and Public Memory at American Historical Sites* (University of Nevada Press: Reno, NV.).

Latour, Bruno. 2004a. *Politics of Nature: How to Bring the Sciences into Democracy* (Harvard University Press: Cambridge, MA.).

Latour, Bruno. 2004b. 'Why Has Critique Run out of Steam? From Matters of Fact to Matters of Concern', *Critical Inquiry*, 30: 225–248.

Lawrence, D.H. 1993. *Selected Poems* (Oxford University Press: Oxford).

Leeming, David Adams. 2019. *The World of Myth: An Anthology* (Oxford University Press: New York).

Lewis, Martin W. 1992. *Green Delusions: An Environmentalist Critique of Radical Environmentalism* (Duke University Press: Durham, N.C.).

Lewis, Simon L. and Mark A. Maslin. 2015. 'Defining the Anthropocene', *Nature*, 519: 171–180.

Lilley, Deborah. 2020. *The New Pastoral in Contemporary British Writing* (London: Routledge).

Linnaeus, Carl. 1747. *Letter to Johann Georg Gmelin*, February 25, 1747. https://www.alvin-portal.org/alvin/view.jsf?pid=alvin-record%3A223725&dswid=2523 Accessed July 5, 2022.

Lomborg, Bjørn. 2001. *The Skeptical Environmentalist: measuring the real state of the world* (Cambridge University Press: Cambridge).

Long, Mark C. 2021. 'Close reading at the end of time.' in Helena Feder (ed.), *Close Reading the Anthropocene* (Routledge: New York, NY.).

Lousley, Cheryl. 2018. 'Spectral Environmentalisms: National Politics and Gothic Ecologies in Silent Spring, Surfacing, and Salt Fish Girl', *Interdisciplinary Studies in Literature and Environment*, 25: 412–428.

Lousley, Cheryl. 2020. 'Ecocriticism', *Oxford Research Encyclopedia of Literature* (Oxford University Press: Oxford) doi:10.1093/acrefore/9780190201098.013.974.

Loxley, James. 2007. *Performativity* (Routledge: London). Kindle book.

Lundgren, Jakob. 2020. 'The Grand Concepts of Environmental Studies: Boundary objects between disciplines and policymakers', *Journal of Environmental Studies and sciences*, 11: 93–100.

Lutts, Ralph. 2000. 'Chemical Fallout: Silent Spring, radioactive fallout and the environmental movement.' in Craig Waddell (ed.), *And No Birds Sing: Rhetorical Analyses of Rachel Carson's 'Silent Spring'* (Southern Illinois University Press: Carbondale and Edwardsville, IL.).

Lynch, Tom, Cheryll Glotfelty, Karla Armbruster and Ezra J. Zeitler. 2012. *The Bioregional Imagination: Literature, Ecology, and Place* (University of Georgia Press: Athens, GA.).

Macfarlane, Robert. 2003. 'Call of the Wild', *The Guardian*, December 6, 2003. https://www.theguardian.com/books/2003/dec/06/featuresreviews.guardianreview34. Accessed June 13, 2022.

Macfarlane, Robert. 2007. *The Wild Places* (Granta: London).

Machin, Amanda. 2019. 'Changing the story? The discourse of ecological modernisation in the European Union', *Environmental Politics*, 28: 208–227.

MacKethan, Lucinda Hardwick. 1980. *The Dream of Arcady: Place and Time in Southern Literature* (Louisiana State University Press: Baton Rouge, LA.).

Malthus, Thomas Robert. 1998. 'An Essay on the Principle of Population [1798]' *Electronic Scholarly Publishing Project*. http://www.esp.org/books/malthus/population/malthus.pdf Accessed August 13, 2022.

Mann, Charles C. 2011. *1491: New Revelations of the Americas Before Columbus* (Vintage: New York).

Manning, Preston. 2007. 'Being as Canadian as possible, under the circumstances', *The Globe and Mail*, September 1, 2007. https://www.theglobeandmail.com/opinion/being-as-canadian-as-possible-under-the-circumstances/article20401133/ Accessed March 10, 2022.

Manolescu, Monica. 2021. '"Arboretum America" in Richard Powers's *The Overstory*', *Polysèmes*, 25. https://journals.openedition.org/polysemes/8565 Accessed July 24, 2022.

Marris, Emma. 2011. *Rambunctious Garden: Saving Nature in a Post-Wild World* (Bloomsbury: New York, NY.). Kindle book.

Martínez-Alier, Joan. 2014. 'The environmentalism of the poor', *Geoforum*, 54: 239–241.

Marx, Leo. 2000. *The Machine in the Garden: Technology and the Pastoral Ideal in America* (Oxford University Press: Oxford).

Masson-Delmotte, V., P. Zhai, H.-O. Pörtner, D. Roberts, J. Skea, P.R. Shukla, A. Pirani, W. Moufouma-Okia, C. Péan, R. Pidcock, S. Connors, J.B.R. Matthews, Y. Chen, X. Zhou, M.I. Gomis, E. Lonnoy, T. Maycock, M. Tignor and T. Waterfield. 2022. 'Summary for Policymakers.' in IPCC (ed.), *Global Warming of 1.5°C: IPCC Special Report on Impacts of Global Warming of 1.5°C Above Pre-industrial Levels in Context of Strengthening Response to Climate Change, Sustainable Development, and Efforts to Eradicate Poverty* (Cambridge University Press: Cambridge).

Maxwell, Richard and Toby Miller. 2012. *Greening the Media* (Oxford University Press: New York, NY.).

McCarthy, Cormac. 2007. *The Road* (Picador: London).

McConaghy, Charlotte. 2020. *Migrations* (Flatiron: New York).

McEwan, Ian. 2010. *Solar* (Jonathan Cape: London).

McFarland, Sarah E. 2021. *Ecocollapse Fiction and Cultures of Human Extinction* (Bloomsbury Academic: London).

McGuire, Richard. 2014. *Here* (Pantheon: New York, NY.).

Meadows, Donella H. *et al.* 1972. *The Limits to Growth: A Report for the Club of
   Rome's Project on the Predicament of Mankind* (Universe Books: New
   York, NY.).

Menely, Tobias and Jesse Oak Taylor (eds). 2017. *Anthropocene Reading: Literary History
   in Geologic Times* (Pennsylvania State University Press: Pennsylvania, PA.).

Menrisky, Alexander. 2019. 'The Natural Death of Alexander Supertramp: Ecological
   Selfhood and the Freudian Rhetoric of Into the Wild', *ISLE: Interdisciplinary
   Studies in Literature and Environment*, 26: 46–64.

Midgley, Mary. 1983. *Animals and Why they Matter* (Penguin: Harmondsworth).

Midgley, Mary and David Midgley. 2005. *The Essential Mary Midgley* (Routledge:
   London). Kindle book.

Millet, Lydia. 2020. *A Children's Bible* (Norton: New York).

Mills, Brett. 2017. *Animals on Television: The Cultural Making of the Non-Human* (Palgrave: London).

Milton, John. 1992. 'Paradise Lost', Project Gutenberg. https://www.gutenberg.org/
   cache/epub/26/pg26-images.html Accessed Aug 19, 2022.

Mitman, Gregg. 2009. *Reel Nature: America's Romance With Wildlife on Film* (University of Washington Press: Seattle, WA.).

Monani, Salma. 2016. 'Feeling and Healing Eco-social Catastrophe: The "Horrific"
   Slipstream of Danis Goulet's Wakening', *Paradoxa*, 28: 1024.

Monani, Salma, Renata Ryan Burchfield, Danika Medak-Saltzman and William
   Lempert. 2021. 'Indigenous Media: Dialogic Resistance to Climate Disrup-
   tion.' in *The Routledge Companion to Contemporary Art, Visual Culture, and
   Climate Change* (Routledge: New York, NY.).

Monbiot, George. 2007. 'The Road Well Travelled', *The Guardian*, October 30, 2007.
   https://www.monbiot.com/2007/10/30/the-road-well-travelled/ Accessed
   August 24, 2022.

Moncion, Laura. 2016. 'Time Frames: Graphic Narrative and Historiography in
   Richard McGuire's Here', *Imaginations*, 7.

Moore, Jason W. 2017. 'The Capitalocene, Part I: on the nature and origins of our
   ecological crisis', *The Journal of Peasant Studies*, 44: 594–630.

Moor, Robert. 2021. 'The German Forester Who Wants the World to Idolize Trees',
   The New Yorker, June 10, 2021. https://www.newyorker.com/books/under-
   review/the-german-forester-who-wants-the-world-to-idolize-trees Accessed
   May 15, 2022.

Morland, Paul. 2019. *The Human Tide: How Population Shaped the Modern World*
   (John Murray: London). Kindle book.

Mortimer-Sandilands, Catriona. 1999. *The Good-Natured Feminist: Ecofeminism and
   the Quest for Democracy* (University of Minnesota Press: Minneapolis, MN.).

Mortimer-Sandilands, Catriona and Bruce Erickson. 2010. *Queer Ecologies: Sex, Nature, Politics, Desire* (Indiana University Press: Bloomington, IN.). Kindle book.

Morton, Timothy. 2007. *Ecology Without Nature: Rethinking Environmental Aesthetics* (Harvard University Press: Cambridge).

Morton, Timothy. 2010. *The Ecological Thought* (Harvard University Press: Cambridge, MA.).

Morton, Timothy. 2013. *Hyperobjects: Philosophy and Ecology After the End of the World* (University of Minnesota Press: Minneapolis, MN.).

Morton, Timothy. 2016. *Dark Ecology: For a Logic of Future Coexistence* (Columbia University Press: New York, NY.).

Muir, John. 1992. *John Muir: The Eight Wilderness Discovery Books* (Diadem Books: London).

Murray, Les. 1993. *Translations from the Natural World* (Carcanet: Manchester).

Nayar, Pramod K. 2019. *Ecoprecarity: Vulnerable Lives in Literature and Culture* (Routledge: New York).

Newman, Sharan. 2010. *The Real History of the end of the World* (Berkley Books: New York). Kindle book.

Nicholson, Christopher. 2009. *The Elephant Keeper* (Fourth Estate: London).

Nixon, Rob. 2011. *Slow Violence and the Environmentalism of the Poor* (Harvard University Press: Cambridge, MA.).

Nordhaus, Ted and Michael Shellenberger. 2007. *Break Through: from the Death of Environmentalism to the Politics of Possibility* (Houghton Mifflin: Boston).

Norgaard, Kari Marie. 2011. *Living in Denial: Climate Change, Emotions, and Everyday Life* (MIT Press: Cambridge, MA.). Kindle book.

O'Brian, John and Peter White (eds). 2007. *Beyond Wilderness: The Group of Seven, Canadian Identity, and Contemporary Art* (McGill-Queen's University Press: Montreal and Kingston, ON.).

O'Brien, Susie. 2020. 'The Story You Don't Want to Tell: Decolonial Resilience in Thomas King's *The Back of the Turtle*' in Ana María Fraile-Marcos (ed.), *Glocal Narratives of Resilience* (Routledge: London).

O'Neill, Saffron J., Maxwell Boykoff, Simon Niemeyer and Sophie A. Day. 2013. 'On the use of imagery for climate change engagement', *Global Environmental Change*, 23: 413–421.

Oelschlaeger, Max. 1991. *The Idea of Wilderness: From Prehistory to the Age of Ecology* (Yale University Press: New Haven, CT.).

Olstad, Tyra. 2020. 'In Search of Bob Marshall's Alaska Wilderness', *ISLE: Interdisciplinary Studies in Literature and Environment* 29:1: 190–209.

Oreskes, Naomi and Erik M. Conway. 2014. *The Collapse of Western Civilization: A View From the Future* (Columbia University Press: New York, NY.).

Outka, Paul. 2008. *Race and Nature from Transcendentalism to the Harlem Renaissance* (Palgrave Macmillan: Basingstoke).

Parham, John. 2010. *Green Man Hopkins: Poetry and the Victorian Ecological Imagination* (Rodopi: Amsterdam).

Parham, John. 2015. *Green Media and Popular Culture: An Introduction* (Bloomsbury Academic: London).

Passmore, John. 1974. *Man's Responsibility for Nature: Ecological Problems and Western Traditions* (Duckworth: London).

Pearce, Fred. 2016. *The New Wild: Why Invasive Species Will Be Nature's Salvation* (Beacon Press: Boston).

Pepper, David. 1993. *Eco-Socialism: From Deep Ecology to Social Justice* (Routledge: London).

Phillips, Dana. 2003. *The Truth of Ecology: Nature, Culture, and Literature in America* (Oxford University Press: New York, NY.).

Phillips, Dana. 2011. '"He ought not to have done it": McCarthy and Apocalypse' in Sara Spurgeon (ed.), *Cormac McCarthy: All the Pretty Horses, No Country for Old Men, The Road* (Bloomsbury: London).

Pinker, Steven. 2007a. *The Language Instinct: How the Mind Creates Language* (Harper-Perennial: New York, NY.).

Pinker, Steven. 2007b. 'Towards a Consilient Study of Literature', *Philosophy and Literature*, 31: 161–177.

Pinto, Juliet, Robert E. Gutsche, Jr and Paola Prado. 2019. *Climate Change, Media & Culture: Critical Issues in Global Environmental Communication* (Emerald: Bingley).

Plumwood, Val. 1993. *Feminism and the Mastery of Nature* (Routledge: London).

Plumwood, Val. 2007. 'Journey to the Heart of Stone' in Terry Gifford and Fiona Becket (eds), *Culture, Creativity and Environment: New Environmentalist Criticism* (Brill: Amsterdam).

Plumwood, Val. 2009. 'Nature in the Active Voice', *Australian Humanities Review*. http://australianhumanitiesreview.org/2009/05/01/nature-in-the-active-voice/ Accessed August 24, 2022.

Powers, Richard. 2018. *The Overstory: A Novel* (Norton: New York, NY.).

Proulx, Annie. 2016. *Barkskins* (Fourth Estate: London).

Pyne, Stephen J. 2019. *Fire: A Brief History* (University of Washington Press: Seattle, WA.). Kindle book.

Pyne, Stephen J. 2021. *The Pyrocene: How We Created an Age of Fire, and What Happens Next* (University of California Press: Oakland, CA.).

Quinn, Paul. 2018. 'It's the Ecology, Stupid: Richard Powers's Rich Literary Canopy, and the Decentring of Mankind', *Times Literary Supplement*, 6004, April 27, 2018.

Rafferty, John P. 2018. 'Anthropocene Epoch', *Encyclopedia Britannica*. https://www.britannica.com/science/Anthropocene-Epoch. Accessed August 24, 2022.

Rebanks, James. 2020. *Pastoral Song: A Farmer's Journey* (HarperCollins: New York, NY).

Reed, T.V. 2009. 'Toxic Colonialism, Environmental Justice, and Native Resistance in Silko's Almanac of the Dead', *Melus*, 34: 25–42.

Regan, Paulette. 2010. *Unsettling the Settler Within: Indian Residential Schools, Truth Telling, and Reconciliation in Canada* (UBC Press: Vancouver, BC.).

Remington, Vanessa, Sally Goodsir and Roy Strong. 2015. *Painting Paradise: The Art of the Garden* (Royal Collection Trust: London).

Ridley, Matt. 2010. *The Rational Optimist: How Prosperity Evolves* (Fourth Estate: London). Kindle book.

Rigby, Catherine E. 2015. *Dancing with Disaster: Environmental Histories, Narratives, and Ethics for Perilous Times* (University of Virginia Press: Charlottesville, VA.).

Rigby, Kate. 2004. 'Earth, world, text: On the (im)possibility of ecopoiesis', *New Literary History*, 35: 427–442.

Rigby, Kate. 2020. *Reclaiming Romanticism: Towards an Ecopoetics of Decolonization* (Bloomsbury Academic: London).

Ritchie, Hannah and Max Roser. 2021. 'Extinctions', Our World in Data. https://ourworldindata.org/extinctions Accessed June 17, 2022.

'Robinson Jeffers'. *Poetry Foundation.* https://www.poetryfoundation.org/poets/robinson-jeffers Accessed July 19, 2022.

Robinson, Kim Stanley. 2020. *The Ministry for the Future* (Orbit: New York, NY.).

Ross, Andrew. 1994. *The Chicago Gangster Theory of Life: Nature's Debt to Society* (Verso: London).

Roughgarden, Joan. 2013. *Evolution's Rainbow: Diversity, Gender, and Sexuality in Nature and People* (University of California Press: Oakland, CA.).

Ruddiman, William. 2017. 'Geographic evidence of the early anthropogenic hypothesis', *Anthropocene*, 20: 4–14.

Ruffin, Kimberly N. 2010. *Black on Earth: African American Ecoliterary Traditions* (University of Georgia Press: Athens, GA.).

Russill, Chris. 2016. 'Earth imaging: Photograph, pixel, program' in Stephen Rust, Salma Monani and Sean Cubitt (eds), *Ecomedia* (Routledge: London).

Sale, Kirkpatrick. 1985. *Dwellers in the Land: The Bioregional Vision* (Sierra Club Books: San Francisco, CA.).

Sandom, Christopher, Søren Faurby, Brody Sandel and Jens-Christian Svenning. 2014. 'Global late Quaternary megafauna extinctions linked to humans, not climate change', *Proceedings of the Royal Society B: Biological Sciences*, 281:1787. doi:10.1098/rspb.2013.3254.

Saunders, Timothy. 2013. *Bucolic Ecology: Virgil's 'Eclogues' and the Environmental Literary Tradition* (Bloomsbury Academic: London).

Savoy, Lauret. 2015. *Trace: Memory, History, Race, and the American Landscape* (Counterpoint: Berkeley, CA.).

Schama, Simon. 1995. *Landscape and Memory* (HarperCollins: London).

Schneider-Mayerson, Matthew. 2015. *Peak Oil: Apocalyptic Environmentalism and Libertarian Political Culture* (University of Chicago Press: Chicago, IL.).

Scott, Heidi C. M. 2014. *Chaos and Cosmos: Literary Roots of Modern Ecology in the British Nineteenth Century* (Pennsylvania State University Press: University Park, PA.).

Scott, Kim. 2010. *That Deadman Dance* (Bloomsbury: New York, NY.).

Scruton, Roger. 1998. *On Hunting* (Yellow Jersey: London).

Serpell, James. 2005. 'People in Disguise' in Lorraine Daston (ed.), *Thinking with Animals: New Perspectives on Anthropomorphism* (Columbia University Press: New York, NY.).

Sessions, George. 1995. *Deep Ecology for the Twenty-First Century* (Shambhala: Boston, MA.).

Seymour, Nicole. 2018. *Bad Environmentalism: Irony and Irreverence in the Ecological Age* (University of Minnesota Press: Minneapolis, MN.). Kindle book.

Shelley, Mary Wollstonecraft. 2020. *The Last Man* (Windmill: n.p.). Kindle book.

Shields, Fiona. 2019. 'Why we're rethinking the images we use for our climate journalism', *The Guardian*, October 18, 2019. https://www.theguardian.com/environment/2019/oct/18/guardian-climate-pledge-2019-images-pictures-guidelines Accessed August 24, 2022.

Silko, Leslie Marmon. 2020. *Ceremony* (Penguin: London).

Singer, Peter. 1995. *Animal Liberation* (Pimlico: London).

Sinha, Indra. 2009. *Animal's People* (Simon & Schuster: New York).

Sismondo, Sergio. 2010. *An Introduction to Science and Technology Studies* (Wiley-Blackwell: Chichester).

Slezkine, Yuri. 2017. *The House of Government: A Saga of the Russian Revolution* (Princeton University Press: Princeton, NJ.).

Smith, Daniel. 2014. "It's the End of the World as We Know It ... and He Feels Fine." *New York Times*, April 17, 2014. https://www.nytimes.com/2014/04/20/magazine/its-the-end-of-the-world-as-we-know-it-and-he-feels-fine.html. Accessed August 24, 2022.

Smith, Felisa A., Rosemary E. Elliott Smith, S. Kathleen Lyons and Jonathan L. Payne. 2018. 'Body size downgrading of mammals over the late Quaternary', *Science*, 360: 310–313.

Smith, Jos. 2017. *The New Nature Writing: Rethinking the Literature of Place* (Bloomsbury Academic: London).

Smits Masten, Sally L. 2016. 'Reworking the garden: Revisions of the pastoral tradition in twentieth-century southern poetry', PhD thesis, University of North Carolina at Greensboro.

Soper, Kate. 1995. *What is Nature?: Culture, Politics and the Non-Human* (Blackwell: Oxford).

Stein, Rachel. 2002. 'Contested Ground: Nature, Narrative, and Native American Identity in Leslie Marmon Silko's 'Ceremony'.' in Allan Chavkin (ed.), *Leslie Marmon Silko's 'Ceremony': A Casebook* (Oxford University Press: Oxford).

Steinwand, Jonathan. 2011. 'What the Whales Would Tell Us: Cetacean communication in novels by Witi Ihimaera, Linda Hogan, Zakes Mda, and Amitav Ghosh.' in Elizabeth M. DeLoughrey and George B. Handley (eds), *Postcolonial Ecologies: Literatures of the Environment* (Oxford University Press: Oxford).

Sterelny, Kim, and Paul E. Griffiths. 2012. *Sex and Death: An Introduction to Philosophy of Biology* (University of Chicago: Chicago, IL.).

TallBear, Kim. 2000. "Shepard Krech's The Ecological Indian: One Indian's Perspective."IIIRM Publications, 1–5. https://www.iiirm.org/publications/Book%20Reviews/Reviews/Krech001.pdf Accessed Jun 23, 2022.

TallBear, Kim. 2015. 'Genomic Articulations of Indigeneity.' in Stephanie Nohelani Teves, Andrea Smith and Michelle H. Raheja (eds), *Native Studies Keywords* (University of Arizona Press: Tucson, AZ.).

Tasker, John Paul. 2020. 'In a major victory for Trans Mountain, Federal Court dismisses Indigenous appeal of project's approval', *CBC News*, https://www.cbc.ca/news/politics/federal-court-appeal-trans-mountain-1.5450748. Accessed May 31, 2022.

Taylor, Jesse O. 2016. *The Sky of Our Manufacture: The London Fog in British fiction from Dickens to Woolf* (University of Virginia Press: Charlottesville, VA.).

Taylor, Sarah McFarland. 2019. *Ecopiety: Green Media and the Dilemma of Environmental Virtue* (NYU Press: New York, NY.).

Theocritus. 1978. *The Poems of Theocritus.* Trans. Anna Rist (University of North Carolina Press: Chapel Hill, NC.).

Theunissen, L.T.G. 2019. 'The Oostvaardersplassen Fiasco', *Isis*, 110: 341–345.

Thomas, Keith. 1983. *Man and the Natural World: Changing Attitudes in England 1500–1800* (Penguin, 1984: Harmondsworth).

Thomashow, Mitchell. 2002. *Bringing the Biosphere Home: Learning to Perceive Global Environmental Change* (MIT Press: Cambridge, MA.).

Thompson, Damian. 1997. *The End of Time: Faith and Fear in the Shadow of the Millennium* (Minerva: London).

Thoreau, Henry David. 1972. *The Maine Woods* (Princeton University Press: Princeton, N.J.).

Thoreau, Henry David. 1992 [1910]. *Walden* (J.M. Dent & Sons: London).

Thorsheim, Peter. 2006. *Inventing Pollution: Coal, Smoke, and Culture in Britain Since 1800* (Ohio University Press: Athens, OH.).

Toomer, Jean and George Hutchinson. 2019. *Cane* (Penguin: New York, NY.). Kindle book.

Trexler, Adam. 2015. *Anthropocene Fictions: The Novel in a Time of Climate Change* (University of Virginia Press: Charlottesville, VA.).

Tsing, Anna Lowenhaupt. 2015. *The Mushroom At the End of the World: On the Possibility of Life in Capitalist Ruins* (Princeton University Press: Princeton, NJ.).

Tuck, Eve and K. Wayne Yang. 2012. 'Decolonization is not a metaphor', *Decolonization: Indigeneity, Education & Society*, 1: 1–40.

Udel, Lisa J. 2007. 'Revising Strategies: The Intersection of Literature and Activism in Contemporary Native Women's Writing', *Studies in American Indian Literatures*, 19: 62–82.

Voie, Christian Hummelsund. 2019. 'Nature writing in the Anthropocene' in Scott Slovic, Swarnalatha Rangarajan and Vidya Sarveswaran (eds), *Routledge Handbook of Ecocriticism and Environmental Communication* (Routledge: London).

Von Burg, Ron. 2012. 'Decades away or The Day After Tomorrow?: Rhetoric, film, and the global warming debate', *Critical Studies in Media Communication*, 29: 7–26.

Waal, Frans B.M. de. 2001. *The Ape and the Sushi Master* (Allen Lane: London).

Walker, Gordon. 2012. *Environmental Justice: Concepts, Evidence and Politics* (Routledge: London).

Wallace-Wells, David. 2019. *The Uninhabitable Earth: Life After Warming* (Tim Duggan Books: New York, NY.).

Walls, Laura Dassow. 2021. 'Earth' in John Parham (ed.), *The Cambridge Companion to Literature and the Anthropocene* (Cambridge University Press: Cambridge).

Warren, Karen J. and Barbara Wells-Howe. 1994. *Ecological Feminism* (Routledge: London).

Watson, Annette and Orville H. Huntington. 2008. 'They're here – I can feel them: the epistemic spaces of Indigenous and Western Knowledges', *Social & Cultural Geography*, 9: 257–281.

Watson, Robert N. 2006. *Back to Nature: The Green and the Real in the Late Renaissance* (University of Pennsylvania Press: Philadelphia, PA.).

Wayne, G.P. 2022. 'How do human CO2 emissions compare to natural CO2 emissions?'. Skeptical Science. https://skepticalscience.com/human-co2-smaller-than-natural-emissions.htm. Accessed April 15, 2022.

Weaver, Jace. 2014. *The Red Atlantic: American Indigenes and the Making of the Modern World, 1000–1927* (University of North Carolina Press: Chapel Hil, NC.).

Weik Von Mossner, Alexa. 2012. 'Facing The Day After Tomorrow: Filmed disaster, emotional engagement, and climate risk perception', in Christof Mauch and Sylvia Mayer (eds), *American Environments: Climate-Cultures-Catastrophe.* (Universitätsverlag Winter: Heidelberg), 97–116.

Weik Von Mossner, Alexa. 2018. 'Engaging Animals in Wildlife Documentaries: From Anthropomorphism to Trans-Species Empathy' in Catalin Brylla and Mette Kramer (eds), *Cognitive Theory and Documentary Film* (Palgrave: London).

Welling, Bart H. 2009. 'On the limits of visualizing the Nonhuman.' in Sidney I. Dobrin and Sean Morey (eds), *Ecosee: Image, Rhetoric, Nature* (SUNY Press: Albany, NY.).

Welling, Bart H. 2014. 'On the "Inexplicable Magic of Cinema": Critical Anthropomorphism, Emotion, and the Wildness of Wildlife films' in Alexa Weik von Mossner (ed.), *Moving Environments: Affect, Emotion, Ecology, and Film* (Wilfred Laurier University Press: Waterloo, ON.).

White, Laura A. 2018. 'Haunted histories, animate futures: Recovering Noongar knowledge through Kim Scott's 'That Deadman Dance", *Commonwealth*, 41: 63–74.

Whittaker, Jason. 2018. 'Blake and the New Jerusalem: Art and English Nationalism into the Twenty-First Century', *Visual Culture in Britain*, 19: 380–392.

Whyte, Kyle P. 2018. 'Indigenous science (fiction) for the Anthropocene: Ancestral dystopias and fantasies of climate change crises', *Environment and Planning* 1(1–2): 224–242.

Williams, David R. 2021. 'The Other Wilderness: Outside the Text', *ISLE: Interdisciplinary Studies in Literature and Environment*, 28: 1310–1326.

Williams, Raymond. 1973. *The Country and the City* (Hogarth, 1985: London).

Williams, Raymond. 1989. *Resources of Hope: Culture, Democracy, Socialism* (Verso: London).

Willis, Roy. 1974. *Man and Beast* (Hart-Davis: London).

Wilson, Alexander. 2019 [1992]. *The Culture of Nature: North American Landscape From Disney to the Exxon Valdez* (Between the Lines: Toronto, ON.).

Wilson, E.O. 2000. *Sociobiology: The New Synthesis* (Belknap: London).

Wilson, Edward O. 2006. *The Creation: An Appeal to Save Life on Earth* (Norton: New York, NY.).

Wilson, James. 1999. *The Earth Shall Weep: A History of Native America* (Picador: London).

Wilson, Shawn. 2008. *Research is Ceremony: Indigenous Research Methods* (Fernwood: Winnipeg, MB.).

Wolfe, Cary. 2003. 'In the shadow of Wittgenstein's lion: language, ethics, and the question of the animal' in *Animal Rites: American Culture, the Discourse of Species, and Posthumanist Theory* (University of Chicago Press: Chicago, IL.).

Wolfe, Cary. 2013. 'Learning from Temple Grandin, or, animal studies, disability studies, and who comes after the subject', in Alfred Kentigern Siewers (ed.), *Re-Imagining Nature, Environmental Humanities and Ecosemiotics* (Bucknell University Press: Lewisburg, WV.): 91–107.

Wolfe, Patrick. 2006. 'Settler colonialism and the elimination of the native', *Journal of Genocide Research*, 8: 387–409.

Wollstonecraft, Mary, William Godwin and Richard Holmes (ed.). 1987. *A Short Residence in Sweden, Norway and Denmark* (Penguin: Harmondsworth).

Wood, Graeme. 2021. '"Land Acknowledgments" Are Just Moral Exhibitionism', *The Atlantic*, November 28, 2021. https://www.theatlantic.com/ideas/archive/2021/11/against-land-acknowledgements-native-american/620820/ Accessed July 3, 2022.

Wordsworth, William. 2001 [1805]. 'The Prelude of 1805, in Thirteen Books', Global Language Resources, http://triggs.djvu.org/djvu-editions.com/WORDSWORTH/PRELUDE1805/Download.pdf Accessed July 19, 2022.

Yearley, Steven. 1996. *Sociology, Environmentalism, Globalization: Reinventing the Globe* (SAGE Publications: Thousand Oaks, CA.).

Yearley, Steven. 2009. 'Sociology and Climate Change after Kyoto: What Roles for Social Science in Understanding Climate Change?', *Current Sociology*, 57: 389–405.

York, Richard and Eugene A. Rosa. 2003. 'Key Challenges to Ecological Modernization Theory: Institutional Efficacy, Case Study Evidence, Units of Analysis, and the Pace of Eco-Efficiency', *Organization & Environment*, 16: 273–288.

INDEX